THE
LESSON
OF THE
SCAFFOLD

DAVID D. COOPER

ALLEN LANE

CONTENTS

LIST OF ILLUSTRATIONS

PREFACE

THE movement to abolish public executions in Victorian England is still treated as part of the movement for the abolition of capital punishment – either as a footnote or as an appendage. Although the efforts to abolish public hangings merged with attempts to reform criminal laws and movements to abolish the death penalty, the struggle to rid the nation of public display of the death penalty had an identity and history of its own. There were critics whose writings condemning public executions were eloquent literary expressions against cruel forms of punishment. There were numerous members of parliament who prodded their fellow members to legislate the public gallows out of existence. And there were newspapers and journals whose articles exposed the horrors of public executions and aroused public opinion against them.

The study of the history of the movement against public executions reveals insights about the conduct, attitudes, prejudices and fears of people in nineteenth-century England; it is social history in the raw. There were sensational crimes and vividly detailed descriptions of executions in the press. The upper classes shared the interest in executions as avidly as the mass of common people, for whom ostensibly the spectacle was provided. Large sums were spent for rooms and seats at windows overlooking the gallows, and opera glasses were employed to view more perfectly the last moment of some poor wretch's life. The penny press sold millions of broadsides purporting to give the lurid details of the crime, and the criminal's own didactic verse written in the condemned cell the night before his execution. Apprehension and indecision impeded reform of public hangings. There was concern that the lower classes would consider private executions as class legislation. There was the belief that the working classes would not accept the fact of execution of a person of wealth and education if it were done in private.

There is the need to document and to examine the history of events and attempts to bring about an alteration of a form of punishment which had become an anachronism in Victorian England. Here is a historical problem of a needed reform which was not considered a reform. The conflict between a moderate reformer like Charles Dickens and a radical reformer like John Bright over the issue of the abolition of public executions as opposed to the abolition of capital punishment was bitter and uncompromising. That one was accused of 'wishing to put someone to death', and the other was described as 'reckless and dishonest' are evidence of irreconcilable attitudes. Although it would be conjecture whether abolition of public executions was responsible for the continuation of capital punishment in England, as the radicals believed but the evidence tends to reject, there is no doubt that the introduction of private executions within the walls of prisons was a valid reform. Abolition of public hangings was what most people of England in 1868 wanted and would accept.

Many rewarding days were spent in numerous libraries both in the United States and England; and in all of them I received pleasant helpful assistance. In particular, I am grateful to the administrators and staff of the Library of the Institute of Historical Research in London where I did a great part of my research. Not only was I permitted to explore the extensive research materials there, but I was always made to feel very welcome. Mr A. Taylor Milne, the Institute's former secretary and Librarian, was very generous to me with his time and knowledge. Miss Nora Harris, reference librarian in the University of London Library, was also unusually accommodating and helpful. I would also like to thank the librarians and staffs at the following institutions for their patience and service: the British Library of Political and Economic Science of the London School of Economics and Political Science; the Reading Room of the British Museum and the British Museum's Newspaper Library (Colindale); the Public Record Office in London; the New York Public Library; the New

York University Library and the Hofstra University Library in Hempstead, New York.

This study relied very heavily on the assistance of Professor John W. Wilkes of the History Department of New York University. His encouragement and ready accessibility sustained me during the periods of research and writing. I am most grateful to my son Matthew Cooper for searching the archives of London for the illustrations in this book. My thanks go also to my wife Joan, without whose advice and forbearance this work could never have been completed.

David D. Cooper
Edinboro State College
Pennsylvania

1

THE LESSON OF THE GALLOWS

DETERRENCE was a one-sided sword. Disposing of offenders vindictively and cheaply was final, and the only rehabilitative object of public executions was to present a fearful example for the assembled audience. The more public the exhibition, the more effective was the lesson; the more awesome the execution, the longer the repressive sense of terror remained to control the passions and tendencies of those inclined to commit crimes. When a miscreant was sacrificed for the preservation of thousands, the punishment was considered humane and effectual. Punishment very often was continued even after the victim's death to intensify its prolonged, repressive terror. 'An Act for the Better Preventing the Horrid Crimes of Murder' (25 George II, C.37, 1752) was passed so that some further mark of infamy would be added to the punishment of death.[1] The murderer's body was to be given over to surgeons for dissection, and to make this innovation consistent with executing publicly, the dissections were often carried out in public.[2]

The Act also gave the judge the discretion to order the body to be hanged in chains, so that it would remain suspended as a grisly warning to the lower orders. Many a strip of green waste by the roadside and many a gorse-covered common had its gibbet, from which swung in the breeze the clanking and creaking iron hoops. There was gruesome aspect enough to a tar-saturated, deteriorating body, but to add to the degrading character of the penalty, gibbets were often placed near the places of crime, and occasionally in front of the criminal's house.[3] But they were always exposed and public.

The day appointed for hanging in chains was a public event, and months later people would still gather around the gibbet.

'The Execution of Palmer' from A. Griffiths *Mysteries of Police and Crime*. William Palmer, the 'Rugely Poisoner', was executed at Stafford on 14 June, 1856.

And on the rare occasion when the gibbetted body was inaccessible for viewing, some profitable arrangement was made for accommodating the curious. Greenwich pensioners on the hill used to exhibit gibbetted pirates on the Isle of Dogs, across the Thames, to be seen through telescopes. When the bodies were removed by legislative enactment, some newspapers made a great outcry that holiday-makers were being deprived of their amusement.*

There was no doubt that the mob enjoyed public executions, and its mood could become ugly if the pleasure of viewing a hapless victim put to death were interfered with by the authorities. When Basil Montagu had obtained the reprieve of two men sentenced to death in 1801 for sheep-stealing, the High Sheriff of Huntingdon strongly advised him to leave the town as speedily and privately as he could to avoid ill-treatment 'from the disappointment he had occasioned'.[4] Bagehot wrote in 1858 that 'the world of . . . frequent executions . . . is so far removed from us that we cannot comprehend it ever having existed'.[5] However, the world of the reaction of mobs to 'disappointments' from thwarted anticipation at executions had not changed too drastically. An execution mob before Newgate Prison in 1864 reacted with almost the same displeasure expected of the crowds in Huntingdon in 1801. The Newgate mob yelled and hissed at the innovation of black cloth draping on the scaffold, designed to hide all but the 'heads of the culprits . . . after the bolt is drawn'.[6]

Burning at the stake was reserved for women. Although it might appear discriminatory, actually the punishment was considered a mitigation from the disembowelling and quartering meted out to men for counterfeiting and forging coin. Perhaps the mitigating factor was that the tarred, fettered woman was strangled by a chain before the flames reached

* John Laurence, *A History of Capital Punishment*, New York: Citadel Press, 1963, p.60. Laurence quoted a letter Walpole had written to Montague, on 16 August 1746, about the execution of the rebels of 1745: 'I have been this morning at the Tower, and passed under the heads at Temple Bar, where people make a trade of letting spy-glasses at a half-penny a look.' p.35.

her. An additional crime for which women were burned was husband-murder. When Phoebe Harris was burned in 1786 before Newgate Prison, 20,000 persons were present.*

Generally punishment by beheading was performed in public too, although some degree of privacy was given the seven more than usually distinguished prisoners executed in the Tower of London. When Lord Lovat, the last person publicly executed on Tower Hill, was beheaded on 9 April 1747, a scaffolding holding nearly 9,000 onlookers collapsed, killing twelve of them.[7] The axe was used infrequently in England; it was for treason and therefore a form of punishment reserved almost exclusively for the nobility. When Jeremiah Brandreth and two other unemployed insurrectionist weavers were convicted of high treason, aristocratic bias was manifested against them. They were first hanged as common criminals and then beheaded. On Friday 7 November 1817, the three condemned prisoners were dragged on a sledge from their Derby gaol-yard to the gallows where they hung for half an hour. Brandreth was first cut down and his head was placed downward on the block. His executioner, a muscular, masked Derbyshire coal-miner, gave Brandreth one stroke. His assistant, also masked, finished the severance with a knife. The executioner held the head by the hair at arm's length, and called out three times, 'Behold the head of the traitor, Jeremiah Brandreth.'[8] The scaffold was surrounded by a large force of cavalry with drawn swords, and several companies of infantry were also there as a precaution against a demonstration by the densely packed spectators in front of the gaol. The crowd, utterly horrified by the scene, reeled and staggered back several yards, its momentum pressing them against the opposite houses.[9]

The history of Tyburn had been for many years the history of the gallows in London, and it was the most frequently used

* The last sentence of this kind was carried out in 1789. Laurence, op. cit., p.104. England was not alone in committing barbarities against women. Basil Montagu cites information from John Howard, the prison-reformer, that in Sweden women were beheaded on a scaffold, which later was 'set on fire at the four corners, and consumed with the body'. *The Opinions of Different Authors Upon the Punishment of Death*, Vol. I, Longman, Hurst, Rees & Orme, 1809, pp. 247–8.

place for executions in the eighteenth century.* Capital convicts of the City of London and the County of Middlesex were drawn in open carts, pinioned ropes dangling necklace-like from their necks, a distance of two miles from Newgate Gaol to Tyburn. A procession led by the City marshal on horseback, the under-sheriff, a group of peace officers and a body of constables with staves accompanied the convict and his executioner who rode in the open cart. A number of javelin-men brought up the rear. If the criminal was well known, the entourage had two sheriffs in their coaches, each holding his sceptre of office. A halt was made before St Sepulchre's Church where a sexton, with bell in hand, delivered a solemn admonition to the condemned.† Then the great bell of St Sepulchre's boomed forth. Down Snow Hill went the cortège, across Fleet River, up Holborn Hill, where the column stopped before the Crown Inn near St Giles's Pound to allow the prisoner a last drink. The gallows stood between Hyde Park and the end of Edgware Road, where Marble Arch now stands. The gallows was a permanent triangular structure called 'The Triple Tree'. The open cart was placed underneath the gallows, and the prison chaplain, who also had ridden in the open cart, adjured the criminal to repent. After the final prayers were finished, the noose was adjusted, the cap drawn over the convict's head and face, the hangman and his helpers lashed the horse, set the cart in motion and left the criminal dangling in air.[10] The

* Other well-known places of execution in London were Putney Common, Kennington Common, St Thomas a Watering on the Old Kent Road, Execution Dock and Smithfield. Portable gallows were drawn from place to place (Laurence, op. cit. p.171). W. Eden Hooper, *The History of Newgate and the Old Bailey*, London: Underwood Press, 1935, p.111, lists the foot of Bow Street and the Haymarket as other important execution places.

† According to G. T. Crook and John L. Rayner, eds., *The Complete Newgate Calendar*, Vol. IV, London: Navarre Society, 1926, p.325, the bellman of St Sepulchre's repeated the following verse while he rang his bell the night preceding an execution: 'All you that in the condemned hold do lie/Prepare you, for tomorrow you shall die./Watch all and pray, the hour is drawing near/That you before the Almighty must appear./Examine well yourselves, in time repent,/That you may not to eternal flames be sent/And when St Sepulchre's bell tomorrow tolls,/The Lord above have mercy on your souls.'

triangular gallows were taken away in 1759 and new mobile gallows were used. The increasing traffic along both the Edgware and Tyburn roads had made necessary the removal of the triangular gallows as an obstacle.[11]

The last public execution at Tyburn was in 1783; the end had become inevitable. The march to Tyburn from Newgate was increasingly disruptive to traffic and business along its route; often the processions were hindered by unruly crowds along the line of march. Jonathan Wild was pelted with stones and dirt and threatened with every conceivable torture by a furious and vengeful mob. Even when he arrived at Tyburn, the implacable throng threatened to hang the executioner if he failed to speed up Wild's execution.[12] Two thousand troops were deployed in Hyde Park to forestall a suspected rescue-attempt when the Reverend William Dodd was executed for forgery on 27 June 1777.* Execution scenes like these concerned the West End neighbourhood which had become fashionable. The sheriffs were insistent on a change of site. They wished to maintain the essentials of public executions, but they feared that the mounting disorderliness of the pro-cession ritual had destroyed the solemnity of the event. Sir Peter Laurie wrote Croker that the change to Newgate was made by the insistence of the sheriffs 'in consequence of the mischiefs which arose from the long parade of criminals from Tyburn to Newgate'.[13] The change to Newgate was not popu-lar. Dr Johnson grumbled that the age was running over with innovation to such a degree that even Tyburn was no longer safe from its fury.

It is not an improvement; they object that the old method drew together a multitude of spectators. Sir, executions are intended to draw spectators. If they do not draw spectators, they don't answer their purpose.[14]

The first execution at Newgate was on 9 December 1783, and on that day ten persons were hanged on the new gallows, a

* Dodd was well connected, and even Dr Johnson made strenuous efforts on his behalf. There was a widespread rumour that the bribed executioner had placed a silver tube in Dodd's throat. After being cut down, he was rushed to an undertaker in Goodge Street, where two waiting surgeons were going to revive him.

solid structure with two parallel cross-beams. The gallows were kept in a shed in the prison, and were dragged out by horses into the street, just outside of Debtors' Door. Executions there proved no more orderly nor controlled than at Tyburn.

The excitement was so great at the execution of John Holloway and Owen Haggerty on 23 February 1807 that an estimated crowd of 45,000 spectators packed the spaces in front of Newgate Gaol, and all adjacent streets. The pressure of the uncontrolled crowds, and the ensuing panic after many people tried forcefully to shove their way out, caused mass hysteria even before the criminals walked on to the scaffold. People from behind, trying to escape the pressure, trampled over spectators in front. A fierce struggle broke out, everyone fighting to escape the crush. After the bodies were cut down, and the gallows were returned to the gaol-yard, the marshals cleared the streets. There lay nearly one hundred persons on the street, either dead or unconscious. Twenty-seven dead bodies were removed to St Bartholomew's Hospital, four to St Sepulchre's Church, and one to a public house. A cartload of shoes, hats, petticoats and other personal objects were strewn over the road. Neighbouring houses took in many of the injured. The public was barred from St Bartholomew's Hospital until the dead bodies had been stripped, washed and placed around a ward on the first floor. Those admitted went up one side of a centre rail and returned on the other, viewing bodies. The coroner later ruled that the deaths were caused by 'compression and suffocation'.[15]

Few gentlemen had been executed since the execution of the Reverend William Dodd in 1777. It is little wonder that Henry Fauntleroy's trial created a sensation in the press. And the evidence of how the banker had swindled the Bank of England of more than £250,000 and the disclosure that Fauntleroy had lived a double life with country homes and a succession of mistresses only added to the intense interest in the case. He had become such an object of curiosity that on Sunday 28 November 1824, two days before his execution, and two hours before the traditional death service in Newgate chapel, a large group of people queued up at the entrance. They were accommodated by the sheriff, anxious to please. An

overflowing crowd of spectators was placed in the public
gallery immediately opposite the condemned Fauntleroy, who
sat in a pew with an entourage of five gentlemen.[16] One newspaper regarded the attendance of the public at the service in
the chapel of Newgate as 'little less disgusting than being
present in the last moments of persons suffering the last ex-
tremity of the law'.[17] His well-publicized career, his position
in society and the tenacious rumour that he would be snatched
from death by a plot drew an estimated crowd of 100,000: a
human chain stretching as a compact mass from Smithfield
to Ludgate Hill.[18] Bookings had been made in advance for
seats in the houses overlooking Debtors' Door. Fourteen
shillings was charged for a place at the 'King of Denmark', but
Luttman's, an eating-house just opposite the drop, charged £1
for its better location. Despite the huge audience, the belief
that a gentleman would not be hanged like a common criminal
at the hands of a hangman continued. A rumour persisted for
many years that Fauntleroy had been resuscitated by surgeons and lived for a long time afterwards on the Continent.[19]

François Courvoisier was another capitally convicted criminal whose service for the condemned at Newgate attracted a
large number of persons, including lords, ladies and Members
of the House of Commons. He was a Swiss butler who had
murdered his master, Lord William Russell, the uncle of Lord
John Russell. So large was the demand to attend the service
at Newgate chapel that the sheriffs were forced to issue tickets
of admission.[20] Six hundred noblemen and gentlemen were
admitted by the sheriff's order into Newgate Prison on the day
of the execution, 6 July 1840.[21] Charles Dickens, Henry
Burnett, Dickens's brother-in-law, and Maclise, the painter,
had rented a room. Dickens saw Thackeray standing below
among the crowd, and he shouted, 'Why, there stands
Thackeray!'[22] However, their attempts to get Thackeray's
attention failed.

Thackeray had come with Monckton Milnes, who had recently voted in favour of William Ewart's motion in the
House of Commons to abolish capital punishment. Milnes was
anxious to observe the reaction of the crowd, but Thackeray
was so disturbed by the entire spectacle that he was unable to

work for days, and was extremely compulsive in recalling all of the disturbing details of the execution.* It was as though the article he wrote on the execution was an act of exorcism; afterwards he never again alluded to this or any other execution. 'Courvoisier . . . walked very firmly,' he wrote.

He was dressed in a new black suit . . . His shirt was open. His arms were tied in front of him. He opened his hands in a helpless kind of way, and clasped them once or twice together. He turned his head here and there and looked about him for an instant with a wild, imploring look. His mouth was contracted into a sort of pitiful smile. He went and placed himself under the beam, with his face toward St Sepulchre's . . . The tall, grave man in black twisted him around swiftly in the other direction, and drawing from his pocket a nightcap, pulled it lightly over the patient Courvoisier's head and face. I am not ashamed to say that I could look no more, but shut my eyes as the last dreadful act was going on, which sent this wretched, guilty soul into the presence of God.[23]

The execution of Maria and Frederick Manning on 13 November 1849, at Horsemonger Lane Gaol, was the first husband-and-wife execution since 1700. Aside from the circumstance of a heinous murder of a friend for his money and bonds, Maria Manning captured the public's imagination. She was a strong-willed, passionate Belgian, who led her weak, indecisive husband into committing murder, and she persisted during the trial in interrupting the court proceedings with such utterances as 'There is no law and justice to be gathered here! Base and degraded England!'[24] Because Mrs Manning was a foreigner, English insularity and prejudice produced a bias against her, but her continued outbursts against English justice intensified public hostility and vindictiveness. One written account referred to her as 'the female prisoner who spoke in quite a foreign accent'.[25] A correspondent to *The Times* wrote to thank God she wasn't an Englishwoman.

* Early in July 1840 Thackeray had written a letter in reference to the execution: 'I have been to see Courvoisier hanged, am miserable ever since. I can't do any work . . . It is most curious the effect his death has on me . . . Meanwhile it weighs upon the mind, like cold pudding on the stomach.' Gordon N. Ray, ed., *The Letters and Private Papers of William Makepeace Thackeray*, Vol. I, Oxford University Press, 1945–6, p.453.

For days before the execution of the Mannings the neighbourhood of Horsemonger Lane Gaol presented the appearance of a fair, with large, excited crowds congregating there. On Sunday throngs of people poured unceasingly towards the gaol. Platforms were put up by enterprising people who charged for a better view of the execution. The authorities, however, took a dim view of the flimsy platforms run up in every direction with no regard for safety. Many of the more dangerous were removed, and barriers were put in their places. Additional barriers were set up in the area before the gallows in further effort to control the mob's movements and as a safeguard against rioting and injuries. Despite these precautions, and 500 police in position, Catherine Read, aged thirty, was crushed against the wood barriers, and suffered a fatal rupture of a blood-vessel near the spleen.* Notwithstanding the interference of the magistrate and the efforts of the police to remove the frail scaffolding the proprietors of these stands were busy throughout the night soliciting the patronage of every decently dressed person who passed by. They chanted the praises of the 'splendid view of the scene that was to be had from them',[26] and they reassured potential patrons of the strength, security and cheapness of a place on one of these structures. The men and women standing on them, safely out of physical contact with the masses, over whose heads they could view the proceedings, had paid the exorbitant price of two or three guineas. These more respectable parts of the assemblage, who had come from the fashionable clubs of the West End, watched the Mannings' final writhings with binoculars.†

* *The Times*, 16 November 1849, p.6. Despite her death the police arrangements at Horsemonger Lane Gaol were superior to those at Newgate. A chief inspector of the police testified that 'the mob has it all in their own way ... people are allowed to occupy ... pens erected in the streets without any control whatsoever ... at Horsemonger-lane the crowd is never allowed to congregate so densely'. *Parliamentary Papers*, Report of the Capital Punishment Commission, Vol. xxi, Cmnd 3590, 1866, p.110.

† *Daily News*, 14 November 1849, p.5. 'As regards the matter of opera glasses,' wrote a correspondent to *The Times*, 'unless the art of witnessing an execution is proved to be discreditable and bad in itself, it is

All arrangements had been completed on the Monday evening, in ample time for the immense streams of people – men,
women and children – who began pouring towards the place
of execution, and this stream of humanity flowed until the
morning sun was well up in the sky. The sea of upturned faces,
all gazing at the scaffold, numbered perhaps 30,000 persons,
although the official figure was far larger than that. Among
them

were the dregs and scourings of the population of London ... the
'navvy' and Irish labourer ... mizzy with beer, pickpockets plying their light-fingered art,* little ragged boys climbing up posts
... In an instant Calcraft withdrew the bolt, the drop fell ...
They died almost without a struggle ... The mob during the
terrible scene exhibited no feeling except one of heartless indifference and levity.[27]

Dickens, who attended the execution of the Mannings and
later used Maria Manning as the model for Hortense, the
murderous Frenchwoman in *Bleak House*, had faired far
better than those on the platforms. He, with four others, had
taken the whole roof and the back kitchen of a house overlooking the gallows for the moderate sum of ten guineas, or
two guineas each.[28] The next day he wrote a powerful letter
to *The Times* condemning the spectacles of public executions. His biographer attributed to this letter the commence-
ment of 'the active agitation against public executions'.[29]
Whether or not this was so, it did become an important
and effective addition to the body of anti-public-execution
literature.

Franz Müller, the first person believed to have committed a

mere trifling to condemn people for employing the best means they can
to enable them to see plainly what they have come to see.' 19 November 1849.

---

* Pickpockets 'plying their light-fingered art' was an old tradition.
The preamble to a law enacted during Elizabeth I's reign read as follows:
'Whereas, persons in contempt of God's commands, and in defiance of
the law, are found to cut pockets, and pick purses, even at places of
public execution, while execution is being done on criminals. Be it therefore enacted that all such persons shall suffer death without benefit of
clergy.' *Eclectic Review*, Vol. LXXXVIII, August 1848, p.146.

LIFE OF THE MANNINGS

EXECUTED AT HORSEMONGER LANE GOAL
ON TUESDAY 13th NOV

SEE the scaffold it is mounted,
And the doomed ones do appear,
Seemingly borne wan with sorrow,
Grief and anguish, care and pain.
They cried the moments is approaching,
when we togather must leave this life,
And no one has the least compassion,
On Frederick Manning and his wife.

Maria Manning came from Sweden,
Brought up respectable we hear,
And Frederick Manning came from Taunton
In the county of Somersetshire.
Maria lived with noble ladies,
In ease, and splendour, and delight,
But on one sad and fatal morning,
She was made Frederick Mannings wife.

She first was courted by O'Connor,
Who was a lover most sincere,
He was possessed of wealth and riches,
And loved Maria Roux most dear.
But she preferred her present husband,
As it appeared, and with delight,
Slighted sore Patrick O'Connor,
And was made Frederick Manning's wife.

And when O'Connor knew the story,
Down his cheeks rolled floods of tears,
He beat his breast, and wept in sorrow,
Wrung his hands and tore his hair,
Maria dear how could you leave me,
Wretched you have made my life,
Tell me why you did deceive me,
For to be Frederick Manning's wife.

At length they all were reconciled,
And met together night and day,
Maria by O'Connor's riches,
Dressed in splendour fine and gay.

Though married yet she corosponded
With O'Conner all was right,
And oft he went to see Maria
Frederick Manning's lawful wife.

At length they plann'd their friend to murder
And for his company did crave,
The dreadful weapons they prepared,
And in the kitchen dug his grave.
And as they fondly did caress him,
They slew him—what a dreadful sight,
First they mangled, after robbed him,
Frederick Manning and his wife.

They absconded, but was apprehended,
And for the cruel deed was tried,
When placed at the bar of Newgate,
They both the crime strongly denied,
At length the jury them convicted,
And doomed them for to leave this life,
The judge pronounced the awful sentence,
On Frederick Manning and his wife.

Return he said to whence they brought you
Arom thence unto the fatal tree,
Find there together be suspended,
Where multitudes your fate may see,
Your hours recollect is numbered,
You betrayed a friend and took his life,
For such there's not one spark of pity,
As Frederick Manning and his wife.

See what numbers are approaching,
To Horsemonger's fatal tree,
Full of bloom in health and vigour,
What a dreadful sight to see.
Old and young pray take a warning,
Females lead a virtuous life,
Think upon that fatal morning,
Frederick Manning and his wife.

HODGES, Printer, (from PITT's) Wholesale Marble Warehouse, 31, Dudley Street, 7 Dials.

'Life of the Mannings – Executed at Horsemonger Lane Gaol'. Broadside from 'Murders – Broadsides and Ballads'. The stock execution scene has been altered by the inclusion of a very crude female figure.

murder on a train, and the first person arrested by use of the Atlantic cable, after he had fled to the United States, was executed on 14 November 1864.[30] He was a quiet young German without any previous record, and he steadfastly maintained his innocence. As a foreigner, like Courvoisier and Maria Manning, his case excited a natural national antagonism which was further exacerbated by the intervention of the German Protection Society, a German organization in England. This society exerted pressure on the Home Office by sponsoring public meetings, delegations to the Home Secretary and petitions to obtain a respite for Müller. It solicited the aid of German rulers to bring diplomatic pressure on the English government. The Duke of Saxe-Weimer telegraphed his consul to make further inquiries about the case; the Duke of Saxe-Coburg and the King of Prussia sent telegrams to Queen Victoria, beseeching her to postpone Müller's execution. The more aggressive the efforts to postpone the execution, the greater became the anti-Müller sentiment in England.*

The sensational crime, the escape and recapture of Müller, the question of a fair trial and foreign and domestic pressures on the condemned's behalf were factors expected to attract a huge crowd to the execution. Barriers to check the crowd were placed across all the main thoroughfares leading to Newgate as early as the Friday, and all through Friday night, Saturday and Sunday a crowd of dirty vagrants hovered around them. Until three o'clock Sunday morning rival factions competed with songs, laughter and shouting; the mood

* *Morning Star*, 14 November 1864. In its leading article on 1 December 1864 *The Times* spoke for English resentment against foreign interference and imputations against English justice: 'A number of these foreigners . . . anxious to show the strength of these organizations . . . set to work to save Müller by any means, and . . . chose to work not only on the Home Office, but on Continental Governments . . . The conduct of the King of Prussia to demand a respite for Müller on the ground that the evidence for the defence had not been heard was a piece of most offensive and insolent presumption . . . Can anything show more the ill effects of their proceedings? For more than a week or two the German papers were raving about England, which had murdered Müller in revenge for a political defeat on the Danish question.'

was ribald, half-drunken and gay. At about three o'clock
Monday morning workmen had come to finish the last barrier,
the gallows having been put in place next to the Debtors'
Door. A crowd of between 4,000 and 5,000 began to fill the
space in front of Newgate. The space between the gaol and the
buildings facing it had been barricaded and partitioned into
immense pens. St Sepulchre's Church was boarded up to a
considerable height to prevent the expected huge crowd from
overflowing into its churchyard. Most of the shop-fronts in the
Old Bailey area were boarded. The crowd began to increase
enormously between six and seven o'clock in the morning, and
continued to grow until the time of the execution. Groups of
men, boys, women, girls and children hurried along the avenues
to the Old Bailey, cabs rattled along and costermongers, their
carts filled with 'cheering, jeering ruffians',[31] raced to the
execution scene.

Müller's minister, Dr Cappel of the German Lutheran
Church, was compelled to complain to the authorities about 'a
cruel and crying evil in Newgate. Again and again on Monday
morning in those last solemn moments our prayers were
interrupted by the savage yells of the multitude assembled to
witness the execution.'[32] During the night the noise of the
hammers raising the scaffold had penetrated into the gaol
cells, and each prisoner knew when the procession with the
pinioned convict was on its way to the press-yard and to the
scaffold. The great bell of Newgate tolled mournfully, like a
church bell during a funeral. As Müller walked through Debtors' Door and on to the scaffold, shouts of 'Hats off!' reverberated through the crowd. The command was not out of
respect for the soon-to-be-dead Müller, but an impatient
demand from those in the rear wanting an unobstructed view.
The crowd of 50,000 again extended from Ludgate Hill
to Smithfield. They had whiled away the hours in rough
play: plucking hats from the well-dressed, robbing them
and tossing hats to raucous laughter. At the appearance of
Müller, however, all gave their undivided attention to the
scaffold.

While the executioner was adjusting the noose, Müller spoke
quietly to Dr Cappel. With lowered head he said, '*Ich habe es*

gethan.'* Thus was English justice vindicated. And when the tolling of Newgate Gaol bell stopped, all the prisoners within knew that Müller was in the agony of death, and that for an hour the body would remain hanging in the street. 'Generally the execution is immediately followed by violent language, threats, brutal oaths, and other savage expressions ... two hours after execution, the prisoners in Newgate have resumed their ordinary pursuits and demeanour.'†

Not since the public hanging and decapitation of Arthur Thistlewood and his four accomplices of the so-called Cato Street Conspiracy on 1 May 1820 had there been an execution of five people at one time. On Monday 22 February 1864 a huge London throng came to see the execution of the 'Five Pirates', the mutineers who had murdered the captain and five crew-members of the ship *Flowery Land* en route to Singapore.‡ From sundown on the Sunday night hundreds had gathered in the pens before the Old Bailey. It was bitterly cold, and the public houses, open after five o'clock, irresistibly invited the many who had begun to congregate. Throngs kept pouring in from

the slums of Southwark, the dens of St Giles, the sinks of Somerstown, and the purlieus of Whitechapel. Costermongers rubbed shoulders with dapper clerks and shopboys ... Hot-potato-men cried aloud, and persons with greasy trays invited the public to buy still more greasy pastry. Roughs reviled each other at safe

* *The Times*, 15 November 1864, p.8. Besides the need for a confession of guilt, whether a criminal died penitent was of great issue in Victorian England. It had been recommended that in a suggested reform, criminals dying impenitent could not be buried in Church ground. *Parliamentary Papers*, Report from the Select Committee of the House of Lords, Vol. VII, 1856, p.3.

† Edward G. Wakefield, *Facts Relating to the Punishment of Death in the Metropolis*, London, 1832, pp. 184–5. Presumably prisoners in 1864 still reacted to an execution of one of their own as they did in Wakefield's time.

‡ Their execution at Newgate rather than at Execution Dock was based on 4 & 5, William IV, c. 36, sec. 32, that 'crimes committed on the high seas are to be tried at the Central Criminal Court'. 'This statute accounts for the execution in the City of London.' *Morning Herald*, 23 February 1864, p.4.

distance and bedraggled women in gaudy rags pushed about with more than masculine effrontery.[33]

While there was yet an hour remaining to the usually quiet English Sunday, four to five thousand persons had collected in the space before Debtors' Door. With each waning hour, as Sunday faded, more additions to the crowd increased 'the blasphemy from the roughs'.[34] A few minutes before three o'clock Monday morning, the cry was raised, 'Here it comes!' Then the yelling was shrill, while the base of the scaffold was dragged out by a team of horses. Hooting, cat-calls and other oaths greeted the men employed to put up the gallows.

From the illuminated windows of the houses facing Newgate the commotion was almost equal. Here the well-to-do, well-dressed men had rented rooms with a commanding view of the gallows. They had been amusing themselves by smoking, drinking, laughing and playing whist or escarte to pass the tedious hours.[35] It had been 'whispered at the clubs' several days before the execution that parties were being formed. On the Sunday night at several West End clubs fowls, hams, tongues, sandwiches, liquors, champagne, sherry and cigars were ready.[36] At the same time these delicacies were being savoured, the other England was patronizing a penny-ice shop in Newgate Street which was doing 'a roaring trade in muddy coffee and sticky cakes'.[37]

Occasionally the 'swells' would open their windows and banter with the mob below; the mob answered with cries of contempt. The occupants of the rooms could observe on the pavement beneath gangs of ruffians hustling and robbing any-one who appeared to be moderately respectable. 'Black, black', was the signal, and in a moment the victim was 'surrounded, hustled, divested of all his valuables, and sent hatless and coatless away. If he resisted he was beaten; if he cried out he was garrotted.'*

The owners of many of the tenements were not content to advertise their window seats by canvassers, to whom they gave

---

* *Daily News*, 23 February 1864, p.5. 'The crowd as an execution crowd was perhaps more orderly than usual.' *Morning Advertiser*, 22 February 1864, p.6.

liberal commissions. They placarded windows with such announcements as 'Seats to Let', 'Good View of the Execution'.[38] Prices ranged from ten shillings to one guinea for a single seat, and the number packed into a room was determined by the conscience of the tenant. Each family, trying to capitalize fully on the execution, had its own tout who yelled, cajoled and bargained with potential patrons. Disputes broke out between vying touts as each tried to ween business from the other by lauding the view and the fairness of the price of their respective premises. The seat-buyers took advantage of the competition, inspected and rejected rooms on the basis of cost, location and numbers in the room.

By four o'clock the scaffold was nearly ready, the lower part covered by a screen of black cloth; this proved very unpopular with the mob. The vendors increased in number and volume of noise, and the shouts of men hawking chestnuts vied with the bawling of the orange-sellers.* Between four and five o'clock 330 policemen, seven inspectors and thirty-seven sergeants of the City police force were stationed near the scaffold under the command of the chief inspector. The City of London police were aided by 800 of the metropolitan police assisted by four superintendents, and a large number of mounted police, under the command of the City police commissioner.[39]

The police stood shoulder-to-shoulder around the gallows to keep the crowd from pressing forward. The metropolitan police, meanwhile, kept open the roads leading to Newgate. Constables in pairs prevented loitering and saw that people who wished to go into the pens were passed along to police appointed for the purpose of packing them in. The crowds

seemed to hold in wholesome respect ... the few members of the city police force ... and when a policeman ordered a few hundreds of them to do this or that they obeyed, and called the constable 'Sir' while they did it.[40]

* 'There were about 23,000 costermongers in London at this time. The costermonger was a peddler who sold vegetables, fruits, game, fowl, ginger beer, nuts. Any merchandise found on barrows and wagons of London peddlers; those hawking these commodities are called by the generic term "costermonger".' Daniel J. Kirwan, *Palace and Hovel*, London: Abelard-Schuman, 1963, published originally in 1870, p.41.

The excellent, well-organized police maintained extraordinary civility under trying conditions. The well-placed pens prevented accidents despite the crush of numbers; in fact, 'there were only two slight accidents, scarcely worthy of notice'.[41]

After six o'clock the crowd grew with increasing rapidity. The Metropolitan Underground Railway and omnibuses incessantly discharged their successive loads of passengers throughout the day. A number of members of the Religious Tract Society mingled among the spectators, inveighing against sin. They distributed tracts in every direction, and some of them succeeded in organizing little knots of people, whose prayers and hymns were drowned out by the cursing mob. Shortly after, at seven o'clock, Calcraft, the executioner, appeared on the scaffold to see the arrangements.

His entrée was hailed with a kind of familiar but suppressed hum of recognition from those in front of the gallows, which was returned by a slight bow and a smile of strange and sinister character. After a close scrutiny of the flooring of the scaffold, and the mechanism of the drop, he quickly retired.[42]

Mr Jonas, the governor of Newgate, the sheriffs and under-sheriffs, accompanied by reporters permitted to hear what took place, went to the cells of the condemned criminals shortly before eight o'clock. Calcraft pinioned each man separately with a harness-like device secured by black leather straps with thongs and buckles. As each man was pinioned he was returned to his cell. Then each prisoner was brought out of his cell, placed between warders and lined up to form a procession. The under-sheriffs led the way, followed by the sheriffs and a dozen other officials and spectators, two by two. They passed from the Sessions House down steps into the courtyard of Newgate, where the roar of the crowd was deafening. They passed through narrow passage-ways; one, a dim, close alley, was the burying place. Here the corpses were thrown naked into graves full of lime, and covered by pavement blocks. Arthur Thistlewood and companions were buried at the opposite end of the alley from where the remains of the 'Five Pirates' were to rest.[43]

The densely packed crowds were hushed; all eyes were on

the Debtors' Door through which the prisoners would walk
one by one to face the now anxious spectators, waiting on tip-
toe. Brief, subdued speculations about the scaffold behaviour
of each criminal broke the tense silence. The windows in the
surrounding houses were filled with eager, expectant faces.[44]
The eaves and roofs of the adjacent houses, the chimney-pots,
and even their spouts had people clinging to them. Round
about the gallows were impatient, well-dressed men pacing
about in comparative comfort in a 'well-kept space . . . much
as members of the Jockey Club'.[45]

The procession had finally reached the press-yard, and
before being taken to the gallows the prisoners were allowed
to rest on a bench. Their strength failed them, and they were
given some brandy. As soon as St Sepulchre's Church clock
struck eight, the Newgate bell began to toll. Blanco was the
first to walk through the black-draped passage into the open.
'Hats off! Hats off! They are coming!' shouted members of
the crowd. Then 'the groans and hisses that arose from the
mob were tremendous'.[46] Blanco collapsed on the scaffold,
but was caught and supported by Calcraft and his assistants.
A chair was immediately obtained, and the prisoner was
seated on it while the rope was fixed around his neck. He was
hanged in that position, the chair falling from under him
when the drop fell.

Lopez, who had danced out of the dock at the trial, was put
on the scaffold last. He nodded and laughed at the crowd, and
they cheered him.[47] Then a buzz ran through the crowd and
after a short interval the mob began to disperse. A costermonger was overheard to tell another, 'So help me, Bill, ain't
it fine; five of them and all darkies.'*

The sheriffs and other officials then returned to the reception room where they sat down to breakfast with the priests
who had attended the prisoners. At nine o'clock the sheriffs
were summoned to witness the cutting-down of the bodies and
to be present at the certification of the surgeon that the condemned 'could never slay or sin again'.[48] At three o'clock the

---

* *Parliamentary Papers*, Report of the Capital Punishment Commission, Vol. XXI, 1866, p. 111. Four of the pirates were natives of Manilla
and one was Levantine.

'Five Pirates' were placed beneath the pavement without any ceremony.

Although Newgate was the publicized focal-point for executions in England, public executions in provincial assize towns rivalled London in numbers of spectators.* These crowds had a similar cross-section of the morbid, the curious, the criminal and the sadistic. The country people's zest for executions was just as keen as those in London, and on Monday, market-day, they would throng into the towns from the outlying rural area.† The town took on the festive air of a local holiday fair. Archdeacon Bickersteth gave evidence in 1856 before the Select Committee of the House of Lords, declaring that at a public execution in Shrewsbury in 1841

the town was concerted for a day into a fair. The country people flocked in their holiday dresses, and the whole town was a scene of drunkenness and debauchery of every kind . . . Children and females contributed to the larger portion of the attendance.[49]

And when four persons were hanged at Liverpool, the railways advertised excursion trains 'or parties of pleasure' from the manufacturing towns.[50]

Executions in the provincial towns were as fraught with hazards to the spectators as those in front of Newgate. Twelve people, mostly women and children, were crushed and trampled to death in Nottingham on 7 August 1844. The Mayor of Nottingham wrote to Sir James Graham, the Secretary for the Home Office:

It is right that I should immediately inform you of a most calamitous occurrence which has taken place in Nottingham today . . . The case has excited extreme interest, and a vast crowd was assembled early in the morning to see the execution . . . It was no sooner over than a tremendous rush of the multitude was made

* In 1856 an estimated 50,000 persons attended the execution of Dr William Palmer, the notorious poisoner, in Stafford. *Morning Star*, 16 June 1856, p.6.

† 'Why was market day usually fixed upon? Under the impression that it leads to a large number of persons being present and that the spectacle will have a deterring effect?' . . . 'Yes,' replied Mr Barber, governor of Winchester Gaol. *Parliamentary Papers*, Report from the Select Committee of the House of Lords, Vol. vii, 1856, p. 23.

from the scaffold down the High Pavement Street. A confusion excited by mischievous persons throwing hats, shoes about originated the general desire to escape from the overpowering pressure. Numbers of persons were thrown down, run over, and trodden upon. The shrieks and cries of the sufferers are beyond description. Altogether it was a most appalling sight.*

Factory hands in Glasgow, disgorged early by their employers, were at the place of execution, swearing and saturated with ale. The lower class of mechanics, mobs of dirty men and tattered women were hurrying at an early hour to the execution. They might have been an unruly mob packed into Newgate Street like cattle going to market, but on this day it was the salt market, wedged full of profane people. The scaffold was set in Gaol Square, not before Newgate Gaol. And little children pulling their mothers by the hand 'to gang awa''[51] and see the sight spoke broad Scots, not Cockney. The execution was in Glasgow in 1853, but it could have been in London.

The art of the executioner was performed in public before multitudes. The minutiae of his skill with the noose, his handling of the criminals on the scaffold, his appearance and conduct at executions were subjects for journals and the press. He was a public celebrity, a recognizable personality. Whether reviled or fawned-over, he was an institutional figure in nineteenth-century England. Perhaps cognizance of the importance of the executioner's role in society was manifested by the solemn ritual of his investiture as public executioner. Calcraft's years of service, from 1829 to 1874, bridged the change from public to private executions. He was sworn into office by the City Recorder of London, assisted by the Lord Mayor, the aldermen of the City and the javelin-men dressed in their liveries.[52]

The wage of an executioner was by no means handsome, but by nineteenth-century standards it was above that of the

* Public Record Office, Home Office 45, No. 05861. Thomas Beggs gave a figure of sixteen or seventeen dead, and fifty or sixty maimed for life. He also suggested that the panic 'was created by a body of pickpockets from Derby'. *The Royal Commission and the Punishment of Death*, London: Society for the Abolition of Capital Punishment, 1866, pp.10–11.

average worker, and just a little below the minimum annual income of the lower middle class.[53] Calcraft, who was also a cobbler, received £50 a year, additional fees of half-a-crown for every man he flogged, and an allowance for birch rods. In addition, he received a retaining fee of five guineas as executioner at Horsemonger Lane Gaol, and the usual guinea for each execution. He was permitted, in addition, to perform executions elsewhere in England for £10 on each occasion.[54] By selling the criminal's clothing and belongings to exhibitions such as Madame Tussaud's he could further supplement his income. The rope with which he hanged the criminal could be sold for as much as five shillings an inch, depending on the notoriety of the criminal. Moreover, he was probably paid to allow superstitious persons to cure skin lesions by touching the hand of a hanged man.*

That most of those he hanged seemed to have been 'violently convulsed' for several moments after he released the trap door indicated that Calcraft was not a skilful practitioner of his art. This ineptness was attributed primarily to his use of a 'short drop'. One performance which gained him considerable criticism and odium was the execution of William Bousfield on 31 March 1856.

Bousfield had to be carried to the scaffold, his face swathed in cloth after he had placed it in the fire in his cell before the turnkey dragged him off. In this state he was seated on a chair above the drop, while Calcraft, frightened by a letter threatening to shoot him on the scaffold, hastily adjusted the cap and rope. Then the executioner ran down the steps, drew the bolt and disappeared. Bousfield, after hanging motionless for a second or two, drew himself up with astonishing strength and rested his foot on the drop. One of the turnkeys rushed forward and pushed him off again, but he succeeded once again to obtain a foothold. The chaplain forced the frightened Cal-

* Laurence, op. cit., pp.111–12. Gathorne Hardy, Secretary of State for the Home Office, while a boy at Shrewsbury saw a man hanged for sheep-stealing and unlawful wounding, and a crowd of people waiting to be touched by the 'dead hand' as a cure for warts. A. E. Gathorne-Hardy, ed., *Gathorne Hardy, First Earl of Cranbrook: A Memoir*, Vol. I, Longman & Co., 1910, p.22.

craft to return. Four times Bousfield raised himself and gained a foothold. The last time he was thrust off; Calcraft threw himself on the suspended Bousfield and mainly by strength and his weight, he strangled him at last.[55]

This dreadful scene produced a profound impression throughout the country. The advocates of the abolition of capital punishment dwelt on the horror of the exhibition. Others appealed to it as an argument in favour of execution within the precincts of the prison.[56]

In addition to the newspaper and magazine accounts of crimes and executions, these events had a literature of their own. These were the penny broadsides, the 'gallows literature' hawked at executions by street patterers. The printers and publishers, despite the cheapness of the broadsides and the low rate of 3d. per dozen to the street patterers, made a good profit by selling them in huge quantities. The Catnach Press, one of the leading printers of cheap literature, sold almost 2,500,000 broadsides of the Mannings' execution.[57]

The contents of the broadsides published by the Catnach Press, printers also of sensational scandals, murders and robberies, were repetitious. There were the usual 'sorrowful lamentations' which the criminal supposedly composed in his condemned-cell before his execution. The street patterers urged the execution crowds to read the criminal's own statement written 'from the depths of the condemned cell with the condemned ink and paper'.[58] The street patterers always claimed that the woodcut was the exact likeness of the murderer, taken 'at the bar of the Old Bailey by an eminent artist!'[59] The 'exact likeness' was probably an old woodcut that had been used for many years.

The last dying speech and confession, too, were staples of the 'gallows literature', and whether the criminal was illiterate or semi-illiterate, the publishers were not deterred from publishing cliché-ridden statements. Robert Peat, a farmer executed at Durham, wrote

I am about to undergo the dreadful sentence of the law, to suffer an ignominious and horrible death, to pass from the wicked, delusive and transitory world to the Realms where through God's infinite mercy, I hope to find eternal rest.[60]

THE EXECUTION AND CONFESSION OF

FRANZ MULLER,

For the Murder of Mr. BRIGGS, November 14th, 1864.

At two o'clock on Saturday afternoon Sir George Grey returned an answer to the memorial presented to him, praying for a respite of the convict Muller, by the German Legal Protection Society. Previous to the delivery of his decision he had a long conversation with the Lord Chief Baron Pollock and Mr. Baron Martin, which terminated in his arriving at the conclusion that the memorial did not warrant his interfering with the verdict of the jury.

Immediately upon the receipt of the letter, Mr. Beard, with Alderman Wilson, proceeded to communicate to Muller the result of the efforts that had been made on his behalf. They were received by Mr. Jonas, the governor of Newgate, who conducted them to the condemned cell. They found the prisoner engaged in writing. He immediately rose, and extended his hand to Mr. Beard, who asked him how he was. The convict said, "I am very well." Mr. Jonas then informed the prisoner of the efforts that had been made to save his life, and that Mr. Beard had just received a reply from the Secretary of State, which he read to him. At the conclusion the convict said, in a low voice, "I did not expect anything else." Mr. Beard then said to the prisoner, "Did you know that any efforts had been made on your behalf?" The prisoner replied, "Yes, I did think so." Mr. Beard then said, "Have you any statement that you wish to make?" The prisoner, "No, nothing." "Because," continued Mr. Beard, "now that all has been done that can be done for you, and there is no hope in this world, if you have anything to acknowledge, you had better do so." In reply to this Muller said, "I should be a very bad fellow if I had done it. I have no other statement to make than that which I have already made." Mr. Beard then asked him if he had made his peace with God. The prisoner said, "Yes;" and in every respect appeared resigned to his fate. Mr. Beard then shook hands with him, and said, "Good-bye Muller; God bless you;" The prisoner returned the pressure of his hand, and was left to himself.

The prisoner on Sunday attended Divine service in the chapel, both in the morning and the afternoon, and listened apparently with deep attention to the discourse delivered by the Rev. Mr. Davis, the Ordinary. He was visited in the evening by Dr. Walbaum and Dr. Cappell.

PREPARATIONS FOR THE EXECUTION.

Up to Sunday night Muller preserved the same quiet, firm demeanour, and although he occupied some of his time in writing, he did not lie down till considerably after his usual time, and slept but little. He rose at five o'clock on Monday in good spirits, and was soon afterwards joined by the Rev. Mr. Davis, the chaplain of the gaol, and the Rev. Mr. Walbaum. He in every respect appeared calm and resigned to meet his fate. He joined devoutly in prayer with the rev. gentleman, and otherwise conducted himself in a manner becoming his awful position. A little before seven o'clock he was visited by Mr. Jonas, the governor of the gaol, to whom he extended his hand, and feelingly thanked him for the kind attention he had received since his incarceration. Calcraft arrived at six, but was not recognised by the mob, and thus escaped the usual hooting.

Although the fixing of the scaffold was completed by four o'clock, still the clang of hammers in putting up barriers continued till day had dawned.

At five o'clock a heavy drenching rain set in, which had the effect of driving the majority of those who during the night had taken up positions, from their strongholds, and to hastily beat a retreat to the now open public-houses and coffee-shops, as well as to other places offering anything like shelter. At this time there could not have been more than five hundred people actually upon the scene. But at six o'clock the rain abated, and from this time the crowd was recruited by an increasing flow of new comers.

At six o'clock the main body of police, under Mr. Inspector Duddy, was stationed at the approaches to, and in the Old Bailey, and preserved throughout the morning in the strictest order.

Soon after seven o'clock, Mr. Alderman and Sheriff Besley, Mr.

Alderman and Sheriff Dakin, and the Under Sheriffs, Messrs. Davidson and De Jersey, arrived at the Sessions House, where they remained until summoned to the prison by the governor. About twenty minutes to eight they were informed that the condemned man would soon leave his cell. Upon receiving this intimation these officials left the Sessions House. A few minutes after this, the procession reached the door which opens into the chapel-yard. Here they awaited the arrival of the culprit.

THE EXECUTION.

While the officials were on their way from the Sessions House to this spot, Mr. Jonas had gone to the cell of the prisoner, and informed him that it was time for him to leave. The prisoner, who was deadly pale, trembled with emotion, but sought to bear the awful announcement with all the fortitude possible. He rose up, shook hands with the gaolers who had been principally with him since his incarceration, and with a firm and rather quick step left his cell, accompanied by Mr. Jonas, followed by two or three other officials. As soon as they left the cell the shouts and cries of "They are coming," "They are coming," "Hats off." At this moment the most intense excitement and confusion prevailed, in the midst of which terrible din reverberated the echoes of the solemn knell, which, from its increased rapid tolling, indicated that the mournful procession had gained the steps of the hideous, cloth-draped gibbet. A moment afterwards Calcraft, the hangman, made his appearance on the scaffold, and then withdrew to see that all was right. He had no sooner disappeared than Muller, accompanied by the Rev. J. Davis, chaplain, and Dr. Cappell, followed by other officials, made his appearance. This was a signal for the renewed excitement and clamour of the swerving multitude, who had largely, and as it were imperceptibly increased, and whose up-turned anxious faces met the gaze at all points.

The culprit ascended the scaffold with a firm step, and placed himself under the drop. He cast his eyes once up towards the beam, and his lips quivered with emotion, but this he evidently sought to check. After the cap had been drawn over his head and the rope put round his neck, Dr. Cappell took hold of his hand and again prayed with him. This he did for some minutes, and concluded by addressing the following words to the now fast dying man:—"In a few moments you will be before your God. I ask you, for the last time, are you innocent or guilty?"

Muller: I am innocent.

Dr. Cappell: You are innocent?

Muller: God Almighty knows what I have done.

Dr. Cappell: Does God know that you have done this deed?

Muller was silent.

Dr. Cappell: I ask you now, solemnly, and for the last time, have you committed this crime?

Muller: Yes, I HAVE DONE IT.

Almost at the same instant, and while the words were upon the lips of the wretched man, the drop fell, and Muller died without a struggle.

Dr. Cappell nearly fainted.

Immediately after the execution the sheriffs despatched a communication to Sir George Grey, informing him that the culprit had confessed. A similar communication was made to Sir R. Mayne, at Scotland-yard.

The following despatch was immediately after the execution forwarded to the Home Secretary:—

"Gaol of Newgate, 14th day of November, 1864.

"To the Right Hon. Sir George Grey, Bart.

"Sir,—By direction of the sheriffs I have the honour to acquaint you that the prisoner Muller has at the last moment, just before the drop fell, confessed to the German minister of religion attending him that he was guilty of the deed for which he suffered.

"I have the honour, &c.,

"SEPTIMUS DAVIDSON, one of the under-sheriffs."

London; Printed for the Vendors.

'The Execution and Confession of Franz Muller.' Broadside from Charles Hindley, *Curiosities of London Street Literature*, London; Reeves and Turner, 1871.

Murder in the Railway Train.

Listen to my song, and I will not detain you
    long,
  And then I will tell you of what I've heard.
Of a murder that's been done, by some wicked
    one,
  And the place where it all occurred ;
Between Stepney and Bow they struck the
    fatal blow,
  To resist he tried all in vain,
Murdered by some prigs was poor Mr Briggs
  Whilst riding in a railway train.

Muller is accused, at present we cannot refuse
  To believe that he is the very one,
But all his actions, you see, have been so very
    free,
Ever since the murder it was done ;
From his home he never went, but such a
    happy time he spent,
  He never looked troubled on the brain,
If he'd been the guilty man, he would have
    hid all he can,
  From the murder in the railway train.

Muller he did state that he was going to
    emigrate
  Long before this dreadful tragedy ;
He often used to talk about travelling to
    New York,
  In the Victoria, that was going to sea.
Mr. Death, the jeweller, said, he was very
    much afraid,
  He might not know the same man again,
When he heard of the reward, he started out
    abroad,
  About the murder in the railway train.

If it's Muller, we can't deny, on the Cabman
    keep your eye,
  Remember what he said the other day,
That Muller a ticket sold for money, which
    seems so very funny,
  When he had no expenses for to pay.
They say his money he took, and his name
    entered on the book,

  Long before this tragedy he came ;
Like Muller's, the Cabman had a hat, and it
    may be his, perhaps
  That was found in the railway train.

Would a murderer have forgot, to have de-
    stroyed the jeweller's box,
  Or burnt up the sleeve of his coat,
Would he the chain ticket have sold, and
    himself exposed so bold,
  And to all his friends a letter wrote,
Before Muller went away, why did not the
    cabman say,
  And not give him so much start on the
    main
If the cabman knew—it's very wrong—to
    keep the secret up so long,
  About the murder in the railway train.

When Muller does arrive, we shall not be
    much surprised,
  To hear that that's him on the trial ;
Give him time to repent, though he is not
    innocent,
  To hear the evidence give no denial.
Muller's got the watch, you see, so it proves
    that he is guilty,
But like Townley don't prove that he's
    insane
For if it should be him, on the gallows let
    him swing,
  For the murder on the railway train.

Now Muller's caught at last, tho' he's been
    so very fast,
  And on him they found the watch and hat,
Tho' across the ocean he did roam, he had
    better stayed at home,
  And hid himself in some little crack,
Tho' he pleads his innocence, but that is all
    nonsense,
  For they'll hang him as sure as he's a man,
For he got up to his rigs, and murdered Mr.
    Briggs
  While riding in a railway train.

London: Printed for the Vendors.

'Murder in the Railway Train.' Broadside from Charles Hindley, *Curiosities of London Street Literature*, London ; Reeves and Turner, 1871.

That there is a thread of didactic quality to the dying speeches and confessions is undeniable. No doubt the broadsides were given a sensational quality to appeal to and be purchased by a popular market, but they also, like the public executions they chronicled, confirmed the lesson of the gallows and warned of the consequences of a life of crime and sin:

> See what numbers are approaching
> To Horsemonger's fatal tree
> Full of bloom in health and vigour
> What a dreadful sight to see.
> Old and young pray take a warning
> Females lead a virtuous life
> Think you of that fatal morning
> Frederick Manning and his wife.[61]

2

THE 'BLOODY CODE'

A VICTORIAN looked back at the early years of his century, decried their bloody criminal laws, and was relieved that they were so remote from his world.

We hanged for everything – for a shilling – for five shillings – for five pounds – for cattle – for coining – for forgery, even for witch-craft – for things that were and things that could not be.[1]

So Charles Phillips, barrister and a commissioner of the Court of Insolvent Debtors, reviewed England's not-too-remote history in 1857; there were many alive for whom hangings for such minor and idiosyncratic offences were still vivid.

During the eighteenth century the number of capital-crime statutes increased at an unprecedented rate. In the reigns of the Tudors and Stuarts no more than fifty offences carried the death penalty, but in the period from the Restoration to the death of George III in 1820, approximately 160 years, statutes defining crimes with capital punishments swelled to over two hundred. During Mary Tudor's reign – the sobriquet 'Bloody' given her for allowing the fires of Smithfield to consume heretics – only four additional statutes were added as capital crimes. In the relatively more enlightened and more recent reign of George III, sixty crimes were added to the death-penalty statutes.[2]

Such a growing need to suppress crime with so much severity was manifested in exaggerated fears and concern for the safe-guarding of property. England had embarked on an industrial expansion during George III's reign. Her economy in comparison with other countries was relatively advanced, and unlike other countries her aristocracy shared with the mercantile class in this enterprise. The wealth and properties accrued from increased agricultural production, trade and finance were

jealously guarded and legislated for by a Parliament domin-
ated by great Landlords and influenced by merchants. Con-
current with the expansion of commerce was an unusual rapid
growth in population. The population increased from approximately 6,000,000 in 1730 to 12,000,000 in 1811.[3] Sheer numbers alone, to a social order still moored to the past in its
policies and solutions to new problems, created wretched
conditions for the new urban poor and dispossessed rural poor.
Food riots, burning, looting, mob violence were commonplace.[4]
These ugly acts – born of despair and greed – had to be suppressed by the militia because the justices, after reading the
Riot Act, had inadequate forces to keep order.*

As predatory acts and crimes increased a generally accepted
belief grew that the laws, despite their harshness, were not repressive enough. If whipping, mutilation and pillorying failed
to restrain, then the gallows would have to be the ultimate
and most fearful punishment. Even hanging was not considered severe enough. Only vindictive cruel, and terror-
inspiring punishments could produce salutary results. A writer
urged aggravated punishment along with hanging. He recommended a little cord about the arms and legs and more 'sen-
sible parts'.[5] This would, he predicted, cause 'keenest anguish
. . . before they expire'.[6] Prescribed punishments exceeded the
'eye-for-an-eye' Biblical injunction. 'If one has . . . mur-
thered [sic] me at last, and burns my house', another writer
entreated that the other 'should be made to feel himself
die.'[7] A prolonged dying should be extended to the thief who
'surreptitiously steals the value of five shillings' – a statute
just enacted at the time.[8]

Some earlier dissent – scattered and disorganized – was
raised against these pervasive, vengeful laws. Uncertainties
were expressed about their efficacy as deterrents. Among the
more prominent dissenters were Sir Thomas More and Sir
Francis Bacon. More condemned inordinate punishments of
thieves which exceeded the limits of justice and were harmful

---

* There is current speculation that an adequate police system would
not have encouraged the growth of such a severe system of law. See
Leon Radzinowicz, *A History of English Criminal Law and its Administration from 1750*, Vol. I, London: Stevens & Sons, 1948.

to the public weal as a result. 'For as the severity was too great, so the remedy was not effectual.'[9] Bacon advocated the repeal of the numerous and unnecessary penal laws 'which now lie . . . upon people as the rain whereof the Psalm speaks'.[10]

Not until after the middle of the eighteenth century was an effective offensive finally launched against the practice and theories of punishments. New, more humane doctrines had a far-reaching influence on English thought and gave fresh impetus to reform. A most profound influence came from the seminal work *Dei Delitti e delle Pene* written by Cesare Bonesana Beccaria (1738–94) and published in 1764. Beccaria's little book, the first to deal exclusively with criminal justice, became famous almost immediately. It was translated into every important language and rulers as diverse as the Empress Maria Theresa of Austria, the Grand Duke Leopold II of Tuscany and the Czarina Catherine the Great 'announced their intentions to be guided by Beccaria's principle in the reformation of their laws'.[11] The first English translation was made in 1767 and its undoubted popularity is shown by the seven editions published between 1769 and 1807.[12] As in other countries, Beccaria's impact was readily discernible in England. Blackstone, Howard, Bentham and Romilly – men whose influences were stamped on English law and penal practices – 'freely acknowledged their indebtedness to him'.*

Beccaria's humanitarianism was repelled by cruelty and injustice. Good laws made men moral and happy, bad laws corrupted men and invited retaliation, and as a consequence evil was perpetuated. Revolted by infliction of punishments imposed by state sadism, he attempted to show how futile were severe disproportionate punishments. As an avowed believer in principles of Enlightenment, Beccaria anathemized cruelty as an affront to reason and humanitarianism. 'The certainty,' Beccaria wrote, 'of a small punishment will make a stronger impression than the fear of one more severe, if attended with the hope of escaping.'[13] Certainty of punish-

---

* Peter Gay wrote that if he could sum up in one phrase the unifying description of the Enlightened philosophers, he would term them 'the party of humanity'. 'The Enlightenment in the History of Political Theory', *Political Science Quarterly*, Vol. LXIX (March 1969), p.389.

ment rather than severity deterred crime. That concept was stated so repetitiously by criminal-law critics that it assumed the validity of a mathematical axiom.* Beccaria rejected the cherished belief that the death penalty was the ultimate punishment and produced the greatest deterrent effect on spectators. The fear of execution never stopped desperate men, whereas the prospect of perpetual loss of liberty preyed on their minds more than the expectation of swift death. A violent scene left only a terrible momentary impression without the sought-after effect. Moreover, the spectators often sympathized with the criminal, reviled the authorities and cursed laws that took life so cheaply.

These philosophical theories about laws and punishments had a great influence on enlightened thought in England. The origin of philosophical and critical opinion about criminal law may have originated with Beccaria, but effective agitation for criminal-law reform in England began with Jeremy Bentham (1745–1832). Bentham provided the thrust and the philosophical elements to English law-reform. His voluminous writing, his pragmatism which harmonized so well with the general tendencies of English thought and his coteries of loyal, dedicated disciples had an almost incalculable effect.† Bentham, like Beccaria, condemned inefficacious punishments.‡ He condemned them because they encouraged the wholesale evasion of the laws, and promoted crime rather than diminished it. Bentham attacked the criminal laws for other reasons

---

* As late as 1856 Beccaria's principle was reverentially restated without qualification. 'Beccaria long ago proved that mild and certain punishments not only tend to increase the popular respect for the law, but are far more effectual as deterrents than enactments of an opposite character.' Henry Mayhew, 'On Capital Punishment', *Three Papers on Capital Punishment*, London: Society for Promoting the Amendment of the Law, 1856, p.39.

† Elie Halévy has put it rather succinctly: 'Bentham gave Mill a doctrine, and Mill gave Bentham a school.' *The Growth of Philosophic Radicalism*, Boston: Beacon Press, 1955, p.321.

‡ Bentham was a disciple of Beccaria. Halévy affirms, however, that he carried the principle of utility to solve judicial reforms further. *ibid.*, p.21. Peter Gay places Bentham firmly in the camp of the Enlightened philosophers. loc. cit.

too. He objected to them on quantitative and utilitarian grounds. Unwarranted severity produced evil and moderate punishments produced salutary results with less suffering and less expense.* Laws will be violated with impunity when they conflict with the nature and sentiments of the people. As a result, 'criminals are pardoned, offences are overlooked, proofs are disregarded and juries, to avoid an excess of severity, frequently fall into an excess of indulgence.'† The paradox that severe laws gave encouragements to criminals would vanish only when Parliament reformed the laws and brought them into conformity with juridical practice. This was a clarion call to overhaul, rationalize and humanize the haphazard accretion of statutes loosely called 'the criminal code'.

Bentham was fortunate to have been aided in his endeavours to reform the criminal law by zealous disciples of great ability – Henry Brougham, Samuel Romilly and Sir James Mackintosh.[14] It was, however, to Romilly that the first period of reform from 1808 to 1818 was almost entirely due. Sir Samuel Romilly (1757–1818), the son of a Huguenot immigrant, was affected by a preoccupation with reading *The Newgate Calendar*, and he was influenced by John Howard, Bentham and Beccaria.‡ He had a most formidable influence on English criminal-law history. Paradoxically, he was unable to carry many reforms in Parliament despite persistent, assiduous,

* Montagu, op. cit., Vol. I, p.220. When Thomas Babington Macaulay was recorder of Bombay, he abolished the death penalty there (except for treason and wilful murder). He did so on the utilitarian principle of 'smallest possible suffering' and 'smallest possible cost of time and money'. See Leon Radzinowicz, op. cit., Vol. I, p.522.

† Jeremy Bentham, *The Works of Jeremy Bentham*, ed. John Bowring, Vol. I, New York: Russell & Russell, 1962, p.430. Lord Suffield submitted in 1833 a list of 555 perjured verdicts over a fifteen-year period at the Old Bailey. The verdicts returned for offences for stealing forty shillings from dwelling-houses were changed to thirty-nine shillings only. Phillips, op. cit., p.13.

‡ Halévy claims a 'direct and profound' influence from Bentham on Romilly, even though Romilly tried to avoid Bentham's taint of radicalism. Halévy, op. cit., pp.229–30. For influences of John Howard (1726–90), the prison-reformer, and Beccaria, see Radzinowicz, op. cit., Vol. I, p.314.

efforts.* Every year from 1810 to 1818 he introduced Bills to abolish capital punishment for the offence of stealing forty shillings in a dwelling-house and five shillings in a shop. Despite his legislative failures, his pervasive ideas left a legacy and an inspiration for his and later generations. Romilly, like Beccaria and Bentham, directed much of his condemnation of severe laws for their inutility; the principle of certainty of punishment was much more effective than any severity of example for the prevention of crime.[15] Romilly marshalled his information, drawn heavily from tables published under the authority of the Secretary of State for Home Affairs, for the seven-year period from 1803 to 1810. He attempted to expose how circumvention of laws occurred. With the thoroughness of a solicitor drawing up a brief – he had been made King's Counsel in 1800 and appointed Solicitor-General in 1806 – Romilly demonstrated how consistently and flagrantly juries shrank from imposing death penalties for minor crimes. He cited the astounding statistic that of 1,872 men and women committed to Newgate for trial under charge of stealing in dwelling-houses during the period from 1803 to 1810 only one person was executed.[16] It was his contention that the unwillingness to convict and execute verified the certainty principle.

Additional dimension was added to Romilly's arguments by William Grant, Master of the Rolls and a supporter of Romilly. He pointed out the futility of imposing laws which could not be enforced. The reluctance of juries to inflict the death penalty for stealing forty shillings was evidence of this fact. The legislature could not arbitrarily make laws without the awareness that 'every law must be faulty which acts so decidedly against the feelings of the whole country',[17] a subtle acknowledgement of the work and influence of public opinion.

Romilly moved early in the parliamentary session of 1810

* In 1808, his first year in Parliament, he succeeded in abolishing the death penalty for picking pockets. C. G. Oakes, *Sir Samuel Romilly: 1757–1818*, George Allen & Unwin, 1935, p.47. He also had death punishments abolished for soldiers and sailors 'found vagrant without their passes' and for stealing from bleaching-grounds in England and Ireland. *Dictionary of National Biography*, Vol. XVII, p.188.

for leave to bring in three Bills to abolish capital punishments; for privately stealing five shillings in shops, for stealing forty shillings in dwelling-houses and for stealing forty shillings on navigable rivers. The weight of his arguments was convincing and effective. In the House of Commons a majority agreed that laws which allowed five-sixths of all persons sentenced to death to escape execution were in need of alteration. Also a telling effect was produced by the disclosure of widespread evasion of law-enforcement. Romilly exposed the legal fiction of how the courts subtly and tacitly circumvented laws by finding crimimals 'guilty of stealing, but not privately'[18] as a means of removing the crime from the capital-offence category. The House of Commons, convinced by Romilly's logical argument and bolstered with revealing statistics about judicial collusion in enforcing the law, voted to abolish the death penalty for stealing privately from shops to the value of five shillings. The bill was defeated thirty-one to eleven in the House of Lords. Seven bishops, including the Archbishop of Canterbury, voted against the bill.* Romilly ruefully commented:

I would rather be convinced of their servility to government than that, recollecting the mild doctrines of their religion, they could have come down to the House spontaneously to vote that transportation for life is not a sufficiently severe punishment for the offence of pilfering what is of five shillings value, and nothing but the blood of the offender can afford an adequate atonement for such transgression.[19]

Six times, in 1810, 1811, 1813, 1816, 1818 and 1820, the House of Commons passed Bills to abolish capital punishment for shop-lifting to the value of five shillings, and six times the House of Lords threw out the Bills.

In 1811 Romilly sought leave to bring in two additional Bills for abolishing the death penalty: stealing to the value of ten shillings from bleaching-grounds in England, and to the value of five shillings from bleaching-grounds in Ireland.

---

* That the Established Church took no lead in reform is hardly surprising considering the ultra-Tory make-up of its hierarchy. In 1815 eleven bishops were of noble family. D. C. Somervell, *English Thought in the Nineteenth Century*, New York: David McKay, 1965, p.16.

He reintroduced as well the three Bills first presented in 1810.

Now at his disposal was concrete corroboration of his allegations. He placed before the House of Commons two extraordinary petitions signed by 150 Irish bleaching-ground proprietors and a number of calico-printers from England urging the repeal of these laws. These petitions contended that the severity of the laws made them unenforceable and hence denied the businessmen protection from the pilfering which plagued them.[20] Significantly then, and for the first time, a section of the community petitioned for the repeal of a law because of its severity.[21] Romilly had his argument reinforced: abolition would not result in increased crime, as his critics and opponents claimed; it might happen in theory but it would not happen in practice.[22] The petitioners had given substance to the principle that unenforceable laws inevitably tend to lower the conviction rate.

The House of Commons passed the Bills. However, the resistance of Romilly's chief antagonists, Lord Chief Justice Ellenborough (1750–1818) and Lord Chancellor Eldon (1751–1838), was consistent and unremitting. Along with a substantial majority in the House of Lords, they condemned his reform Bills as dangerous innovations. These reforms, they cautioned, would endanger the existing system of criminal law sanctified by time and experience and which had withstood the test of a century.[23] Some lords dissented from this line of reasoning. Some, like the Marquis of Landsdowne, stung by allegations of endangering the law, demurred: 'I should,' he replied in support of the Bills, 'be the last man in the world to countenance it if, as it has been insinuated, it led to any loose or dangerous innovation.'[24]

Others seized upon the arguments used so effectively by Romilly in the House of Commons. Lord Holland reiterated the charge that the courts meted out punishment inconsistently out of fear and abhorrence for the laws they were sworn to uphold. It was not on speculation that he advocated repeal of these laws, nor was it on any general theory. 'It is notorious that the practice of our courts is at variance with the laws they profess to administer.'[25] That laws were not enforced but ignored was the essence of Holland's contention.

Lord Ellenborough was distressed by such condemnations of the courts. He was fearful that such talk would encourage the public to believe 'prosecutors, witnesses and juries are deterred from doing their duty'.* He was, along with Lord Eldon, committed to the principle of allowing the judges to exercise their discretionary selection in handing down verdicts. It was an awful but necessary power given to them, but one that they could better exercise than anyone else because of their experience with criminals. There was, and still is, the belief that judges were best equipped to cope with criminals because they knew and understood the problems of crime best.† Ellenborough and Eldon insisted that all criminal-reform Bills must be submitted for prior approval to the judges. Romilly considered this form of judicial review unconstitutional. He had – and with good reason – no hope that the judges, as a group, would support reform.[26]

Lords Eldon and Ellenborough continued obdurate and remained inured to all arguments. Eldon thought the imaginary terror of the gallows on men's minds was reason enough to retain capital punishment.[27] It was the salutary influence of terror, not the consistent application of the law, that produced the wanted reluctance to commit crimes. This terror principle

---

* Montagu, *Opinions of Different Authors Upon the Punishment of Death*, Vol. III, p.270. There was greater currency to these charges than Ellenborough admitted. Such a venerable source as Blackstone lamented these alleged legal deceptions. 'It is a melancholy truth,' he wrote, 'that no less than one hundred and sixty laws have been declared . . . to be worthy of instant death. So dreadful a list . . . increases the number of offenders. The injured, through compassion, will often forbear to prosecute; juries, through compassion, will sometimes forget their oaths, and either acquit the guilty or mitigate the nature of the offence; and judges, through compassion, will respite one-half of the convicts, and recommend them to royal mercy.' William Blackstone, *Commentaries on the Laws of England*, 15th ed. Vol. IV, London: A. Strahan, 1809, p.18.

† The question of whether judges understood criminal behaviour and disposition was brought up at a Cambridge conference held the first week of July 1968. Mr Justice Lawton in a speech alluded to a current belief that judges did not know what criminology was and would not understand it if they did. C. H. Rolph, 'Should Britain Have a Criminal Code?', *New Statesman*, Vol. LXX (July 1968), p.43.

was stated with great exactitude by William Frankland, a
law-reform opponent, in the House of Commons. He asked,
'Is it not better that the laws should operate by terror than
by punishment?'[28] For Lord Ellenborough the laws were a
bulwark between order and ruin. 'Repeal these laws,' he
warned during the debate considering repeal of the shop-
lifting statute in the House of Lords, 'and see the difference –
no man can trust himself for an hour out-of-doors.'*

While stubborn opposition resisted Romilly's efforts, no
such restraint impeded passage of additional capital-punishment laws. Shaken by the Luddite disturbances in 1812,
death-sentence laws were sped through Parliament to suppress
them. Conversely, there was no such haste to rid the country
of barbarous, anachronistic laws like that reserved for high
treason.† Romilly pleaded in vain for its repeal, but he was
not surprised when the Bill was lost by twelve votes. He had
heard the same fears and similar arguments expressed in
defence of burning women as a necessity to safeguard society
and to preserve its institutions. Romilly promised that again
and again he would appeal to the good sense and right sentiments of Parliament and people. Whatever might be his fate,
he prophesied, 'the seed which is scattered has not fallen
upon stony ground'.[29]

Events which followed Romilly's death on 2 November
1818 almost made him into a seer. On 25 January 1819, the
sheriffs of London presented a petition to Parliament from the
Corporation of London. The petition requested a revision of

* *Hansard*, Vol. xix (1811), appendix cxix. Lord Eldon remained
inordinately concerned that any amelioration of the criminal laws would
bring about an apocalypse. When abolition of capital punishment for
cutting down trees was debated, he was opposed. He conceded that
death was an undoubted 'hardship' for cutting down a single tree; but
if the bill was passed 'a person might root up or cut down whole acres
or plantations . . . without being subject to capital punishment'. ibid.,
Vol. ii (1820), col.495.

† A traitor was to be 'dragged to the gallows . . . hanged by the neck
and then cut down alive . . . his entrails be taken out and burned while
he is yet alive . . . his head cut off . . . his body divided into five parts
and his head and quarters be at the King's disposal'. ibid., Vol. xxviii
(1813), appendix lxxxi.

the criminal code. It stated that the inordinate number of capital-punishment laws created 'the widespread disinclination to put these statutes into effect' and was partly responsible for the 'rapid increase in crime'.[30] Sir James Mackintosh (1765–1832), Romilly's supporter and successor in criminal-law matters in the House of Commons, moved swiftly to take full advantage of the petition's effect. On 2 March 1819 he carried a motion over the Liverpool government's opposition for the establishment of a 'Select Committee appointed to consider so much of the criminal law as relates to capital punishments in felonies'.* Despite the initial governmental opposition, the 1819 Committee's importance soon made it evident that the Home Office would have to take the lead in reforming the criminal code.[31]

England in the early nineteenth century was in a state of rapid transition. Even after the fears caused by the excesses of the French Revolution had disappeared and the pervasive-ness of its revolutionary zeal had subsided, fear grew in retrospect. The reform work of Romilly and Mackintosh was retarded because they had been early and enthusiastic suppor-ters of the French Revolution.[32] During the last decade of the eighteenth century and the early part of the nineteenth any reforms, regardless of how innocent, were considered dangerous by a state policy committed to crush revolution. The exigen-cies of England's wars against the French Revolution and Napoleon increased the nation's industrial production. Society, too, had noticeably changed. The old feudal ties had begun to break down in the new manufacturing districts, and a new independence sprang up divested of the old deference towards traditional authority.

Luddite mobs, 'Captain Swing' and his incendiaries, and

---

* *D.N.B.*, Vol. xii, pp.617–22. Sir James Mackintosh was a lawyer, statesman and supporter of liberal principles. Like Macaulay, Mackin-tosh experimented with withholding the death penalty while serving in Bombay. The stated purpose of the Select Committee was to determine 'whether in the present state of the sentiments of the people of England, Capital Punishment in most cases unattended with violence, be a neces-sary or even the most effectual security against the prevalence of crime'. *Parliamentary Papers*, Report from the Select Committee on Capital Punishments, Vol. viii, 1819, p.4.

Peterloo 'massacres' created an apprehension about the continuance of the old social order. The safety of the upper classes' property and the honour of their sisters had to be defended against the violent and the dispossessed. The deep-rooted fear and aversion many of the upper classes felt towards the lower classes was manifested by the attitudes revealed by Mrs Trimmer. Compulsive in her Christian charity, she nevertheless felt a physical revulsion towards those she aided. She encouraged the giving of more than just money, even to visiting the poor in their cottages, yet she viewed them as 'little better than savages and barbarians with whom any familiar intercourse would be degrading, if not dangerous'.[33]

The suspension of the Habeas Corpus Act in 1817, symptomatic of panic legislation, drove the powerful pamphleteer William Cobbett into refuge in America. Coincidental with Cobbett's return to England in 1819, like a harbinger announcing change, Romilly's prediction that his efforts would not fall on barren ground was being belatedly realized. In 1811, when Romilly had introduced his Bill to abolish capital punishment for stealing in dwelling-houses, only sixty-seven members were present in the House of Commons; in 1819, when the same Bill was introduced, 275 members were there. In 1810 Lord Ellenborough had dismissed the reform as a system of innovation upon criminal law by persons speculating in legislation.[34] In 1819 Lord Castlereagh, the Foreign Secretary, previously an avowed opponent of criminal-law reform, referred to reform of the criminal law as 'this grave and most important business'.[35]

Much of the atmosphere conducive to change had been anticipated and prepared by the reform work of diverse groups of Benthamites, Evangelicals, religious dissenters, Whig philanthropists and Tory humanists. The matrix that held such groups together was a common dislike of cruelty that was transformed into a social creed for every form of humanity. They cooperated in different shifting alliances: on factory-reform, prison-reform, free trade, religious liberty and education for the underprivileged. Humanitarianism often cut across party and religious lines. The anti-slavery movement

was supported by William Wilberforce, an Evangelical leader
of the saintly 'Clapham Sect', William Allen, a prominent
Quaker philanthropist, Charles Fox, Whig leader, and Henry
Brougham who had been one of Bentham's disciples.[36] An
aspect of the criminal-law reform which held common interest
was the rehabilitative element. The Quaker reformers, the
Benthamites and the various religious denominations were
agreed 'that just as crime was a deliberate act, so reform was
an equally deliberate step the offender ... could himself
take'.[37]

The number of capital offences was reduced by a series of
individual Acts beginning in the second decade of the nineteenth century. The old story of English reform successfully
resisting change in favour of gradual evolution was really the
newer story of old biases eroded by once-denied principles, by
amorphous but emerging public opinion, and by intelligent
self-interest. Robert Peel (1788–1850), during whose tenure as
Home Secretary more than three quarters of the criminal laws
was revised,[38] had sensed the change of mood and opinion in
the nation. He wrote in 1822:

Do you not think that the tone of England – of that great com-
pound of folly, manners, prejudice, wrong feeling, right feeling,
obstinacy – and newspaper paragraphs which is called public
opinion – is more liberal to use an odious but intelligible phrase,
than the policy of government?[39]

Peel took the lead from Mackintosh in reforming the criminal code, and in the two months remaining before the end
of the parliamentary session in 1823 he pushed through the
two Acts abolishing death penalties for stealing forty shillings
in shops and from ships in navigable rivers.* The speed with
which Peel carried out the two reforms that Romilly, Mackin-

* Among others, Peel obtained repeal of the Waltham Black Act, an
Act to execute for any crime committed wearing a mask, and abolished
capital punishments for breaking river banks, cutting down hop-vines,
impersonating Greenwich pensioners and destroying textile machinery.
The custom of burying suicides on the high road with a stake driven
through the body was also abolished. Gash, *Mr Secretary Peel*, p.329. The
year 1823 also saw the parallel penal-law reform bear the fruit of the

tosh and Sir Thomas Fowell Buxton* had so long sought demonstrated how necessary was the support of the Home Secretary and the government. Peel was still cautious and deliberate. With meticulous care and thorough preparation he consulted the judges, gauged their and Parliament's dispositions towards projected reforms, and obtained opinions from the important business community. The result of exhaustive consultations and numerous and lengthy communications was the repeal of 278 Acts and the consolidation of their provisions into eight Acts.[40]

Peel had deprived Mackintosh of the glory of having executed reforms when he undertook the reform of the criminal laws in 1822,[41] but in 1830 Mackintosh had begun to reclaim his leadership. Seeing no reason for continuing the death penalties for forgery which were rarely inflicted at that time, Peel claimed that he had used the opinion of the 1819 Committee as a guideline in following such a course of reform. He proposed, therefore, to abolish capital punishment for all forged receipts of money and goods, stamps, deeds, bonds and bank paper.[42] Overall Peel sought the consolidation of 120 statutes dealing with public and personal forgeries to be reduced to four clauses for which capital punishment was to be retained. Mackintosh immediately moved to amend Peel's Bill and sought to substitute transportation for all cases of forgery except for wills.[43] An irreconcilable conflict developed between Peel and a strong party in the House of Commons

---

labours of John Howard, Elizabeth Fry and others. Systematic legal steps were taken to segregate the criminals. Previously the debtor, pickpocket, burglar, coiner, poacher, highwayman, vagrant, prostitute and murderer were placed together in the 'Common Gaol'. Henry Mayhew and John Binny, *The Criminal Prisons of London and Scenes of Prison Life*, London: Griffin, Bohn, 1862, p.80.

* Thomas Fowell Buxton (1786–1845) through marriage with Hannah Gurney, became associated with John Gurney, a distinguished Quaker, and was influenced by Elizabeth Gurney Fry, the prison-reformer. He succeeded William Wilberforce as the leader of the anti-slave party in Parliament. Supporting Sir James Mackintosh on criminal law reform, he seconded Mackintosh's motion to form the 1819 Select Committee on the Criminal Laws. See Cowherd, *The Politics of English Dissent*, pp.52–4 and *D.N.B.*, Vol. III, pp.559 ff.

headed by Mackintosh, Buxton, Henry Brougham and Lord John Russell. Mackintosh insisted that the laws against forgery were untenable because the public was unwilling to prosecute and juries were reluctant to convict. The arguments hardly convinced Peel: 'Fear of trouble and expense,' he insisted, 'was a more powerful deterrent to prosecution than an inherited dislike for the death penalty.'* Claiming that neither transportation nor any other forms of secondary punishments were sufficient deterrents, Sir Robert Peel persistently opposed further reduction of capital punishment.†

The parliamentary controversy aroused great interest throughout the country. Brougham presented a large number of petitions from over 1,000 bankers and directors of joint-stock companies, including the heads of Rothschild and Overend, Gurney & Company, urging the abolition of the death penalty for forgeries. Their motivation, they insisted, was primarily concern for their property. The forgery laws deprived them of the means of protection because the laws prevented the prosecution, conviction and punishment of forgers. 'Your petitioners ... earnestly pray,' stated their petition, 'that your Honourable House will not withhold from them that protection ... they could derive from a more lenient law.'‡

* Gash, op. cit., pp.482–3. Edward Gibbon Wakefield, a critic of Peel and an advocate for further repeals of death-penalty statutes, agreed: 'Time and peace of mind incurred in bringing felons to justice, according to the law of England, caused the escape of many notorious criminals.' E. G. Wakefield, *Facts Relating to the Punishment of Death in the Metropolis*, London, 1832, p.7.

† Peel's opposition hardened to such a degree that he apparently advocated executions for the criminally insane as well. After his attempted assassination on 20 January 1843 by Daniel MacNaghten, an anti-Catholic bigot, he wrote Queen Victoria that it was lamentable that 'a man may be at the same time so insane as to be reckless of his own life and the lives of others, and be free from moral responsibility'. John Raymond, ed., *Victoria's Early Letters*, 2nd edn., New York: Macmillan & Co., 1963, p.85. The Queen argued, 'The law is perfect ... and why could not the Judges be found to interpret the law in this and no other sense to the Juries?' ibid., p.86.

‡ Charles Brixton, ed., *Memoirs of Sir Thomas Fowell Buxton*, J. M. Dent & Sons, 1925, p.113. In 1844 all cases for forgery were removed as capital crimes. The number of convictions for forgery rose from 404 to 781 during the five years following final removal. How much of this was

Some of the business community's antipathy towards the death penalty for forgery was probably influenced by abolitionist propaganda. John Thomas Barry, a philanthropist and reformer, was very energetic in his activities on behalf of Mackintosh's amendment. He corresponded with the provinces, prepared and arranged statistics, and pressured Members of Parliament through their constituents. He estimated that he had sent out a vast amount of anti-forgery-law literature under the franking privileges of friendly Members of Parliament to the value of £1,000.[44] Despite government opposition, Mackintosh's amendment passed the House of Commons by thirteen votes; it failed in the House of Lords. Yet Peel's victory over Mackintosh was a Pyrrhic one. His cautious administrative approach was being outpaced by public feelings.*

Sydney Smith, in a remarkably acute prediction, augured that political reform would bring an end to 'cruel and oppressive punishments'.[45] In the five years between 1832 and 1837 the reformed Parliament abolished a number of anachronistic laws previously punishable by death: coining, horse-stealing, sheep-stealing, cattle-stealing, stealing letters from the Post Office, sacrilege and rick-burning. An influx of politically independent-minded men entered the House of Commons as a result of the Reform Bill. John Bright approximated the number of independent members at 100;[46] they helped tip the scale in favour of law-reform. Earl Grey, the Prime Minister, and Viscount Melbourne, the Home Secretary, had little interest in penal questions and 'the pressure to examine and reform the criminal laws came almost entirely from private members'.[47]

Prominent utilitarian–radical Members of Parliament were

attributable to the greater certainty of conviction after the removal of capital punishment would be difficult to determine. See *Analysis and Review of the Blue Book of the Royal Commission on Capital Punishment*, London: Society for the Abolition of Capital Punishment, 1866, pp.8–9.

* Peel's biographer, Norman Gash, reached the following conclusion about Peel's role in this episode in the history of criminal-law reform in England: 'In 1830 he had his way, but only with the help of the peers . . . As soon as the Whigs came into power, they accelerated the process on which Peel had tried to place a restraining influence.' op. cit., p.485.

Sir William Molesworth, George Grote, Arthur Roebuck and Charles Buller.* Among them William Ewart emerged as the foremost proponent of criminal-law reform; it was he who kept the issue before Parliament and the public.† Ewart carried the Act which provided for the bodies of executed criminals to be buried within the prison precincts. In 1834 he carried an Act which discontinued the practice of dissecting executed murderers before exposing the body to public view.[48] In the same year he sponsored the Act that abolished capital punishment for felons returning from transportation. Perhaps Ewart's most important Bill gave persons charged with crimes the full protection of a learned counsel. Before enactment of Ewart's Act, counsel could raise only legal points and examine witnesses; the accused had to comment on the evidence himself.[49] Ewart's Act corrected this and removed the disabling part an inarticulate, uneducated accused person had to play in his own trial. Henceforth, counsels, wise in the ways of courts and familiar with legal precedents and terminology, could speak in a client's defence. It is little wonder that Ewart earned lavish praise from contemporaries favourable to reform of the criminal laws. One zealous, devoted abolitionist thought if he wrote a history of criminal-law reform he would 'attempt to erect a fitting memorial to the quiet and unostentatious labours of Mr Ewart in the cause of human legislation'.[50]

Ewart's devotion to criminal-law reform brought him into conflict with Lord John Russell, Home Secretary in the second Melbourne cabinet. Russell had sought in March 1837 to reduce the death penalty severely. Ewart immediately moved to amend the proposed Bill so that it would abolish capital

---

* Molesworth, Grote, Roebuck and Buller called themselves 'utilitarians'. Young intellectuals had gathered around James Mill, Bentham's closest friend, and among them the above were the most important. See David Roberts, 'Jeremy Bentham and the Victorian Administrative State', *Victorian Studies*, Vol. II, March 1959, p.197.

† William Ewart (1788–1869) was the son of a prominent Liverpool businessman who was William Ewart Gladstone's godfather. The younger Ewart succeeded to Huskisson's seat from Liverpool in 1830. He is also important for introducing the first Public Library Act in 1850. William A. Munford, *William Ewart, M.P. 1788–1869: Portrait of a Radical*, London: Grafton & Co., 1960, p.70.

punishment for all crimes except murder, carefully emphasizing that he had not 'expressed himself in favour of total abolition'.[51] Despite government opposition and the activity of the Whig whips to muster a comfortable majority, Ewart's motion was defeated by one vote: seventy-four to seventy-three.[52] Russell, William Gladstone and Sir Robert Peel voted with the majority.[53] Harriet Martineau chided Ewart and the radicals: she thought they should have given more consideration to secondary punishments to allay the fears of the opposition. However, as a perceptive observer of events, she did praise Ewart for pressuring the government to bring in more ambitious criminal-law reforms than it had at first proposed.*

John Sydney Taylor (1795–1841), prominent barrister and editor of the *Morning Herald*,† was elated by how narrowly the government scraped through the vote and wrote:

What a change has taken place since we first began to demand regularly and systematically the expiration of punishments of blood! Ten years have scarcely elapsed since we entered the field, prepared to avail ourselves of every fair opportunity to expose the barbarous and prove the inutility or rather the pernicious effects of a state of law, under which judicial homicide was carried to a most frightful extent. Romilly's honest and able efforts to civilize our penal code had proved abortive in all but comparatively unimportant instances ... Now we have to record the gratifying fact of a majority of the independent members of the House of Commons having voted for the abolition of capital punishments in all cases except that of wilful murder.‡

* Martineau, *The History of England During the Thirty Years' Peace*, p.420. Interestingly the author gave the abolitionists' litany, revealing the pervasiveness of their trenchant ideas. 'From the days Sir Samuel Romilly began his disclosures of the effects of severity of punishment,' she wrote, 'there has been a growing conviction that severity of punishment tends to increase crime.'

† *D.N.B.*, Vol. xix, pp.450–51. The *Morning Herald* was 'the conspicuous organ of Clarkson and the humanitarians'. ibid.

‡ Taylor, *Selections from the Writings of John Sydney Taylor*, London: Charles Gilpin, 1843, p.259. Ewart was listed as a friend in the dedication. Charles Gilpin, M.P., the publisher, was active as a member of the Committee for the Abolition of Capital Punishment. The *Eclectic Review*, Vol. lxxxviii (1848), p.148, called him 'the Cobden of the Abolition Movement'.

On 5 March 1840 William Ewart rose in his seat to make a historic resolution to abolish capital punishment entirely.* Conscious of the conspicuous importance of the occasion – no other motion for total abolition had ever been made in the history of Parliament – Ewart was careful to reassure the more than 150 Members that his resolution was not without precedent. He invoked the hallowed names of 'Mr Burke, Mr Wilberforce, Mr Canning and Sir Samuel Romilly' as illustrious predecessors who had 'advocated the discontinuance of capital punishments'.† Speaking with unaccustomed eloquence, eschewing his usual monotonous, inaudible speech, he pleaded the urgency that capital punishment should be abolished. He denounced the demoralizing, degrading spectacles of public executions; he described the shocking scenes of dissipation and ribaldry. Repellent jests and profane language were all that could be heard at the 'Saturnalia of the Gallows'.[54] Not only were they reprehensible in themselves, but they augmented crime rather than discouraged it. As evidence, Ewart cited the testimony of Reverend J. Roberts of Bristol who had positively ascertained that of the 168 criminals he attended at the place of execution, 164 had previously witnessed at least one other execution.[55]

Henry Goulburn, who had been Home Secretary in Peel's

* A large number of capital punishments had been abolished in 1837 by Lord John Russell's Acts, a generic, collective title for individual acts. Attempted murder, robbery, burglary and arson were abolished. By 1840 execution was reserved by practice only for murder. The number of persons sentenced to death was reduced from 438 in 1837 to fifty-six in 1839. See Dymond, *The Law on Trial,* pp.38 ff.

† *Hansard,* Vol. LII (1840), col.914. Burke was emphatic about the urgency of repealing obsolete statutes and revising capital punishments. Pitt had been described as a 'Whig philanthropist with a detestation of cruelty'. Canning believed in reforming the penal laws and adapting them to the sentiments of the community. See Radzinowicz, op. cit., Vol. I, p.339; A. V. Dicey, *Lectures on the Relation Between Law and Public Opinion in England During the Nineteenth Century,* 2nd edn, Macmillan & Co., 1914, p.106. Canning had no dread of innovation in regard to reform of the penal laws 'after it had been seen that in the course of a century that crime and punishment were so seldom found together'. *Hansard,* Vol. XVI (1810), col.778. He voted in favour of Romilly's Bill in 1810.

first cabinet in 1834, granted the injurious nature of public executions, but he would not concede that capital punishment was ineffective. Goulburn betrayed the ambivalence of those who wished to retain executions, but shied away from the ultimate question concerning private executions as the alternative. He considered the possibility that executions might be 'inflicted in a mode otherwise than that calculated to produce those effects', but hastily added that he 'was not for a moment going to say that secret punishments were not objectionable'.[56]

Inexorably the debate was concentrating on the very related matter of public executions. Sir Stephen Lushington sought to counteract Lord John Russell. Russell had insisted that objections to the brutalizing effects of public executions would be removed by the decreasing number of executions reserved 'now only for grave and atrocious crimes'.[57] Lushington argued rather ingeniously that if one hundred executions in a year brutalized the public mind, 'six would do so in a twenty-fold greater degree'.*

The problem of public executions had become inextricably part of the debates. Since most of the anachronistic laws had been repealed, and barbarous punishment had become part of criminal-law history, the abolitionists now focused on total abolition for all crimes. The usual arguments of deterrence and non-deterrence remained. Recourse could still be given to the tables and statistics to show how severity tended to diminish the certainty of conviction. Murder, however, unlike the anomalous crimes that had been abolished, was still the most abhorrent and threatening. It was still the ultimate crime which had to be suppressed by the ultimate punishment. If it could be shown that public executions, the spectacle of the ultimate punishment, did not deter people by its terrifying and grisly scenes, then obviously capital punishment did not deter murderers. The abolitionists, as an integral facet of their anti-capital-punishment crusade, had to discredit public exe-

---

* *Hansard,* Vol. LII (1840), col.933. Sir Stephen Lushington (1782–1873) supported liberal causes throughout his long life. He was one of the founders of the Society for the Diffusion of Useful Knowledge; he supported Buxton's anti-slave efforts and Grote's resolution of the ballot. *D.N.B.,* Vol. XII, pp.292–3.

cutions in a number of ways: they were futile; they were in-
decent and immoral; they were abominations in a civilized
country; they hardened people to accept violence, and they
encouraged and excited criminal passions. But the dilemma of
the abolitionists was the possibility that their vivid denunciations of executions might influence retentionists, unhappy with
the institution of the public execution. They walked a tight-
rope.

Ewart's motion for abolition of capital punishment reached
a high-water mark with ninety Members of the House of
Commons voting for its passage. However, 161 Members voted
against it, and the motion was defeated.* Two days later, the
ever-optimistic Sydney Taylor wrote in a state of euphoria:
the doom of capital punishment was at hand; such a large vote
for abolition foreshadowed the end of capital punishment. He
was happy about the movement public opinion was taking
away from 'blood-stained' legislation; he was astounded at
the swift progress of the abolitionist reform movement:

When I started writing on 7th June, 1830, upon the question of reform of the criminal law . . . we little thought that within ten years
the anticipation thus indulged in would have been brought so
near fulfillment.[58]

Criminal-law reform advocates immediately seized what
appeared to be a most propitious time to push for further
reduction in capital crimes. Sir Fitzroy Kelly,† a law-reformer
and loyal supporter of Ewart, sought leave to introduce a Bill
to abolish the death penalty for all crimes except murder and
high treason; for all practical purposes, it would have limited
capital punishment to murder alone. Just five months after

---

* *Hansard*, Vol. L (1840), col.946. It was remarkable that Ewart's
motion received ninety votes in face of government opposition. Since
1832 the 100 to 120 independent radical Members had dwindled. Only
eight Members were estimated in 1840 to be radicals separate from the
government party. See Norman Gash, *Reaction and Reconstruction in
English Politics, 1832–1852*, Clarendon Press, 1965, p.88.

† Sir Fitzroy Kelly (1796–1880) sat in Parliament from 1834 to 1852.
He served as Solicitor-General, Attorney-General and Lord Chief Baron
of the Exchequer. His most famous case was the defence of John Frost,
the Chartist. *D.N.B.*, Vol. X, p.1236.

Ewart's motion to entirely abolish capital punishments received ninety votes, Kelly's more moderate Bill received only thirty-one votes on its third reading on 29 July 1840. Sydney Taylor, dismayed by the sudden reversal in the fortunes of criminal-law reform and in its severely reduced support in the House of Commons, sought explanations. He attributed the defeat of Kelly's Bill to the absence from London of most of the independent Members at the time of the vote.[59] He also blamed government influence – 'treasury circulars having been issued expressly for that purpose'.[60] There is the possibility that a particularly sensational crime dissuaded some Members from supporting Kelly's motion. François Courvoisier had, on 10 May 1840, murdered his employer, Lord William Russell, in bed at his Park Lane residence.* Five days later Charles Greville wrote about the event's impact on London society:

Just after I got back to Newmarket, the intelligence arrived of the extraordinary murder of Lord William Russell, which has excited prodigious interest and frightened all London out of its wits.[61]

The butler of the deceased victim was hanged on 6 July 1840, just twenty-five days before Kelly's motion was defeated; the trauma of the murder still reverberated.

Again, in 1841, Kelly sought to restrict capital punishments. Lord John Russell attempted to extend the scope of Kelly's motion by amendment. Russell's attempt to extend the Bill to include the abolition of death for arson of Her Majesty's ships and rape was defeated, and he then announced his opposition to Kelly's original Bill.† On 3 May 1841 Kelly

---

* John Cam Hobhouse (later Lord Broughton), President of the Board of Control in Melbourne's second cabinet, wrote about the way Lord John Russell was affected by his uncle's murder. At a cabinet meeting on 13 May 'we ... had some conversation on Mr Kelly's motion to abolish capital punishment, except for murder and high treason, a disagreeable subject for Lord John who, however, treated it very calmly and said he should request Mr Kelly to put off his motion for a short time. He looks very affected and worn by the death of his uncle.' Lord Broughton, *Recollections of a Long Life*, ed. Lady Dorchester, Vol. v, J. Murray, 1911, p.273.

† Spencer Walpole, *A History of Great Britain from the Conclusion of the Great War in 1815*, Vol. iv, Longman & Co., 1912, p.424. Lord

succumbed to the whole force of government opposition and withdrew his Bill.*

Between 1841, when Kelly introduced the last abolition Bill, and the introduction of the next attempt at abolition in 1849 England was stirred by the Anti-Corn Law League agitation and survived Chartist threats of revolution. In 1849, against continuing government opposition and decreasing parliamentary interest in criminal-law reform, Ewart again sought to abolish capital punishment. In the debate Ewart recalled an Act, passed during Queen Elizabeth's reign, which prescribed executions for pickpockets plying their trade among the crowd at the foot of the gallows – possibly at the very moment a pickpocket was writhing from a rope.[62] This, Ewart didactically pointed out, was 'the early proof and inefficacy of the demoralizing tendency of public executions'.[63] Sir George Grey had become Home Secretary in Russell's first cabinet formed in 1846; he was of the firm conviction that no further reduction in capital crimes should be made,[64] and he reminded Ewart that some years ago (in 1841) when a Bill was introduced to alter public executions no one protested against it more than Ewart, and yet, he continued, 'my honourable Friend has made the evils arising from public executions his strongest argument'.[65] Grey had exploited and exacerbated the raw, vulnerable area of the abolitionists' argument.

John Russell's position on capital punishment was very ambiguous. He had been one of the earliest supporters of Romilly; he had been a member of Sir James Mackintosh's Committee on Criminal Law in 1819; he supported the reform movement throughout its early uphill fight. Radzinowicz, op. cit., Vol. IV, p. 309. Later, he opposed all of William Ewart's reform efforts. This ambivalence is heightened by his professed opposition to capital punishment: 'I come to the conclusion that nothing would be lost to justice, nothing lost in preservation of innocent life if punishment of death were altogether abolished.' John Russell, *An Essay on the History of the English Government and Constitution from the Reign of Henry VIII to the Present Time*, Longman, Green, Longman, Roberts & Green, 1865, introduction, p.1.

* Broughton, op. cit., Vol. VI, p.18. More important than Kelly's own government's opposition was the attitude of the opposition party. Sir James Graham, who became Home Secretary in Peel's second cabinet, formed in September 1840, had privately told Hobhouse that he was 'opposed to any further reduction in capital crimes'. ibid., p.273.

The motion was rejected in a very small total vote in which was further evidence of decreasing interest. Among the seventy-four voting against the motion – only fifty-one voted for it – was Anthony Ashley Cooper, seventh Earl of Shaftesbury. The same zealous Christian morality which made him pity the exploited also directed him to punish the sinful. 'I have very strong feelings on the subject,' he wrote. 'I wished publicly to record my opinion that the word of God does not permit but commands, "He that sheddeth man's blood by man shall his blood be shed."'[66]

Sir George Grey made a most remarkable concession in the 1849 debate, stating that 'a public execution is not absolutely necessary. If that question comes before the House to be discussed on its merits, I shall be prepared to give my opinion.'[67] No previous Home Secretary had ever before admitted the possibility of abolishing public executions. Reaction was swift and strong. The *Eclectic Review*, a supporter of radical causes, religious liberty and abolition of capital punishment, condemned his conciliatory attitude towards altering public executions and accused him of wishing to substitute 'secret strangulation' for public executions. 'A large portion of his speech was devoted to a description of the depraving tendency of public executions,' it declared.

He spoke with manly and honest disgust of the evils incidental to such scenes, and hinted that if private executions were proposed, he would not object to the alteration. Now it is not our intention to discuss the propriety of substituting secret for public strangulation ... For on what grounds does Sir George Grey defend the punishment of death? 'On the grounds of its exemplarity ...' Yet Sir George Grey decries the 'exhibition' of the punishment which he approves![68]

The retentionists, like the abolitionists, were also caught up in a dilemma. They agreed that public executions were 'depraving', 'ugly', 'disgusting', 'evil', 'brutalizing', but retentionists had to accept their existence and continuance as necessary and exemplary.

In 1850 Ewart introduced another motion to abolish capital punishment. Disregarding his usual tactics, for he avoided discussing the futility and brutalizing effects of public executions, he concentrated his indignation on private executions. He insisted that these were merely substitutes for public executions and not cures; they were, in fact, greater evils. Government could not exclude the press from attending private executions, and reports about them would be more lurid and incite greater morbid curiosity throughout the nation. Moreover, the English people would not accept private executions. 'They were contrary to the genius of the constitution and the habits of the people.'[69]

Joseph Hume, who had seconded Ewart's motion, also attacked secret executions. How could a Home Secretary who believed that 'public executions tend to promote crime' carry one out to its fullest severity?[70] And John Bright, one of the chief speakers in favour of Ewart's motion, doubted whether 'it would be possible to propose much less carry out private executions in the country'.*

Bright noted how judiciously Sir George Grey avoided the question of private executions,[71] and how he had indeed dropped the matter. His vague concession about considering the question of private executions the previous year was attacked – although for different reasons – by the radical and conservative press alike.† *The Times* opposed any alteration in the mode of execution, stating in its leading article:

The question of capital punishment appears likely to be closely associated with the question of public executions . . . We are willing, on the contrary, that the two questions should for all purposes of argument be identified, for we are convinced that the same considerations which warrant the assumption of power over

* *Hansard*, Vol. cxii, col.1278. John Bright's biographer wrote, 'There's one subject on which Mr Bright has always felt strongly . . . the abolition of capital punishment.' J. Barnett Smith, *The Life and Speeches of the Right Hon. John Bright*, Vol. i, Hodder & Stoughton, 1881, p.18.

† The *Daily News*, however, under Charles Dickens's editorship, supported Sir George Grey and advocated private executions. See Dickens's powerful Letters to *The Times* on 14 and 19 November 1849, describing his position. The retentionist, conservative *Law Magazine* replied to Ewart that the only part of society which could object 'would be the vile mob'. Vol. xliv (1850), p.121.

life and death do also imperatively command that the exercise of this power should be a public solemnity.[72]

If Sir George Grey had sent up a trial balloon, it was pricked by the furore that raged over public executions following the hanging of the Mannings on 13 November 1849. Anger at that spectacle provoked bitter letters and articles in the press and periodicals, and produced vicious denunciations at public meetings. Sir George was caught between radical and conservative opinion. There was to be a long interval of six years until Parliament was again willing to look into the problem of public executions.

Ewart's motion to abolish capital punishment was defeated by forty-six votes to forty. That only eighty-six Members chose to vote showed the erosion of interest in Parliament over the issue. Many members probably had their reforming instincts blunted since executions had now become reserved entirely for murders. Some sparkle of interest might be rekindled by some sensational, well-publicized execution; but then it would flicker and sputter out. The repetitious arguments had become tedious, and some aversion to philanthropists had set in. England in the 1850s had begun to tire of being improved.

The avidly abolitionist *Eclectic Review* continued to breathe life into the movement. It was critical of absented Members, claiming that had at least half of Ewart's supporters been present, as they ought to have been, 'the cause would have been an actual as well as virtual triumph'.[73] The legislators needed to be pressured and coerced to achieve this elusive triumph; an obvious admission that the initiative and thrust for abolition was no longer in Parliament. 'The Society for the Abolition of Capital Punishment,' warned the *Eclectic Review*, 'will not fail to remind the constituents of these defaulters.'[74]

In its 'notices for the evening' on 23 April 1850 *The Times* noted 'the conspicuous space occupied by Mr Ewart's annual motion on the total abolition of capital punishments ... All questions must ultimately rest on the decision of public opinion, particularly true of that proposition Mr Ewart has taken under his care.'[75] Thus, *The Times*, a critic of Ewart and an opponent of his cause, had set forth the challenge. With

obviously depleted numbers and obvious lack of initiative on
the side of abolition, the government saw no pressing need to
change its position. Government, particularly that part which
still possessed an aristocratic caste, tended to make decisions
not on the basis of compulsion, but from a paternalistic sense
of greater wisdom and duty than the rest of the nation in
regard to national interest.

The abolitionists, supported by sympathetic newspapers,
journals and societies, were a vocal minority. They produced
the illusion of public opinion without the substance. Nourished
by the illusion, and by the certainty of the rightness of their
cause, the abolitionist movement limped on. Ewart, and other
reformers, refrained from pushing the issue again until 1856,
then 1864 and finally 1868, and each time without success.
The Times never wavered in its editorial policy; it remained
adamant in support of the retention of capital punishment for
murder; perhaps, better than radicals and reforming societies,
it reflected the attitudes of a retrenched, stable and prosperous
England as it entered the decade of the 1850s.

3

STIRRINGS FOR REFORM: SOCIETIES, PAMPHLETS AND JOURNALS

ATTITUDES had been progressively changing in the country and the legislation enacted reflected the compromise between prejudices and enlightenment. Dicey thought the failure of Parliament during the eighteenth century to introduce reasonable reforms was due far less to the prejudices of that body than to the deference 'paid to the dullness or stupidity of Englishmen'.[1] The development of public opinion as an influence on the legislature had accordingly been slow but continuous.* In the nineteenth century criminal-law reform proceeded as the conviction grew among a majority of those citizens effectively involved in public life that change was necessary and advisable. As the nineteenth century wore on, and as the old criminal-law structure was being dismantled piecemeal, the demand to repeal remaining anachronistic laws grew incessantly shriller and found greater acceptance. The gradual diminution of fear – fear of revolution, physical fear of the depraved, sullen masses, fear of incendiarism and destruction of property, fear of all kinds of lawlessness and violence – induced a parallel diminution of laws needed to repress by severity and terror.

Enlightened, dedicated men who organized societies, got up petitions, exposed abuses, published pamphlets and flooded

* The steady pressure of emerging public opinion on the legislature can be revealed by the number of petitions presented to Parliament. '880 petitions relating to all matters were presented to the House of Commons in the five years ending 1789; 1,206 in the five years ending 1805; 4,498 in the five years ending 1815; 24,492 in the five years ending 1831'. Leon Radzinowicz, *The History of English Criminal Law and its Administration from 1750*, Vol. I, London: Stevens & Sons, 1948–68, p.528.

the press with letters were important in this progress of reforming society. William Allen (1770–1843), chemist, Fellow
of the Linnean Society and the Royal Society, was a fine
representative of the committed reformer, deeply involved
and active in work to transform society. Sensitized by his
Quaker religion to abhor cruelty and to respect the sanctity of
human life, Allen was one of many of his own sect who had
shown great zeal in attempts to lessen the severity of the
criminal laws, especially the amelioration of capital punishment.*

In 1809 he founded the first society for the abolition of capital punishments, the Society for the Diffusion of Knowledge
Respecting the Punishment of Death and the Improvement of
Prison Discipline. He was aided by his co-religionist neighbour
Peter Bedford. Both men were as interested in removing unnecessary cruelty from the penal laws as they were in reducing
the causes of crime. Accordingly, William Allen and Peter
Bedford were also very involved with the Society for Lessen-
ing the Causes of Juvenile Delinquency in the Metropolis.[2]

Another staunch opponent of capital punishment was Basil
Montagu (1770–1851), son of the fourth Earl of Sandwich and
a friend of Bentham and Romilly. Montagu, a non-Quaker
collaborator with William Allen, was particularly instrumental in bringing before a larger audience the ideas and arguments of Sir Samuel Romilly. Under the aegis of the Society
for the Diffusion of Knowledge Respecting the Punishment of
Death, Basil Montagu published those proceedings of 1810 and
1811 of both Houses of Parliament which contained the
debates of Romilly's proposed amendments of the criminal
law.

In 1828 another and succeeding anti-capital punishment
society, the Society for the Diffusion of Information on the
Subject of Capital Punishments, was organized. Its London

* Hope was expressed in the 1881 Yearly Meeting of the Society of
Friends, and reported in the annual *Epistles* that 'as religion took a
deeper hold on the nation, the popular demand for the abolition of
capital punishment would gradually become too strong to be withstood'. Auguste Jorns, *The Quakers as Pioneers in Social Work*, New
York: Macmillan & Co., 1931, p.192.

chairman was the ubiquitous William Allen, and among its
members were Sir Thomas Fowell Buxton, Thomas Clarkson,
Leonard Horner, the Reverend Daniel Wilson (afterwards
Bishop of Calcutta), Stephen Lushington, Lord Suffield and
J. Sydney Taylor. The Society sponsored and organized lectures, published a series of five tracts on 'The Punishment of
Death', and sponsored the publication of valuable articles
from the *Morning Herald*. The Society also acted as a pressure
group on Parliament and was responsible for procuring in
1830 the signatures of 1,000 bankers to a petition for reform
of the laws on forgery.[3]

The Society for Promoting the Abolition of Capital Punishment – formed in 1846 – replaced the old society. Its founders
were Charles Gilpin, William Ewart, Frederic Hill and Thomas
Beggs.* John Thomas Barry (1790–1864), close associate of
William Allen and Basil Montagu, had an active share in its
formation and in its activities. It was Barry, along with his
old friend Peter Bedford, who raised funds to circulate several
thousand copies of Charles Phillips's *Vacation Thoughts on
Capital Punishment*. The volume cost one shilling and had 'a
very extensive circulation'.[4] Barry also promoted the abolitionist cause in the columns of the *Morning Herald*.

The Society for the Abolition of Capital Punishment prose-
lytized others to its cause. Charles Gilpin, Thomas Beggs and
Alfred Dymond visited the principal towns of England and
held meetings where 'the expediency of totally abolishing the
death penalty was brought prominently and repeatedly before
the public mind'.[5] Members of the Society, motivated by
humanitarian impulses, were eager to intercede between the
harshness of the law and its victims. Deputations of members
visited Home Secretaries to plead for reprieves from execution
for those criminals convicted under some special or extenuat-

* See Gordon Rose, *The Struggle for Penal Reform: The Howard
League and Its Predecessors*, London: Stevens & Sons, 1961, p.26, and
Alfred H. Dymond, *The Law on Trial, or Personal Recollections of the
Death Penalty and Its Opponents*, London: Society for the Abolition of
Capital Punishment, 1865, p.244. Dymond is a good source of first-hand
information of the abolitionist movement: its personalities, events and
methods. Dymond, a Quaker, was the secretary of the Society for the
Abolition of Capital Punishment.

ing circumstances. Spencer Walpole, Home Secretary in 1852, 1858 and 1866, was considered 'earnest and just'.[6] Sir George Grey was also thought of as a man of humane spirit, assiduous in his duty, but forced by his position to refuse the alteration of capital punishment even though he was in agreement with every criterion.[7] Grey's long tenure as Home Secretary, and as the holder of that office whenever Ewart's motions were introduced in Parliament, made him the symbol of obstruction and the backbone of the opposition against criminal-law reform.

The pressures placed on home secretaries were so intense and unremitting that even such a dedicated and vigorous opponent of capital punishment as Dymond could sympathize with the burdens placed on them. 'Truly,' Dymond empathized, 'the post is no sinecure.'[8] He has left a vivid description of how members hounded the Home Secretary:

In London deputations hunt him down like a deer; they watch the private entrance to the Home Office like revenue officers snaring a false coiner. They sight his exit as he escapes by the front stair case; raise the hue and cry down Parliament Street; circumvent him as he darts through the members' entrance and buttonhole him in the lobby.[9]

The Society for the Abolition of Capital Punishment used other methods to pressure the Home Secretary besides harassment by deputations. Some sensational case, or a controversial circumstance relating to the verdict or the execution itself, would lead the Society to bombard the press with letters and otherwise funnel their cause to sympathetic newspapers. They also called frequent public meetings at which memorials and petitions were circulated, signed and then presented to the Home Secretary. Public opinion could be a force even in the mid-century. Charlotte Harris was convicted in 1848 of murdering her husband; she was pregnant and her sentence was respited until after she gave birth. Some 40,000 women appealed to the Queen, and Charlotte Harris was reprieved.*

Occasionally the abolition societies would coordinate public meetings to coincide with abolitionist efforts initiated in the

---

* Dymond, op. cit., p.156. In the case of George Hall, however, despite 60,000 names on memorials and other pressures Sir George Grey refused to interfere in his execution. ibid., p.296.

House. The Society for the Abolition of Capital Punishment held a meeting in London the evening before William Ewart was scheduled to sponsor a motion for the creation of a select committee 'to inquire into the operation of the existing law imposing the punishment of death'.[10] Public pressure and agitation were continued: Charles Gilpin and Alfred Dymond spoke at a public meeting in Manchester at the Free Trade Hall; a motion was unanimously carried there 'to agitate parliamentary inquiry for the abolition of capital punishment'.[11] Dymond also spoke in Rochdale at a heavily attended meeting presided over by John Bright.[12] 'Educate, proselytize and agitate' was a formula used by the abolitionist societies to keep the issue alive and to mobilize public opinion.

The Howard Association, founded in 1866 in a Stoke Newington Friends' Meeting, superseded the Society for the Abolition of Capital Punishment. William Tallack, who had been the paid secretary of the Society for the Abolition of Capital Punishment, assumed the same position with the Howard Association, although the other organization, under the leadership of Thomas Beggs, lasted 'another two or three years until the money originally subscribed gave out'.[13] The Howard Association advocated abolition also, but it had as a goal the wider scope of criminal rehabilitation and penal reform. Among its patrons were Lord Brougham, Stephen Lushington, Sir John Bowring, William Ewart and John Hibbert, M.P.[14] Like its predecessors, it had important links with the business world, the press, Parliament and other societies. Sir John Bowring was editor of the *Westminster Review* and Lord Brougham was one of its chief contributors. Brougham, like Tallack, had close ties with the Social Science Association.*

Known officially as the National Association for the Pro-

* Rose, op. cit. The first meeting of the Social Science Association took place under Lord Brougham's 'roof and patronage in 1856'. B. Rodgers, 'The Social Science Association, 1857–1866'. *The Manchester School of Economic and Social Studies*, Vol. xx, September 1952, p.223. William Tallack had been influenced by Thomas Barwick Lloyd Baker, a Gloucestershire squire, in penal reform. Baker was instrumental in founding the Social Science Association. Rose, ibid., pp.22–3.

motion of Social Science, the Social Science Association was for nearly thirty years a force in Victorian England. It was a pressure group as well as a forum, and exerted an influence on the legislation of the day. It brought social reformers, lawyers, social workers, doctors and businessmen together at an annual congress. Divided into different departments, it was presided over by well-known figures, many of whom presented papers which were later published in the annual *Transactions of the National Association for the Promotion of Social Science.** The General Committee of the Social Science Association was composed of an impressive array of important and influential people in Victorian England. Of the 139 members of the General Council, no less than nineteen were peers or sons of peers; twenty-seven were Members of Parliament, ten were Fellows of the Royal Society. Also serving were such eminent people as Edwin Chadwick, Charles Kingsley, John Stuart Mill, John Ruskin and James Kaye-Shuttleworth.[15] Most of the lawyers in the Association were also members of the Law Amendment Society, founded by Lord Brougham in 1844 expressly to reorganize the legal system of the nation.[16]

Both the Society for the Abolition of Capital Punishment and the Howard Association used the annual congresses of the Social Science Association as effective public platforms. The congresses were held in major cities and their meetings were civic events,[17] reported in *The Times* and the *Guardian*.[18] Alfred Dymond, secretary of the Society for the Abolition of Capital Punishment from 1854 to 1857, valued the relationship with the Social Science Association. 'The appearance . . . of the Honorary and Acting Secretaries of the Society for the Abolition of Capital Punishment at Social Science meetings has been of great value to the cause.'[19] Also valued was the prestigious name of the National Association of the Social Sciences. Articles advocating abolition of capital punishment

* *Transactions of the National Association for the Promotion of Social Science* was published in London between the years 1857 and 1884, and in 1886. See James D. Stewart, Muriel E. Hammond and Erwin Saenger, eds., *British Union Catalogue of Periodicals: A Record of the Periodicals of the World from the Seventeenth Century to the Present Day, in British Libraries*, Vol. iii, Butterworth, 1964, p.299.

were first placed in the *Social Science Review*, the Association's journal, and then published later by the Society for the Abolition of Capital Punishment.* Thus, the views against capital punishment in the Social Science Association's publications guaranteed them a wider circulation and the attention of an important group of readers.

How effective were these multifarious activities of the abolitionist societies, and the Society for the Abolition of Capital Punishment in particular? The Society for the Abolition of Capital Punishment never achieved its goal. When the Royal Committee in 1866 recommended the abolition of public executions, the Society disbanded and reconstructed itself on the broader lines of the Howard Association.† It did, however, receive some belated, grudging acknowledgement for its achievements from *The Times*, its chief critic and nemesis. In a leading article in 1868, following the debate in the House of Lords on the second reading of the Bill amending the law of capital punishment, *The Times* was to marvel at the remarkable advance in public opinion on capital punishment.

If we go still further back, though not beyond the reach of living memory, we find eminent Judges solemnly protesting, in name of religion and on behalf of society, against the substitution of any secondary punishment for offences now considered almost trivial.[20]

The Times could not precisely account for what had quickened the reforming spirit and had turned much of the public opinion and so many of its leaders against enormous punishments for petty crimes. With some condescension it had to give some tentative credit for the change in climate for reform to the Society against which it had so long fought. 'The labours of

* See Thomas Beggs, *The Royal Commission and the Punishment of Death*, London: Society for the Abolition of Capital Punishment, 1866; *Analysis and Review of the Blue Book of the Royal Commission on Capital Punishment*, London: Society for the Abolition of Capital Punishment, 1866, and Tallack, op. cit. All three were reprinted from the *Social Science Review*.

† Collins, *Dickens and Crime*, Macmillan & Co., 1962, pp.247–8. Collins states categorically that 'by the 1860s the abolitionist movement was dead. In 1862 The Society for the Abolition of Capital Punishment was a very small society which previously had suspended its operations several times owing to lack of support.'

the Society for the Abolition of Capital Punishment may perhaps,' it stated clumsily and cautiously, 'have contributed to it.'[21]

The nineteenth century saw a proliferation of pamphlets and shilling magazines which attempted to influence attitudes on economic, social, religious and political matters, and much of the content was frank propaganda.* A propagandist in this tradition was Edward Gibbon Wakefield (1796–1862), an early and very influential critic of the penal code. Despite the exaggerated assertions of his biographer, who claimed Wakefield was responsible for reshaping the criminal code of England,† his role was essentially that of a pamphleteer whose writings provided the substance for arguments and insights used by later penal-reformers; they refined Wakefield's ideas and mined his uniquely intimate knowledge of criminals and their crimes.

Wakefield condemned punishments on the familiar principles of severity and futility espoused by Buxton, Bentham and Romilly whom he fully credited for his conversion to their doctrines.[22] He was, however, more important as an observer of criminal behaviour; his ability to capitalize on his own

---

* Broadsides, too, were important forms of propaganda. Charles Gilpin published an unabashed propagandistic broadside under the flamboyant title 'Grand Moral Spectacle'; it is with a collection of other gallows-literature in the British Museum in a volume of the originals previously cited as British Museum, *Murders*, p.102. 'Under the Authority of the Secretary of State for the Home Department this Saturday, April 17, 1847, a young girl, seventeen years of age is to be strangled in front of the County Gaol, Bury St Edmonds. She will appear attended by a minister of the Church of England, clad in his robes Canonical; also by the hangman, the Great Moral Teacher, who after fastening her arms, and putting a rope around her neck . . . and if the neck of the wretched victim be not by this shock broken, the said Moral Teacher will pull the legs of the miserable girl until by his weight . . . he strangles her.'

† See Irma O'Connor, *Edward Gibbon Wakefield, the Man Himself*, London: Selwyn & Blount, 1928, p.53. She wrote that Wakefield was responsible for the abolition of the death penalty for most serious crimes and for initiating agitation against the transportation of convicts. Wakefield must have come by his social conscience by example and inheritance. His father, a friend of Francis Place and James Mill, served on a parliamentary committee investigating mendicancy and pauperism; Elizabeth Fry, the saintly prison-reformer, was his cousin. ibid., p.21.

first-hand association with criminals added to the literature of crime.* Such accessibility to criminals made it possible for Wakefield to record an extraordinary conversation with a criminal whose execution had just been remitted. Wakefield's intent was to demonstrate the inefficacy of capital punishment as a deterrent when confronted by the criminal mentality with its curious blend of optimism and fatalism.

Q. Now, when you have been going to run a great risk of being caught and hanged, did the thought never come into your head that it would be as well to run the risk?

A: Never!

Q: Not when you remembered seeing men hanged for the same thing?

A: Oh! I never remembered anything about it; and if I had, what difference would that make? We must all take our chance. I never thought it would fall on me, and I don't think it ever will.

Q: But if it should?

A: Then I hope I should suffer like a man. Where's the use of sniffling?[23]

Wakefield's intimate knowledge of the criminal permitted him to write authoritatively about the criminal's attitudes and habits. His style was so assured that his observations took on a heightened sense of reality.

I feel assured that a considerable portion of the crowds which assemble to witness executions in London, consist of thieves. From all I could learn, I am inclined to believe that the criminals of London, spoken of as a class and allowing for exceptions, take the same sort of delight in witnessing executions as the sportsman and soldier find in the dangers of hunting and war.[24]

Wakefield excoriated judges, clergymen and executioners alike; they were the powers who sanctified sadistic repressions and imposed cruel injustices. He delighted in demolishing

* Edward Gibbon Wakefield served three years in Newgate from 1826 to 1829 for the abduction of the daughter of a wealthy manufacturer. Wakefield had persuaded the girl to marry him under false representation and the legality of the marriage was later struck down by a special Act of Parliament. *Dictionary of National Biography,* Vol. xx, Oxford University Press, 1959–60, pp.449–52.

them with satire and audacious irreverence for their persons and positions. The English judge condemned like a savage seeking murderous revenge. 'He has killed, strike him with the laws of vengeance.'[25] The awe of the judge and the majesty of the law were maintained by hanging. 'What,' Wakefield asked rhetorically, 'would the judge be without his black cap?'[26] The common people instinctively identified the judge's crimson robes with blood, and they reacted when they saw a judge: 'They draw in their breath and whisper, shuddering.'[27] Equally detestable to Wakefield was the hangman; he was hand-in-glove with the judge, a mercenary with a vested interest in putting people to death. The clergyman was exposed: he was sanctimonious and hypocritical; his wink from the scaffold, the usual signal to the hangman to release the drop, was symbolic of the entire clergy's cynical approval of brutal hanging laws designed solely to 'frighten the people and to beat them hollow'.[28]

Wakefield described a compulsively shocking and frenzied reaction to hanging – not any in particular, but a composite scene of horror and hate – that left no doubt about how execrable public executions were to him.

You will see such flashing of eyes and grinding of teeth; you will hear sighs and groans and words of rage and hatred, with fierce curses on the judges and hangman; and then laughter, such as it is after an unnatural kind; that will make you start; jests on the dead to turn you sick.[29]

Nor did the genteel middle classes escape Wakefield's satiric wrath; they were as guilty as the judges, clergymen and even the iniquitous executioner because of their indulgence and indifference to public executions and suffering. The newspaper-reading public read the following morning the usual account of an execution between bites of buttered toast and quaffs of strong tea. Details of the execution were always explicit and curiously familiar, as though from the same script but with a different cast. 'How this man seemed resigned to his fate,' Wakefield wrote, 'and that woman half with terror; how the necks were haltered and the faces capped; how he died without a struggle and she struggled for a while.'[30]

To contrast French and English reactions to public executions, an allegorical device was used by Wakefield in *Terror-struck Town*. The people of Dunkirk were gentle and humane, like Quakers; their children were well-behaved, not out of fear but from love. This idyllic life was shattered suddenly when a murder committed by two Paris swindlers transformed the town. The Douay court ordered a public execution for the two convicted murderers and these formerly gentle people were 'corrupted by the law'.[31] Now they were filled 'with a beastly curiosity so that they resembled an Old Bailey mob'.[32] Thereafter terror and dread pervaded Dunkirk's inhabitants. Some townpeople sent their families into the country; some prayed continually; some cursed the government; some talked incessantly about the horrid exhibition either from curiosity, compassion, anger or disgust. The reactions of the English residents, however, were markedly different from the local inhabitants.

Some of these could not imagine why the Flemings made such a fuss about nothing; and some engaged windows in the market-place, curious to see the difference between hanging and the guillotine.[33]

Another pamphleteer sharing Wakefield's opinions about capital punishment, although not in quite so doctrinaire a manner, was George Jacob Holyoake (1817–1906).* He anathemized public executions and savagely denounced them as did Wakefield. He also fought the hangman for many years with the intention of abolishing 'him'. He intended to expose the fatuity of the spectacle, but unlike Wakefield he was willing to compromise, expressing the opinion that if capital punishment could not be abolished he 'would be content to repress public executions as a public teacher'.[34]

Holyoake exaggerated his influence on the trend of reform, claiming that he had fought capital punishment and public executions before public opposition to them had become so

---

* G. J. Holyoake engaged in a variety of propaganda through books, pamphlets and voluminous correspondence with the press. He was the last person in England imprisoned for blasphemy. Stanley J. Kunitz and Howard Haycraft, *British Authors of the Nineteenth Century*, New York: H. W. Wilson Co., 1936, p.30.

widespread.[35] Newspapers, Holyoake asserted, were influenced by his writings and many of them, which had never written against public executions before, were now 'against the spectacle'.[36] When *The Times* wrote a leading article about the execution of Franz Müller, Holyoake claimed that it was inspired by his letter in the *Morning Star* on 16 November 1864.[37] Holyoake assumed much of the credit for the 'distrust of public killing which had crept into many minds'.[38] His views inveighed upon the Grand Jury at Manchester to protest against executions in that city, he said.[39]

Audacious exaggeration aside, his writings, both as a newspaperman and pamphleteer, provide a fine example of radical opinion, and his flamboyant, hyperbolic style was forceful, vivid and evocative.

The condemned has been kept a fortnight within hearing of the very footstep of death daily coming nearer and nearer to him. He is brought out alive and well and conscious upon the scaffold. Twenty-thousand strange eyes glare upon him with hungry, terror-striking warning. He is shown to the excited mob before his face is covered ... The wretch stands face to face with inevitable, piti-less, premeditated death. Not the scythe, but the strange cold cord of death strikes against his ear, and the crowd knows he knows it. They see the neck. The noose is adjusted, the click of the drop is heard by the hushed throng and the wretch descends still in sight; and then the rain, the cold, the damp, the struggling of the night is all forgotten in the coveted gratification of that horrible moment.*

Holyoake could be moved to strident moral indignation. 'Why did the Archbishop of York condemn sensational novels,' he wondered, 'and not utter one word against this vile, this real, this overriding villainous sensation provided by the government in every country of the Kingdom?'[40]

That he was no humanitarian, Holyoake readily admitted. He promised he would, if given the responsibility, make short work of the 'right knave' to protect society from further harm. Although his position on capital punishment was blurred and ambivalent, he continued to condemn it, and almost by the

* George Jacob Holyoake, 'Public Lessons of the Hangman', London: Farrah, 1864, pp.2–3. This pamphlet was sold for one penny or four shillings for one hundred.

ritual of radicalism, continued to insist that experience had already condemned hanging and that 'murder will be regarded with greater horror'[41] when executions are done away with. There was no such ambivalence in regard to public executions: Holyoake predicted unequivocably that 'it will be better for society when public killings are at an end'.*

Few articles about capital punishment and public executions appeared in respectable middle-class magazines.[42] Journals like the radical, non-conformist *Eclectic Review*, and *Punch* which had listed the abolition of capital punishment as one of its avowed goals, struck vigorously at the institution of the gallows. *Punch*, in the very first article of its first issue in 1841, announced as part of its manifesto, entitled 'The Moral of Punch', its opposition to capital punishment.

We now come to the last great lesson of our motley teacher – the gallows; that accursed tree which has its roots in injuries. How clearly *Punch* exposes the fallacy of that dreadful law which authorizes the destruction of life.[43]

One of *Punch*'s most prolific and influential contributors during the 1840s was Douglas Jerrold, and he was very instrumental in its campaign against capital punishment and public executions.[44] He sanguinely predicted that 'the gallows is doomed, is crumbling, and must down – overthrown by no greater instruments than a few goose quills'.[45] Henry Mayhew,

---

* ibid. As a counterpoise to the radical ideas of Wakefield and Holyoake, the opinions of Joseph Kingsmill, chaplain of Pentonville Prison, represent that part of England which took the Bible literally and applied its lessons to society. The Bible authorized executions for murder – 'the land cannot be cleansed of the blood that is so shed therein, but by the blood of him that shed it'. Death penalties are sanctified by God and form part of the code of laws God himself gave to his chosen people. Kingsmill insisted that the state had the same right of self-defence that any threatened person had against attack, and could resort to violence to protect itself. Only the terror of the gallows was sufficient to deter the wicked, and very many semi-insane people from the commission of violence and murder. Kingsmill was contemptuous of those misguided people who showered more mercy on the murderers about to be executed than on those about to be murdered. See Joseph Kingsmill, *Chapters on Prison and Prisoners and the Prevention of Crime*, 3rd edn, Longman, Brown & Green, 1854, pp.377 ff.

famed author of *London Labour and the London Poor*, and one
of the founders of *Punch*,[46] must have decisively influenced
Punch's editorial policy on capital punishment. Mayhew was
a writer of anti-capital-punishment literature and an active
member of the Committee for the Abolition of Capital Punishment, and he remained a firm, consistent abolitionist.

Also important in *Punch*'s efforts to bring down the gallows
was John Leech. His Hogarthian cartoon, 'The Great Moral
Lesson at Horsemonger-lane Gaol',[47] depicted the raucous,
drunken, carnival-like atmosphere that surrounded the execution of the Mannings. Under the cartoon was a poem, 'The
Lesson of the Scaffold, or the Ruffian's Holiday', which
described the reactions of two illiterate Londoners who had
spent a jolly night waiting for the execution to take place. The
lesson of the gallows was wasted on the two who shrugged it
off as a 'tumble and a kick'.[48] When their time came, they
boasted, they would die just as game.

By 1850 *Punch*'s crusade against capital punishment had
petered out.* The journal had grown so increasingly conservative that on *Punch*'s fiftieth anniversary in 1891 *The Times*
smugly commented, 'May we be excused for noting the fact
that he [*Punch*] has generally, in regard to public affairs, taken
his cue from *The Times*.'[49]

On the other hand, the *Eclectic Review* continued, with
moderation, as an outspoken, implacable organ for the abolitionist point of view,† still optimistic in 1848 that capital
punishment was soon to follow the rack, the inquisition and
the Smithfield fires, never to return. Its optimism sprang from
its conviction that 'the defenders of the pain of death are
daily becoming fewer, and only a very limited portion of the

---

* W. L. Burn observed that '*Punch*, which had been a better Radical
journal under Douglas Jerrold's influence, changed its tone when his
influence was superseded in 1847–48 by that of Thackeray and Leech.'
The Age of Equipoise: A Study of the Mid-Victorian Generation, New
York: W. W. Norton & Co., 1964, p.13.

† Some of the articles in the *Eclectic Review* in 1848 were written by
members of the Society for the Abolition of Capital Punishment.
Frederick Rowton, Secretary of its London Society, contributed 'The
Punishment of Death Reviewed' and Lord Nugent wrote 'Crime and
Punishments'. *Eclectic Review*, Vol. xxi, April 1848, table of contents.

community can now be found to maintain it, even for the extreme crime of murder'.[50] It cited a large number of books and articles written in Great Britain and abroad as tangible evidence of the widespread concern with the problem of capital punishment and the increasing disenchantment with it.

The books before us show that the question of capital punishment has penetrated into every class of the civilized community. We have here, not merely the extremes, but every gradation of the social scale. A monarch, a nobleman, a doctor of divinity, two Edinburgh baillies, a popular novel-writer, a theological tutor, a chartist, and a country-gentleman are amongst the writers who present themselves for review. Moreover, the subject is discussed in parliament; public meetings are held to debate it; our newspapers take it up; our magazines, legal and literary, gravely consider it. What clearer proof could there be that the time for its final discussion and settlement is come?[51]

Soon the *Eclectic Review* was drawn into the acrimonious debate over the apostate, Charles Dickens, whom it had previously and approvingly referred to as 'the popular novel-writer'. Dickens had fallen, by 1850, from the inspired ranks of the faithful; he was branded now as a man blinded by Sir George Grey's vague suggestion of the possible alteration of public executions. The defection of such an eminent man as Dickens rankled the *Eclectic Review*; it accused him of his willingness to hide executions on any terms, and 'to forego his well-known desire for the abolition of the death punishment altogether'.[52] Although it agreed with Dickens's denunciation of public executions as judicial homicide performed in public view, it was unwilling to accept his alternative of private executions. It was the open and public nature of proceedings in England, the *Eclectic Review* contended, which produced that quality in the English people which contrasted so favourably with the 'dark, deadly characteristics of people under inquisitorial government'.[53] There was no doubt that abrogation of any of the forms of open and public proceedings in England would establish a precedent that could lead only to tyranny and accordingly the *Eclectic Review* raised the alarm.

The necessity which now exists for displaying before the public every exercise of the power of life and death is unquestionably a check upon the State ... We could not safely entrust the power of secret extermination to the State because of the likelihood that the power would be abused by over-exercise, by unconcern and by official hardness of heart. Not only should we suspect that many were hanged who ought not to be, but we should also suppose that many were not hanged who were sentenced to die.[54]

Thus, the radical, abolitionist *Eclectic Review* found itself strangely in agreement with the conservative, retentionist *Times.* By the paradox of such an unusual editorial agreement, the *Eclectic Review* was able to quote *The Times* for support against the abolition of public executions.

As *The Times* very truly said in one of its powerful articles on the subject 'The English are too jealous a people to permit such a law and if they did not see the execution, they would not believe that it had taken place, the more especially if the culprit were a rich, a noble or a well-connected one.'*

Fraser's Magazine joined the anti-capital-punishment ranks in the early 1840s when it published a bitter rejection of capital punishment written by Thackeray after he attended the execution of Courvoisier on 4 July 1840. 'It seems,' Thackeray wrote, 'that I have been abetting an act of frightful wickedness and violence performed by a set of men against one of their fellows.'[55]

Forty thousand persons – say the Sheriffs – of all ranks and degrees, mechanics, gentlemen, pickpockets, members of both houses of parliament, street walkers, newspaper writers ... Pickpocket and peer, each is tickled by the sight alike, and has the hidden lust after blood which influences our race.... Monday morning at eight o'clock this man is placed under a beam, with a rope connecting it and him; a plank disappears from under him, and those who have paid for good places may see the heads of the

* ibid., Vol. xxiii, p.42. Reviving old rumours as reinforcement of the belief that criminals had been – and would be – treated preferentially, the *Eclectic Review* retold the old stories about Dr Dodd, the minister friend of the influential, cheating the gallows by a silver pipe inserted in his throat to prevent strangulation, and Fauntleroy, the errant banker, who was hanged in effigy and permitted to escape as did Tawell, the Quaker, who was supposedly seen later in America.

D

government agent, Jack Ketch, coming up from his black hole, and seizing the prisoner's legs, and pulling them until he is quite dead – strangled.[56]

When Monckton Milnes and he came upon two girls, about eleven and twelve, in the enormous mob at the place of execution, one of them was crying hysterically and begged the men to take her away. They asked the older girl, a very pretty one, what had made her come there in the first place. She grinned and said, 'We've koom to see the mon hanged!'[57] 'Tender law,' Thackeray commented with didactic sarcasm, 'that brings out babes upon such errands and provides them with such moral spectacles.'[58]

By 1864 the position of *Fraser's Magazine* on capital punishment changed drastically, reflecting a growing conservatism and changed attitude to hanging. Contents of a magazine in the nineteenth century usually revealed editorial policy; James F. Stephens, the noted lawyer and criminal-law historian, authored a hard-line, retentionist article for the June issue. The purpose of criminal law, Stephens wrote, was to control and suppress passions. 'If we in England,' he stated, revealing some defensiveness about the harshness of English justice, 'are more alive to this than other people, so much the better for us, and so much the worse for them.'[59] Moreover, Stephens was convinced that no other punishment but the death penalty deterred men effectively from committing murder and no other punishment gratified and justified in so emphatic a manner the 'vindictive sentiment'.*

The *Spectator* pursued a consistent but moderate position. It

* Stephens, 'Capital Punishment'. This argument reinforces Karl Menninger's observation that 'the public has a fascination for violence and clings tenaciously to its yen for vengeance'. Karl Menninger, 'The Crime of Punishment', *Saturday Review*, Vol. LI, 7 September 1968, p.55. The craving for vengeance persists even to the degree of sadism. A letter in the *Huddersfield Daily Examiner* stated quite unabashedly, and apparently published in the same vein, that 'for murderings of policemen, prison officers, security men, and murderings for robbery, I would support amputations of both legs up to the body, plus prison for ten years, with no artificial limbs in the offing ... Further violence, if any, could be dealt with by further deformities.' Quoted in 'This England', *New Statesman*, Vol. LXIX, 15 January 1965, p.70.

deplored public executions but never freed itself from a dis-
quieting uncertainty about the proper remedy. It seriously
questioned the policy of inflicting death before vast audiences
and alluded to Dickens's letter to *The Times* about the executions of the Mannings when it editorialized that 'hardly any
benefit can be conferred on the criminal and the ragamuffin
public by witnessing the compulsive kicks of a suspended
human being'.[60] The *Spectator* veered away from the obvious
conclusion of advocating private executions, and preferred to
permit the issue to remain clouded and inconclusive. It con-
signed the public-execution-versus-private-execution controversy to the state of limbo and hoped, in an evasive way, that
the stir which had set men thinking 'may bring about substantial conclusions'.[61]

Hesitancy and timidity to advocate private executions
sprang, in the *Spectator*'s case, from fear that private executions would turn into 'a small tea party selected from certain
official circles'.[62] There was a real underlying anxiety that private executions might be retrogressive and arbitrary; that
hierarchical government could be reimposed as a result. A
pattern of concern developed about the possible chain of
events should public proceedings be made private. The *Spectator* faced a dilemma; its choice was between public executions which excited 'wild and vehement passions among the
vagabond sections of our population'[63] and private executions
which the magazine still regarded as a form of 'private
assassination'.[64]

As late as 1864 the *Spectator* remained troubled about the
potential dangers of private executions, but by then it no
longer considered these incipient dangers irremovable.
Sufficient experience in other countries indicated that private
executions were feasible and did not lead to government
tyranny. Yet the *Spectator* demurred from giving private
executions its total endorsement; there was that prolonged, lurk-
ing suspicion that Englishmen would trust no government –
even under a judge's sentence – to execute anyone privately
before government witnesses alone. Executions must be performed under certain rigidly prescribed conditions in order
to allay public hostility and suspicion. Thus, the *Spectator*

suggested that executions should be carried out in a hall especially added to Newgate, and these conducted

with the solemnity of an act of religion and only in the presence of a clergyman, a surgeon, and a body of witnesses especially admitted to testify to the identity and to the fact of death, and the absence of all cruelty.[65]

The *Spectator* rejected the suggestion that the jury should be present at the private execution. It thought the idea bad because it was self-defeating; forcing juries to be present at executions would result in seldom getting convictions in capital cases.[66]

'The hour is surely at hand,' pronounced Henry Rogers in *Good Words*, 'when England must abolish either public executions or capital punishments.'* He attributed this point of decision principally to the interest raised by the press in public executions and capital punishment, and cited the painfully vivid photographs of executions. 'Without their aid,' Rogers wrote, 'the mass of people would never have had their minds sufficiently possessed of the facts to form a judgement.'[67]

Rogers accepted the fact that the majority of the people were pretty well agreed about the retention of capital punishment for cases of clear murder,[68] but he warned that unless the plausible arguments against private executions were not removed, the uproar about them could readily jeopardize the retention of capital punishment altogether. He urged guarantees to counteract the suspicion that executions would not be carried out impartially within prison walls. The presence of proper officials, he thought, would go a long way in removing lingering vestiges of doubt.

Rogers favoured private executions because he thought they would have a beneficial effect on the 'criminal class', removing the theatrical bravado before multitudes that had transformed many of the executed into heroes.[69] But what effect would private executions have on the people in general?

* Henry Rogers, 'On Public Executions', *Good Words*, Vol. VI, April 1865, p.104. Rogers was not about to give up supposed deterrents easily; he was openly delighted with the reintroduction of corporal punishment for garrotting and public destruction. ibid.

Rogers believed that private executions inflamed the imaginations and increased 'the awe and mystery which would be associated with that terrible and silent scene'.[70] These would more powerfully affect people than 'the heterogenous reminiscences of a public execution'.[71]

All the Year Round, the weekly journal published by Charles Dickens,* included an article by an anonymous clergyman who had attended a criminal on the scaffold. From this, his first and only experience at a public execution, he denied the accuracy of reports about executions that he had read previously in the press. They did not, he said, resemble his observations of the execution he attended. 'I have never yet read,' he stated categorically, 'what has impressed me as a truthful account of any such a scene.'[72] Then departing from the usual practice of calumning the executioner, Calcraft, he instead dealt with him kindly and almost sentimentally. 'I can see him as I write, a mild, gentlefaced man, his eyes full and grey, though small and sweet in their expression.'[73]

While Calcraft was pinioning the victim, the chaplain had already begun the solemn service for the dead. 'I am the Resurrection and the Life' – the big bell of St Sepulchre Church was tolling slowly and deeply – 'Whoever liveth and believeth in Me shall never die.'

'It's my own invention,' Calcraft whispered with some modesty. 'The old pinions used to hurt the poor fellow so ... This waist strap answers every person and is not the least uncomfortable.'... Then he fixed the rope with long pains to arrange the knot in the most merciful place. ... And there was a fall and something was swaying to and fro, till at last it became steady. ... And there was the noise of the crowd ... and it woke up into life to go about its business.[74]

That such an account could be published was extraordinary in the face of public and private condemnation; and that it was in a journal published by Charles Dickens was very revealing.

* Dickens had begun publication of *All the Year Round* in 1859; it contained many articles on social issues, and on crime and punishments. Although Dickens wrote some articles, many were written at his suggestion and according to his instructions – and always subject to the power of his veto. Collins, op. cit., p.12.

A complex man of strong emotions and intense feelings, Dickens did not, obviously, mirror the sentiments of moderate people who instinctively sought the middle ground and veered away from the extremes.* It was the moderates who had begun to accept the abolition of public executions on principle. Retention of capital punishment for murder was no longer in doubt. The only questions which remained were how and when abolition of public executions was to take place.

* Dickens's enormous influence as a journalist and prolific writer of letters to the press will be considered in Chapter 4, and his metamorphosis from abolitionist to retentionist will also be traced there.

4

CONTROVERSY OVER PUNISHMENTS: THE PRESS AND PUBLIC OPINION

IN the nineteenth-century magazines, particularly the respectable middle-class ones, slight heed was given to public executions and the problems of capital punishment, but newspapers pandered to their readers' taste for gore, printing detailed, grisly descriptions of murders and executions. In the first quarter of the nineteenth century, the economics of newspaper finances had changed drastically; newspapers had begun to depend on their sales for profit rather than on government subsidies for existence.* They found profit in exploiting public interest in sensation. Fulfilling the morbid curiosities of their readers about the dark, violent recesses of their society helped increase their circulation. Moreover, a new class of readers had begun to emerge. Working-class literacy had developed so much that in 1849 there were 5,260 pubs and 2,748 beer-shops in England which served as reading-rooms for working-men, and it was in these places that newspapers were read.† Nineteenth-century moralists deplored working-class reading

* In 1795 the editor of *The Times* had supported the government in return for a pension of £600; by 1815 such an offer would have been ludicrous. Lord Liverpool, the Prime Minister in 1815, petulantly remarked to Lord Castlereagh: 'No paper of character, consequently one with an established sale, will accept money from Government; and indeed their profits are so enormous in all critical times, when their support is most necessary, that no pecuniary assistance that government can offer would really be worth their acceptance. The truth is they look only to their sale.' D. C. Somervell, *English Thought in the Nineteenth Century*, New York: David McKay, 1965, p.56.

† R. K. Webb, *The British Working Class Reader, 1790–1848*, George Allen & Unwin, 1955, p.33. The most popular working-class newspaper was the *Morning Advertiser*, for which Karl Marx wrote in the 1850s.

habits; they had 'a very licentious tendency sufficient to excite evil passions'.[1] Newspapers found it profitable and necessary to accommodate the tastes of this new class of readers.

As newspapers grew independent of government and looked to their circulation for profit, their editorial policies and the slant of their news-coverage reflected this liberty. Many newspapers became critics of government; others became agitators for reform; some became both. Lord Liverpool complained that the newspapers now took their lead in editorial policy from the readers.

They make their way like sycophants with the public by finding out the prejudices and prepossessions of the moment and flattering them; and the number of soi-disant government or opposition papers abound as the government is generally popular or unpopular.[2]

Newspapers often took the lead in reform, and enjoyed some success in effecting the changes for which they agitated. John Stuart Mill credited John Black, the editor of the *Morning Chronicle*, with a great share in reforming the laws and courts. 'He kept up,' Mill wrote, 'an incessant fire against ... the absurdities and vices of the law and courts of justice until he forced some sense of them into the people's mind.'*

The press was often more radical than the advanced liberals in the House of Commons. The *Morning Advertiser* in 1837 – acknowledging the debt owed William Ewart for reducing the number of death penalties – felt obliged to rebuke Ewart for his moderation, pointing out that he should have pushed for total abolition of capital punishment.

---

* John Stuart Mill, *The Autobiography of John Stuart Mill*, New York: New American Library, 1964, p.80. The *Morning Chronicle* was also sympathetic to reform of capital punishment; its Paris correspondent wrote, 'Oh! If the people of England did but know one-thousandth part of what is said and thought throughout civilized Europe of these periodical executions in London, and at the county assizes; I cannot but think they would demand the abolition of capital punishment with the same unanimity and energy as they now display for a reform in Parliament.' J. S. Taylor, *Selections from the Writings of John Sydney Taylor*, London: Charles Gilpin, 1843, p.44.

Deeply indebted as we consider ourselves and the good cause to Mr Ewart . . . we do not hesitate to say that we go farther than he does in our view of that complete reform of the code which is justified at once by expedience, by humanity and by reflecting the spirit of the age.[3]

Also hammering away at the criminal code was the *Morning Herald* under its editor, J. Sydney Taylor. An indication of this newspaper's crusading effectiveness was the endorsement of a resolution at a meeting of the Committee for the Diffusion of Information on the Subject of Capital Punishments, on 30 November 1835, which cited the *Morning Herald* for its contribution to criminal-law reform.

Resolved – that the articles upon criminal law, which have appeared from time to time for several years past in the columns of the *Morning Herald*, are of a character to especially call for the grateful acknowledgment of this Committee as having materially contributed to promote the recent amelioration of the penal code.[4]

As outspoken as many newspapers were against the continuation of capital punishment, the press was generally hostile to the suggestion of abolishing public executions. Speaking for almost the entire press in its astringent comment on Rich's motion on 16 February 1841 to abolish public executions, the *Morning Post*'s leading article stated:

The Honourable Member does not seem to entertain any abstract objection to the punishment of death. He simply proposes to convert it into a luxury to the enjoyment of which a select few distinguished amateurs are to be admitted by tickets.[5]

But the press's assault on Rich's proposed reform of public executions was academic; he had withdrawn his motion almost immediately after its cold reception in the House of Commons.

Of importance were letters written in the *Daily News* by its editor, Charles Dickens, on 28 February and 9, 13 and 16 March 1846. Dickens had gone to the execution of Courvoisier and was appalled and disgusted with what he had seen there. He had previously written to Macvey Napier on 28 July 1845 of his intense hatred of public hangings:

I believe the punishment of death to have a horrible fascination for many of those persons who render themselves liable to it, impelling them onward to the acquisition of a frightful notoriety ... I presume this to be the case in very badly regulated minds, when I observe the strange fascination which everything connected with this punishment, on the object of it, possesses of tens of thousands of decent, virtuous, well-conducted people, who are quite unable to resist the published letters, anecdotes, smilings, snuff-takings of the bloodiest and most unnatural scoundrel with the gallows before him ... Regarding it to do harm to both these classes (criminal and gentle), it may even be right to enquire whether it has any salutary influence on those small knots and specks of people ... who actually behold its infliction ... Again, it is a great question whether ignorant and irresolute persons (ever the great body of spectators, as few others will attend), seeing that murder done, and not having seen the other, will almost of necessity, sympathize with the man who dies before them, especially as he is shown a martyr to their fancy, tied and bound along with every kind of odds against him.[6]

It was the letters following the Courvoisier hanging that initiated his public entry into the controversy over capital punishment and public executions and created a greater public debate than any previous condemnations.*

In the *Daily News* letters Dickens wrote at great length; possibly at greater length than about any other social question.[7] Not only were they long, but in them Dickens used every conceivable argument against hanging – psychological insights, emotion, statistics and references to contemporary literature on the subject. Dickens wondered whether it was an insatiate craving for notoriety which produced the 'incentive and impulse'† to commit murder; he cited the familiar statis-

* Philip Collins wrote about Dickens: 'How and when he came to oppose capital punishment is uncertain. He was sympathetic to the cause, at least in May, 1840, when he wrote the prominent abolitionist Henry Gilpin, "I should be most happy to promote your object, but I fear it is not in my power to do so. The worthiness of your work, no one, I imagine, can question for a moment."' *Dickens and Crime*, Macmillan & Co., 1962, pp.223–4.

† Charles Dickens, *Miscellaneous Papers*, ed. B. W. Matz, Vol. I, Chapman & Hall, 1908, p.30. Dickens was very interested in the psychological compulsion to commit murder. 'I have made an enquiry,' he wrote, 'and am assured that the youth now under sentence of death in Newgate ... was a vigilant of the last public execution in this City.' ibid., p.48.

EXECUTION

OF COURVOISIER,

Who was Executed on Monday July the 6th, 1840, for the Wilful Murder of Lord William Russell, on Wednesday, May 6th, at his Residence, 14, Norfolk-Street, Park-lane, London.

Since the period of his condemnation the convict Courvoisier, maintained the same apparent indisposition to the dreadful death he was about to undergo as he had previous to his trial, and appeared to have had an amusement in inventing various and false versions of his confessions; the one day declaring that Lord Russell caught him in the act of plundering, the next that his Lordship never left his bed, and the third that he had buried some money in the cell, at Bow-street, so that at length nothing could be relied upon in any of his statements, except the fact of his having committed the murder; his confessions being so various, and proved to contain so many falsehoods. This hardihood continued until the visit of his Uncle, with whom he had two interviews, in the presence of the Chaplain of Newgate.

His Uncle is a person of great respectability, and has been for eighteen years in the service of Sir George Beaumont; these interviews there is every reason to believe, were productive of the most beneficial results, as the convict appeared awakened to his awful situation and explained many of the inconsistences in his confession.

On Sunday the Rev Mr. Carver, the Ordinary of Newgate, preached the condemned Sermon, in the Chapel of Newgate, to the prisoner, and a very crowded auditory; taking his text from Job, chap. xxiv., ver 21, 22

The Rev. Gentleman entered in the most full manner into the enormity of the prisoner's crime, who from motives of avarice and plunder had shed the blood, not only of an aged and unoffended nobleman but that nobleman his kind and indulgent master, who intrusted his life in his hands, yet, whom he murdered while in the calm repose of sleep. After warning the other prisoners from the commission of so heinous a crime and detailing by the prisoner's example the certainty of guilt, however cunningly devised and speedily punished by Law, he endeavoured to awaken in the Culprit that although here death was certain, yet, however enormous his guilt, by throwing himself by due repentance upon the mercies of the Redeemer, he might still inherit everlasting life in the world to come. The prisoner appeared to feel deeply throughout, and there was scarcely a dry eye among the crowded congregation. During the last night for the unhappy malefactor he slept for about three hours, and on awaking, anxiously enquired what time it was.

THE OLD BAILEY

From an early hour this morning the workmen where busily engaged in making the necessary preparations for the awful ceremony which was about to take place; barriers were placed at the end of Newgate Street, and in all the other thoroughfares to prevent accidents from the denseness of the crowd, and at about 6 o'clock, the engine of death was wheeled out of the great gates and placed in front of the Debtors door; large bodies of police also now marched to various stations in order to preserve order. The crowd now began to assemble and the whole of the area was speedily filled by the dense multitude; every avenue, window, and house-stop, which could command a view of the place of execution, being crowded with spectators.

THE GAOL.

At ten minutes past 7 o'clock, the Sheriffs and other authorities arrived at the Gaol and having proceeded to the press room, the culprit was summoned from his cell and conveyed to the Chapel, where he received the Sacrament, having declared his deep penitence for his crime; he was then conducted to the press-room, where the awful preparations for death, by pinioning his arms, placing the fatal cap on his head, &c , commenced, The prisoner appeared overcome by his situation and wept bitterly.

The Prison Bell now began to toll, and the preparations being complete, the last procession moved towards the drop, the Chaplain reading the Funeral Service. Upon the prisoner's arriving on the drop an audible shudder ran throughout the crowd. He took his stand on the drop, the fatal noose was shortly adjusted, the bolt drawn, and the unhappy man was launched into eternity, and in a few minutes ceased to exist.

John Bonner, Printer, 31, Back Street, Bristol.

'Execution of Courvoisier.' Broadside – John Bonner, Bristol, 6 July, 1840. Francois Courvoisier was convicted and executed for the murder of Lord William Russell.

tics of the 167 persons under the sentence of death of whom
only three had not previously witnessed an execution;[8] he
quoted the Reverend Henry Christmas's recent pamphlet
'Capital Punishments Unnecessary in a Christian State' to re-
fute the 'whoso sheddeth man's blood' argument as justification for putting murderers to death.[9]

What made Dickens's letters to the *Daily News* so important and effective – aside from his enormous prestige – was his
skill as a novelist in recreating the scenes of executions and in
communicating his detestation of them so vividly and drama-
tically.

I was present myself, at the execution of Courvoisier. I was pur-
posely on the spot from midnight of the night before, and was a
near witness to the whole process of the building of the scaffold,
the gathering of the crowd, the gradual swelling of the concourse,
with coming on of the day, the hanging of the man, the cutting of
the body down, and the removal of it into Prison. From the
moment of my arrival when there were but a few score boys in the
street, and those all young thieves, and all clustered together
behind the barrier nearest the drop – down to the time when I saw
the body with its dangling head being carried on a wooden bier into
the gaol – I did not see one token in all the immense crowd of any
emotion suitable to the occasion. No sorrow, no salutary terror, no
abhorrence, no seriousness, nothing but ribaldry, debauchery,
levity, drunkenness and flaunting vice in fifty other shapes. I should
have deemed it impossible that I could have ever felt any large
assemblage of my fellow-creatures to be so odious.*

In the last of the three letters Dickens urged total abolition
of death penalties on the general principle that society would
benefit and crime would be prevented. He was emphatic that
his decision to oppose capital punishment was neither from
squeamishness nor from an effusive sentimentality for murderers. He made his personal violent hatred for murderers
quite clear. An uneasy tension existed within him about his
decision against capital punishment; his reason supported abolition but his deep-rooted revulsion toward murderers created
an uneasy ambivalence within him.

* Charles Dickens, 'A Letter to the *Daily News* 28th February, 1846',
The Law as Literature, ed. Louis Blom-Cooper, Bodley Head, 1961, p.385.

A recent speech in Parliament, on 10 March 1846, by Macaulay had made Dickens self-conscious of his position and very defensive. Macaulay had accused proponents of the abolition of capital punishment of being victims of 'effeminate feelings'.[10] The more Dickens tried to avoid the taint of 'effeminacy' the more punitive his prescription became for suppressing crime. The criminal will be punished if found guilty; there was to be no mawkishness about that. But Dickens reverted to his theme of the need to destroy morbid preoccupation with criminals caused by public executions.[11] He had increasingly begun to concentrate his ire on public executions as his chief argument against the ineffectiveness of capital punishment itself.

No more false letters, portraits in print shops, autographs stuck up in shop windows, elaborate descriptions of their breakfasts, dinners and luncheons, no waxen images in Bakerstreet, no sale of their clothes at Newgate, no profiteering from tolls to their houses and scenes of the crime.[12]

The execution of the Mannings on 13 November 1849 revived the flagging interest in capital punishments started by the Dickens letters in 1846. 'The disgusting eagerness of the people to witness the execution of Manning and his wife last week in London,' wrote a Quaker, 'has again turned public attention to the question of capital punishment.'[13] As in 1846 after the execution of Courvoisier, Dickens raised the intensity of the debate to a high pitch of concern and acrimony. But now he wrote the editor of *The Times* to denounce public executions alone and not to 'discuss the abstract question of capital punishment'.[14] Since 1846 Dickens's focus had shifted entirely to the remedy and reform of executions; his internal conflict about abolishing capital punishment had pretty much been resolved. All that remained of his former feelings about the matter was a residue of ambivalence towards the dedicated abolitionists with whom he had associated himself on behalf of their cause.

In his letter to *The Times* Dickens gave concrete evidence of the direction his feelings had taken; he was publicly willing to advocate private executions which the abolitionists condemned in their lexicon as 'private strangulation', 'secret murder' and other stronger and more sinister descriptions.

I simply wish to make some account for the general good, by taking the readiest and most public means of adverting to an intimation given by Sir George Grey in the last session of Parliament, that the government might be induced to give its support to a measure making the infliction of capital punishment a private solemnity within the prison walls (with such guarantees for the last sentence of the law being inexorably and surely administered as should be satisfactory to the public at large), and a solemn duty which he owes to society, and a responsibility which he cannot for ever put away.*

When Dickens went to Horsemonger Lane Gaol to the Mannings' execution he saw the dawn break on droves of thieves, low prostitutes, thugs and drifters. He thought the thousands and thousands of upturned faces, gilded by the bright, gold sun, brutal and inexpressibly odious. The sight was so macabre, and the people were so obscene in their mirth, that he felt 'a man had cause to feel ashamed of the shape he wore'.[15] He became obsessed by this vision, wishing to destroy all traces of these hideous events; to get rid of the squalid, dissolute onlookers and to banish their victim–heroes, whom he loathed, to lonely, sombre deaths. Now he waged war on public executions, and in return he was singled out by the abolitionists as one of the major obstacles in their crusade. A bitter, personal battle had begun.

On 15 November 1849, just a day after his letter appeared in *The Times*, Dickens crystallized his views on capital punishment. In replying to Charles Gilpin's invitation to appear at an abolitionist meeting, he expressed the urgent need to rid

* *The Times*, 14 November 1849, p.4. Dickens's letter received many varied responses. One letter-writer to *The Times* stated, 'I could as easily conceive of water to run uphill as the sight of an execution to be in itself in the slightest degree an incentive to crime.' Another wrote, 'The evidence of Mr Dickens at the execution of the Mannings is powerfully and truthfully given . . . I am afraid he was not so placed that he could look into the rooms of the Winter-terrace where the moral sewerage of respectable society used opera-glasses to assist their sight in watching the agonies of a man and wife strangled a few yards from them.' *The Times*, 17 November 1849, p.5.

the nation of public executions; no such priority was given the abolition of capital punishment. 'We know,' Dickens wrote to Gilpin, 'what a fearful and brutalizing sight a public execution is, and when we know that we must do a great national service by bringing it to pass that such a sight shall never take place again.'[16] He predicted that abolition of capital punishment would never be accepted in England, and therefore the abolitionists would be well-advised to assist in destroying the public gallows. 'The right course,' he urged Gilpin, 'is to enlist this help in causing capital punishment to be privately and solemnly inflicted.'[17]

The Times still tenaciously supported public executions and defended them against Dickens's attacks in his letter. Treating Dickens gingerly and somewhat deferentially, the newspaper alluded to 'a great novelist' whose language excited its imagination. It was prepared to accept the scene of the execution witnessed by Dickens as horrid and most hardening beyond imagination, but was unwilling to follow Dickens to his conclusion. 'It appears to us as a matter of necessity,' it stated, 'that so tremendous an act as a national homicide should be publicly as well as solemnly done. Were it otherwise, the mass of people would never be sure.'* *The Times* reassured its readers 'of even the most morbid conscience' that although an act of judicial slaughter was performed, some consolation should be derived 'from the infrequency of these acts'.[18]

Writing to *The Times* again on 19 November 1849, Dickens publicly split with the abolitionists and condemned them. He regarded them as obstructionists who were too inflexible and doctrinaire to modify their goals; they would accept nothing less than total abolition of capital punishment. Although the abolitionists understood the fearful influence of public executions, they would prolong them rather than jeopardize total

---

* *The Times*, 14 November 1849, p.3. A reader of *The Times* agreed that the lower classes would regard private executions as class legislation. 'You have properly stated,' he wrote in reply to the 14 November article, 'the strongest objection to such a plan is that suspicion which the ill-formed public would be likely to feel that justice had not been done on offenders rich enough to buy life, or well-connected enough to have friends to "job" their necks out of the halter.' *The Times*, 17 November 1849, p.6.

abolition. Dickens dismissed them as pure-intentioned, unreasonable dogmatists.[19]

Dickens proposed a precise procedure for carrying out private executions. He took great pains to reassure the public and his critics that the treatment of criminals and impartial justice would be rigidly and scrupulously safeguarded.

From the moment of a murderer being sentenced to death, I would dismiss him to the dread obscurity ... I would allow no curious visitors to hold any communication with him; I would place every obstacle in the way of his sayings and doings being served up in print on Sunday for the perusal of families. His execution within the walls of the prison should be conducted with every terrible solemnity that careful consideration could devise. Mr. Calcraft the hangman (of whom I have some information in reference to this last occasion), should be restrained in his unseemly briskness in his jokes, his oaths, and his brandy. To attend the execution I would summon a jury of 24, to be called the Witness Jury, eight to be summoned on a low qualification, eight on a higher; eight on a higher still; so that it might fairly represent all classes of society. There should be present likewise, the governor of the gaol, the chaplain, the surgeon and other officers. All these should sign a grave and solemn form of certificate (the same in every case) on such a day on such an hour, in such a gaol, for such a crime, such a murderer was hanged in their sight. There should be another certificate from the officers of the prison that the person hanged was that person and no other; a third that the person was buried.[20]

Defection from abolitionist orthodoxy brought wrath on Dickens's head. Abolitionists were outraged at his apostasy and angered that his support of the limited reform of abolishing public hangings would sabotage their goal. Their acrimonious feelings towards him were soon exposed at public meetings and in the press.* The day following Dickens's last letter in

* Of course, Dickens was criticized as well by those wishing to maintain both public executions and capital punishment. A critic of his views wrote to the *Daily News*, 'Although, no doubt, there may exist among us many a man of mawkish sensibility who ... may desire that our criminals should be secretly strangled, yet I trust, sir, that instead of "earnestly supplicating Sir George Grey" for this indulgence, will you with your usual power, urge him on no account whatever to attempt to abrogate the inalienable right which every member of our Christian

'Last Dying Speech and Confession' by Thomas Rowlandson, c. 1810.
Street hawkers selling crude broadsides of the condemned's 'last dying speech
and confession' or 'full account of the crime, trial, and execution' were
standard figures at the execution scene.

'Execution Scene Outside of Newgate' by Thomas Rowlandson, *c.* 1810.
Rowlandson's drawing captures much of the bawdy, circus-like atmosphere
which surrounded public executions.

'Hanging in Chains of Francis Fearn, on Loxley Common, Near Sheffield.'
This execution scene with its tents and flags resembles a country fête more
than a solemn and sobering spectacle of justice.

'Preparing for an Execution', a print from A. Griffiths, *Chronicles of Newgate*,
1884. This unsigned print of a riotous scene outside Newgate was widely
circulated. Note the vendor and his cart of 'Bang Up Ginger Pop'.

The Times a large crowd of abolitionists assembled at the
Bridge House Hotel, Southwark. Dickens was roundly condemned and his intentions impugned. Charles Gilpin, the chairman of the meeting, addressed them. 'The friends of the
movement assembled together that night,' he said emphati-
cally, 'were not labouring to substitute one kind of strangulation for another. They would never advocate assassination
instead of public execution.'[21] The crowd roared its approval.
Then Gilpin read letters addressed to the meeting from Richard
Cobden and John Bright. Cobden linked Dickens with the
'Calcraft party'; he cautioned the members to 'take heed of
the new dodge – private executions'.[22] Bright unequivocally
accused advocates of private executions of being motivated by
'a mere longing to put someone to death'.[23] Then William
Ewart addressed the meeting. He spoke of his own feeling of
repugnance towards public executions, but declared that he
must reject private executions as an 'evasion of the main
principle for which they were agitating – the abolition of capital punishment without any qualification whatever'.[24]

In its leading article of the following day *The Times* objected to the language used by the abolitionists against Dickens
and expressed shock at the vicious insinuations made about
his motives and intentions. The mob at the anti-capital-
punishment meeting, according to *The Times*, acted as badly
as the rabble at public executions; the speakers and the
audience 'made a joke of the awful subject'.[25] Although *The
Times* could never agree with Dickens's letters in regard to
private executions, it thought they deserved respect because
of their single-minded honesty. Richard Cobden and John
Bright were severely censured for the unwarranted suspicions
they spawned and spread about Dickens actually 'possessing
a homicidal disposition and sort of monomania to take some-
body's life'.[26] Bright was particularly reproached.

If Mr Bright does not mean this, we think that he would consult
his respectability by saying more explicitly what he really does
mean; for at present he stands in the predicament of having

community ought to maintain of witnessing, whenever his conscience
prompts him to do so, the legalized execution of his fellow creature.'
21 November 1849, p.2.

charged one of the most humane and sympathetic men of our day with a morbid liking for the slaughter of his species.[27]

Bright denied that he had either questioned Dickens's good faith or imputed that the author had any homicidal preoccupation. 'The observation in his letter,' Bright protested, could not possibly apply to Dickens because 'he is well-known to hold the strongest opinions against capital punishment, whether in public or private.'[28] Bright obviously was attempting to smooth over the rash, bold comments he had written about the novelist. Cobden, however, was another matter. There was no tone of conciliation in a later letter he sent to Gilpin. It was subsequently inserted in *The Times* along with Gilpin's own comment that 'it does in some degree reply to the letters of Charles Dickens which you had admitted in your column'.[29]

Your opponents are half ashamed of their cause, but seem not to be aware that when they denounce the evils of public executions, they are abandoning the chief arguments with which they have defended the halter in calling out for secret hanging (which sounds to my ears very much like private assassination) they have delivered themselves into your hands.*

'A roaring sea' was Dickens's description of the response his two letters to *The Times* had whipped up, and he ruefully added he could see 'no hope of land'.[30] He became embittered; he had hoped his letters would produce enough agitation to abolish public executions; but he had no confidence now that any change would be made. 'The total abolitionists,' he complained, 'are utterly reckless and would play the deuce with any such proposition in Parliament.'[31] Impatience and hosti-

---

* *The Times*, 24 November 1849, p.5. In addition to the unpleasant, vindictive campaign waged against him by the abolitionists, his *Times* letters produced an estrangement with his friend Douglas Jerrold. Jerrold bitterly resented Dickens's compromise of the principle of total abolition; Dickens, for his part, was critical of Jerrold's doctrinaire inflexibility. 'My dear Jerrold,' he wrote, 'in a letter I received from Gilpin this morning, he quoted a recent letter from you in which you deprecate the "Mystery" of private hanging ... I wish I could induce you to feel justified in leaving that world to the platform people.' Dexter, ed., *The Letters of Charles Dickens*, Vol. ii, pp.185–6.

lity towards his critics were swelling within him. 'I am waiting to explode the fact on the first man of mark who gives me the opportunity,' he wrote, 'that under the British govern-ment in New South Wales . . . executions take place within the prison walls with decidedly improved results.'*

Dickens's opinions on capital punishment and public exe-cutions changed rapidly. In 1846 he opposed capital punish-ment in his *Daily News* letters. By 1849 in his letters to *The Times* he modified his point of view sufficiently to fix his opposition only on public executions and not on capital punish-ment. As Dickens aged, his beliefs about crime and punish-ment became increasingly reactionary and repressive. In 1846 he opposed capital punishment, but in 1859 he threatened to hang any Home Secretary who stepped in between one par-ticular 'black scoundrel' and the gallows.[32] In 1852 he rejec-ted whipping as a penalty to suppress crime, but in 1869 he would have the back of a street ruffian 'scarified often and deep'.[33]

The stormy debates Dickens had stirred in 1846 and 1849 soon began to subside, leaving *The Times* still poised opposite the forces of abolition and opponents of public executions. It spoke for that larger body of opinion in the country which still thought it impossible to eradicate 'blood-for-blood punish-ments' that had to be re-enacted periodically in public places.

The annual controversy on capital punishment [*The Times* article began] had a double turn last year. A powerful letter from Mr Charles Dickens in these columns was the means of exciting a wide feeling of disgust at the scene of their terrible exit. The description we think, was exaggerated, and not altogether fair; nor can we

* ibid. The abolitionists, for their part, later forgave Dickens his gross defection, and reverted to the earlier Dickens inspiration, and the prestige of his name in support of their cause against capital punishment. William Tallack, the arch-abolitionist secretary of the Howard Associa-tion, conjured Dickens's name at a later debate in support of his cause. 'Mr Dickens' five letters to the *Daily News* on January, February and March, 1846,' Tallack wrote, 'gave a masterly exposition of the impo-tence of the extreme penalty of the law.' Tallack, *A General Review of the Subject of Capital Punishment*, London: Society for the Abolition of Capital Punishment, p.8.

allow the inference to be sound. Grant that all the pickpockets and ruffians of every degree were assembled on that occasion, and that a great deal of heartlessness was shown to a class of spectators from whom more decency might have been expected. That only shows, what everyone is aware of, that a capital execution is to the popular sense a most striking, appalling and in the sense most interesting event, exciting feelings of mixed curiosity, horror and disgust, of doubtful import indeed to that large class of minds that are incapable of distinct or wholesome moral impression, but nevertheless forcing itself on them as a hideous fact, which they can never efface from memory, or jest away from reason . . . But even if the mob be ever so rough, flippant or brutal, and many of it actually engage in the trade of crime, it does not follow that all of them will not learn from the ocular demonstration before them to hesitate before they commit a deliberate murder.[34]

Another literary figure, with even greater international stature than Dickens, became embroiled in the capital-punishment and public-executions dispute. Victor Hugo had written an eloquent letter to Lord Palmerston, the Home Secretary, in *The Times* of 20 February 1854; he lamented the hanging of Tapner, a murderer, on the Island of Guernsey on 10 February 1854. The letter caused not even a brief flurry of letters to the press. English insularity and zenophobia perhaps explained the lack of response to a Frenchman's criticism of English justice.

Public pressure had forced Lord Palmerston to respite Tapner three times. Eventually Tapner's stay of execution was permitted to lapse and he was hanged in a quasi-private execution in a garden adjoining the prison where a scaffold had been erected. Two hundred privileged residents of the island were admitted into the garden to witness the execution.

Victor Hugo, popular revolutionary hero, equated the abolition of capital punishment with freedom; capital punishment was the means of enslavement by repressive, anti-democratic governments.

You Palmerston have yielded to no influence. You simply said 'Let justice take its course.' You gave this order as you would have done any other; the prolonged discussion concerning capital punishment do not interest you . . . At times it is impaling; with the Czar the knout; with the Pope it is the garrot; in France the guillotine; in England the gallows; in Asia and America the slave market. All this will be swept away . . . Democracy yesterday took the name of France; tomorrow it will take that of Europe.[35]

By 1856 the fears of the tumultuous years of 1848–9 had receded, and innovation became less suspect.* On 8 May 1856 the Bishop of Oxford introduced a motion in the House of Lords to inquire into the mode of carrying into effect capital punishments.[36] Previously, in 1854, he had merely questioned the conduct of public executions; now his motion for a select committee, and the subsequent appointment of one, initiated new interest in public executions and in capital punishment in general. The concern about crime and punishment was further intensified by William Ewart's unsuccessful attempt to obtain the approval of the House of Commons on 10 June 1856 to appoint a select committee to look into 'the operation of the law imposing the punishment of death'[37] – ostensibly as the first step towards total abolition of capital punishment.

The execution of the notorious Dr William Palmer at Stafford, on 14 June 1856† brought the issue to the forefront and disturbed many of the abolitionists. John Bright and Alfred Dymond had exhorted a Rochdale meeting on 21 January to petition the Home Office for a commutation of Palmer's sentence.‡ As late as 11 June a densely crowded meeting in

* It was in that year that Polish and Hungarian insurgents were officially granted amnesty by the Romanov Czar and the Hapsburg Emperor.

† Palmer was executed for the murder of a racing associate. It was believed he murdered at least thirteen persons by administering strychnine and antimony for their insurance to cover gambling debts.

‡ *The Times* sardonically commented: 'In these days, if you wish to be an object of public interest, you must at least deserve hanging; never allow a moment's delay to your cupidity, your vengeance, or your lust and you soon have crowds of pious people dawdling and twaddling and snuffing and slobbering at the door of your cell. We are not all ambitious of Mr Bright's affectionate interest, for it is quite clear that in order to obtain it, we must first procure strychnine, arsenic, a revolver, or at least a stout bludgeon. When we have selected the object of our regards, should the deed be discovered, we shall at least have Mr Bright interceding with the Home Secretary on our behalf.' *The Times*, 23 January 1856, p.8.

St Martin's Hall, Longacre, considered 'the propriety of arresting the execution of the convict Palmer on the ground of doubtful and conflicting evidence'.[38]

On 7 July the Select Committee of the House of Lords on Capital Punishment gave its report after a two-month period of hearing witnesses and considering their evidence; the majority of the witnesses presented testimony against the propriety and efficacy of public executions. The Select Committee recommended that 'execution should in the future be carried into effect within the precincts of the prison, or in some place securing similar comparative privacy'.[39] Despite its recommendation, the House of Lords took no action. The weight of opinion from the press, the government and the radicals operated against any hopeful action towards the abolition of public executions.

Once again *The Times* felt compelled to defend public executions; in its lead article of 17 July the paper restated the credo that publicity was a sacred adornment of English justice; without publicity English liberties would be subverted by furtive secrecy, and tyranny would be reimposed. It boasted that the people reign in England through its hallowed constitutional organs of Queen, Lords and Commons, and consequently 'it is the people that inflict the last penalty of the law in this country and the publicity of the process is significant'.[40] Furthermore, public executions were one of the vaunted bulwarks of English freedom, and it warned that these freedoms were jeopardized by 'men in their country, very good men in their own way, who would shut the door of parliament, of every court of justice, police courts and even vestry meetings'.[41]

The report of the noble and right reverend Lords, *The Times* thought, was ambitious enough to rival Dickens's picturesque account of an execution. It refused to accept the conclusion that execution mobs behaved any differently from or more atrociously than persons congregated for any other event in contemporary England.

As for the statement that the whole town, after an execution is a scene of drunkenness, rioting and debauchery – we have heard precisely the same arguments used against country fairs, Michaelmas hirings, national holy days, the observance of Christmas day, and even confirmations.[42]

Then *The Times* used the recurrent arguments against private executions: they would be construed as class legislation against the common people;* the working-class would refuse to believe that influential, well-to-do offenders would not escape punishment; the lower classes were addicted to a belief in the immense idea of the influence of wealth and interest in high places. The old rumours were revived that Dr Dodd had been hanged with a silver tube in his throat and that Fauntleroy was alive in America.†

The common people have a feeling that publicity is their only guarantee for fairness. We will venture to say that common people will never believe a man to be really hanged who had friends to get him off or money to bribe his gaolers. They will lose confidence in the perfect impartiality of the law. This respect is the greatest hold we have on our masses, and it would be endangered by the sentimental process recommended in their Lordships' Report upon Capital Punishment.[43]

The year 1864 was a crucial one: a year in which three sensational, controversial executions brought the long

* There was some reason for *The Times* to fear the lower classes' hostile reaction to class legislation. Workingmen regarded the bill suppressing Sunday trading, including the sale of beer, as class legislation. On Sunday 24 June 1855 a mob destroyed property in Mayfair in protest against the bill; it was subsequently withdrawn in Parliament. W. L. S. Burn, *The Age of Equipoise: A Study of the Mid-Victorian Generation*, New York: W. W. Norton Co., 1964, pp.82–3.

† ibid. There was more than just a rumour concerning the methods used to escape death on the gallows; a broadsheet described the execution of John Tidwell, a Quaker, paralleling the long-rumoured method used to save Dr Dodd. Moreover, Tidwell, the Quaker, resembles Tawell, the Quaker, who it was believed also escaped death on the gallows. The broadsheet related how 'I have arranged with Hallcraft, the executioner . . . I shall bring the silver tube. The lowness of the drop and the shortness of the fall were themes of general conversation . . . the fall was so short it was impossible that the criminal's neck could be broken . . . Hallcraft cut the body down . . . Hallcraft drew a long silver tube from the throat . . . the convict's chest expanded, he gave a compulsive sigh, and then his eyes partially opened.' British Museum, *Murders*, p.176.

discussion about public executions and capital punishments to a climax and a point of decision. It was a year that saw, also, a Grand Jury request the end of public executions; that witnessed two separate motions introduced in the House of Commons related to the abolition of public executions and capital punishment, and that saw a Royal Commission appointed to investigate the whole problem of public executions and capital punishment.

The first of the controversies arose over the sentencing to death of Samuel Wright, a bricklayer, convicted of murder. Because of the doubtful sanity of Wright, and the haste in which sentence followed the verdict, efforts were made to commute his sentence. Before Wright's conviction the sentence of George Townley, from a well-to-do family, had been rescinded on the grounds of insanity, and suspicion grew that the equality of justice for the rich and poor had been violated in Wright's case. Attempts were made to have the Wright verdict changed to manslaughter, but these were ignored by the Home Secretary, Sir George Grey. Memorials to set aside the conviction were presented to Sir George Grey from visiting justices of Horsemonger Lane Gaol, and Lambeth tradesmen circulated petitions appealing for clemency for Wright.

Feelings were running so high against the execution that the authorities set up extra security precautions for Wright's execution, scheduled for 12 July 1864. About 1,000 metropolitan policemen were posted and held in reserve in the neighbourhood of Horsemonger Lane Gaol. A handbill with a black border was circulated in the area as a 'solemn protest against the execution of Wright'.[44] It urged the men and women of London to boycott the execution.

Let Calcraft and Co. do their work this time with none but the eye of heaven to look upon their crime ... Englishmen, shall Wright be hung? If so there is one law for the rich and another for the poor.[45]

Loud cries of 'Shame', 'Judicial murder', 'Where's Townley?' and an increasing din of yelling and hooting were let loose as Wright appeared on the scaffold. Seemingly touched by the expressions of sympathy, he bowed repeatedly to the crowd.[46]

One month later, before the tumult and protest over Wright's execution had died down, the 'Five Pirates' were sentenced to die. When they were hanged, the reaction from the press was generally critical and denunciatory. The *Morning Herald*, disquieted by the event, pointed out that, rather than striking terror into the breast of the wicked, it was just another amusement of the metropolis – noisy, ribald, swearing and drunken crowds packed into the great open space by St Sepulchre's Church. It was a grand, gala affair, a new sensation well worth seeing at any price. The *Morning Herald* could find some excuse for the 'uneducated and vicious mob', but what could it say about the gentlemen who 'descended in parties on the scene of the execution as avidly as for the Derby'?* Its suggested remedy for 'such disgraceful scenes' was the secrecy of keeping the public in ignorance of the precise spot where executions were to take place.[47] The difficulty of finding suitable sites for executions was recognized, but the paper thought the problem could be overcome by erecting the scaffold silently and suddenly in a spot selected by the authorities.[48] Thus, the *Morning Herald* ingeniously avoided advocating 'secret executions' by keeping executions quasi-public.

Reaction to the hanging of the 'Five Pirates' was instantaneous in the House of Commons. On the day they were hanged, John Hibbert moved to abolish public executions. The *Morning Star* regretted that Hibbert had not tried to do away with capital punishment altogether, but it commended his action as useful in drawing urgent attention to the debasing effects of public executions.[49] Undeviating in its support of the

---

* *Morning Herald*, 23 February 1864, pp.4–5. A letter-writer signed 'Vigil' wrote to *The Times* dissenting from the *Morning Herald*'s observations of the execution: 'I am not ashamed to avow that I went this morning to the hanging of the five pirates at Old Bailey, and I'm concerned to state my impressions at this public spectacle, because they were so utterly different from all which I have heard or read, or which it is the current fashion or folly to express at exhibitions. It was to me the most solemn sight I ever witnessed. . . . I am satisfied that at the last moment the better nature of all responded in concert to the terrible appeal.' *The Times*, 23 February 1864, p.8.

abolition of capital punishment, the *Morning Star* predicted
the end of the gallows because the English people would never
consent to private executions.[50]

The *Morning Post*, Tory and retentionist, made a remarkable concession as a consequence of the hanging of the pirates
and admitted that 'there might be some more satisfactory
mode of execution well worth consideration'.[51] The growing
clamour against public executions had evidently begun to
diminish opposition and resistance by sheer attrition and
volume, but the *Morning Post* remained immovable on the
issue of capital punishment.

Hang criminals in private and much that is revolting and demoralizing may be prevented; but cease to hang and murder will
become as common as other offences; justice will have given place
to mawkish sentiment, and a spurious sympathy for the wrong-
doer.[52]

On 3 May 1864 William Ewart once again urged the appointment of a select committee to inquire into capital punishment.
Instead, the government created a Royal Commission whose
scope was broadened to inquire into the matter of public
executions as well. But Parliament was still more conservative
than large segments of the press. John Roebuck spoke for a
retrenched, predominant majority in the House of Commons
when he there debated capital punishment with Charles Gilpin.
Gilpin had cited Dickens – apparently enough time had elapsed
since 1849 to restore Dickens to the panoply of abolitionist
saints – as the incontrovertible authority to prove that innocent men had more than once been executed.[53] To loud cheers
of 'Hear! Hear!' Roebuck retorted:

The Home Secretary would undoubtedly say that he had more
difficulty in hanging a man now than former secretaries had trans-
porting one ... Not withstanding the writing of Mr Dickens, and
others who attempted to mislead mankind on the subject. It was
much more merciful to hang a man at once than to condemn him
to insanity and life-long solitary confinement.[54]

But even the Tory *Morning Post* admitted that there were
many instances when capital punishment could be remitted

advantageously.[55] And *The Times* was amenable to accepting some reductions in capital punishments,[56] but it continued to oppose efforts by Ewart and Bright for total abolition. 'Murder ought to bear a stigma,' was *The Times*'s conclusion, 'and the stigma in the mind of the mass is the retribution of death.'[57]

Responsible, solid middle-class public opinion had begun openly to express discontent with public executions and to agitate to terminate them. The Grand Jury for South Lancashire made a presentment on 29 July 1864 to Sir Gillory Pigott, Her Majesty's Judge of Assize presiding in the Criminal Court at Manchester for the southern division of the county of Lancashire. It was submitted by Algernon Egerton, M.P., the foreman of the Grand Jury, and signed by him.

They deem this, the first occasion of holding a criminal assize for the hundred of Salford, to be a fitting opportunity to present to your Lordship the importance and desirableness of making an early change in the mode of carrying out capital punishment, that they deem such changes to be desirable on account of the pernicious and demoralizing effects which public executions have upon those who from time to time, congregate to witness them. That having in view these effects, and taking with consideration the large population resident in this district, they are impressed with the inexpediency of carrying out capital punishment in public, and are convinced that great advantage would result if the law were so altered as to permit executions to be carried out into effect under proper regulations and securities for due fulfillment of the sentence, within the respective prisons of the United Kingdom. And the jurors aforesaid respectfully desire your lordship to forward their said presentment to the Right Honourable Sir George Grey, Bart., M.P., Her Majesty's principal Secretary of State for the Home Department.[58]

The Times did not underestimate the weight to be attached to the presentment from the Grand Jury, because it was composed of men 'of old descent and men of new fortunes . . . representing good sense and intelligence of educated Englishmen'.[59] Their positions and stature in society added substance to their petition, and made it welcome by *The Times*, especially for those 'not sufficiently advanced in opinion as the abolition of capital punishments'.[60] *The Times* indulged in critical reminiscence of those public writers who had consciously anticipated the abolition of capital punishment: 'Mr Thackeray's description of Courvoisier's execution and Mr Dickens's later narrative of the execution of the Mannings were sentimental pleas for that end.'[61] The newspaper rejoiced that rougher and stronger habits of thought now prevailed; it stubbornly supported the necessity to execute and insisted that hanging should take place in public so that the common people would be satisfied of that fact. However, public executions could be modified somewhat; it was quite feasible in the days of the railroad to execute criminals in solitary spots, far away from town, in the early morning so that spectators might attend if they wished. The terrible spectacle need 'not be thrust upon any unwilling to encounter it',[62] wrote *The Times*.

The excitement and wide publicity of Franz Müller's execution on 14 November 1864 – just fourteen days before the first session of the Royal Commission on Capital Punishment – further exacerbated attitudes towards public executions. The *Daily News*, no longer abolitionist, was appalled by the continued existence of public executions.[63] Dickens, no longer editor of the *Daily News*, did not share that newspaper's empathy towards Müller. 'I hope that gentleman will be hanged, and have hardly a doubt of it – though croakers contrariwise are not wanting,' he gloated.[64] Although the *Morning Star*, which John Bright helped to found,[65] still supported abolition of capital punishment, it condemned the policy that used public hanging as an instrument for public instruction.[66] So did the *Morning Herald* which printed a didactic poem, 'The Gallows Tree', personifying the gallows as a teacher.

> The Gallows Tree, what is its plea
> What lesson does it teach,
> That it should stand on every land
> Where Christ's message preach?
> Your tolling bell, what does it tell
> Of death solemnity
> Of that fond crowd, who laughed aloud
> Beneath the gallows tree?[67]

Over twenty years had passed since the first attempt to abolish public executions was introduced in Parliament on 16 February 1841; its hostile reception made the sponsoring Member withdraw his motion immediately, to the satisfaction of the entire House, the government, the press and every shade of political opinion in the country. Paradoxically, one year before, on 5 March 1840, William Ewart's more extreme motion to abolish capital punishment totally was given over ninety votes in the House of Commons; in addition, he received the plaudits and backing of much of the press, and the support of reform-minded persons throughout the nation. By 1864 attitudes had changed so drastically that newspaper lead articles advocated alterations in public executions, and sympathy in Parliament was growing to discontinue these grotesque spectacles. It was becoming increasingly clear and reasonable to anticipate that it would be the end of public executions which the public was willing to accept and not abolition of the death penalty.

That the role of the newspapers in preparing the public to expect the reform of public executions was important, there can be no doubt. Full and graphic descriptions of public executions made a deep impression on their readers, and made many of them doubt their value and caused others to consider the harm that public hangings caused. It was these middle-class readers, growing in numbers, power and wealth, and not the scruffy execution crowds, which influenced public authorities and helped affect legislative reforms. Finally, newspapers served as an important public forum for the prolonged debate about public executions and capital punishment, and this protracted debate helped mould the opinions and attitudes that made reform both necessary and acceptable.

CHAPTER

5

ATTEMPTS IN PARLIAMENT TO ABOLISH PUBLIC EXECUTIONS: 1841–56

DEEP concern about public executions became manifested in the eighteenth century and foreshadowed the mounting criticism which was brought to bear against them the following century. Foremost, and most literate, of the early critics was Henry Fielding, who when appointed police magistrate for Westminster in 1748 brought to his office an awareness of the social evils about which he had written in his novels. He felt a deep concern for the poor wretched thieves who were hauled before him, later to be prosecuted, convicted and hanged. These were the less practical, the less spirited and the less dangerous rogues of society, seduced into committing crime by the example of those more hardened and fearless who consciously sought and savoured the role of heroes on the scaffold. 'The thief who is hanged today,' Fielding observed, 'hath learned his intrepidity from the example of his hanged predecessors.'[1]

The day appointed by law for the thief's shame is the day of glory in his own opinion. His procession to Tyburn, and his last moments there, all are triumphant; attended with the compassion of the meek and the tender-hearted, and with the applause, admiration, and envy, of all the bold and hardened. His behaviour and his present condition, not the crimes, how atrocious soever, which brought him to it, are the subject of contemplation. And if he hath sense enough to temper his boldness with any degree of decency, his death is spoken of by many with honour, by most with pity, and by all with approbation.[2]

How far public executions were objects of terror Fielding was willing to leave to the consideration of every rational man; and from the examples he described, there was little margin of choice, except condemnation. He felt it was imperative that expressions of dissatisfaction with these spectacles and their pernicious influences must be communicated to the authorities. Executions produced more executions because crime battened on them despite 'the design of those who first appointed executions to be public, [which] was to add the punishment of shame to that of death'.[3] They failed, Fielding contended, in making the example of execution in public an object of greater terror. Experience, he submitted, revealed the event to be directly contrary to this intention.

To prove this, I will appeal to any man who hath seen an execution; let him tell me when he hath beheld a poor wretch, bound in a cart, just on the verge of eternity, all pale and trembling with his approaching fate, whether the idea of shame hath ever intruded on his mind? Much less will the bold daring rogue, who glories in his present condition, inspire the holder with any such sensation.[4]

How can the cycle of crime and punishment be broken? How could punishments be inflicted and yet deprive the criminal of public pity, admiration and emulation? The remedy, Fielding thought, lay in executions which were private in some degree.* 'If executions therefore were so contrived that few could be present at them,' he wrote, 'they would be much more shocking and terrible to that crowd without doors than at present, as well as much more dreadful to the criminals themselves.'[5] The criminal would die silently before his avowed enemies, the enforcers of law and order; deprived by an unheralded death without a sympathetic mob, with no opportunity for theatricality and no hope for martyrdom, the criminal's boldness would wane, his spirits would flag and his moment of glory would vanish. Conversely, without the hero–victims with whom they identified, both incipient and hardened criminals who congregated at executions would lose a source of inspiration for the commission of crimes. Fielding

* Fielding drew from his knowledge of literary devices to demonstrate this point of view. 'Foreigners had found fault with the cruelty of the English drama, in representing frequent murders upon the stage. In fact, this is not only cruel but highly injudicious: a murder behind the scenes if the poet knows how to manage it, will affect the audience with greater terror than if it was acted before their eyes.' ibid., p.123.

believed his prescription of privacy, along with celerity and solemnity, would effectually remove all the evils produced by public executions.

Despite such strictures about the total – and injurious – ineffectiveness of public hangings, they continued unabated and well-attended.* Public executions were ingrained as a way of life, as something accepted except by cranks and eccentrics; they were sanctified by the state as well as by tradition; they had become part of a crime-and-punishment ritual. And public executions were just one aspect of a society which still had its roots in the countryside where life was often brutal and sordid, where manners were rough and heavy-handed, and where even horse-play was indulged in with cruelty. In the towns, even in London, persons and property were under constant threat by crimes of violence, seemingly undeterred by ferocious laws.

When Fowell Buxton spoke in debate on 2 March 1819, to urge adoption of Sir James Mackintosh's motion for the formation of a select committee on criminal law, he voiced one of the first dissenting opinions of public executions in Parliament. They did not, as popularly believed, reduce the incidence of crime. In fact, if anything they encouraged crime and created many other problems. Buxton challenged any member who might scoff at his assertions to see for himself. All he had to do was expose his feelings to the pain of witnessing a public hanging.

There he will see how little solemnity and how little seriousness accompany this awful exercise of power. Sir, it is notorious that executions very rarely take place without being the occasion on which new crimes are committed. On the very last, a pickpocket

* Many enlightened reformers such as William Eden and Jeremy Bentham could not agree with Fielding; they believed in the deterrent value of punishments which would be vitiated if they were not public. Bentham even advocated a more awe-inspiring ritual to strike terror into the hearts of the criminal and onlookers alike. A black scaffold, officers of justice bedecked in black crêpe, a masked executioner and sombre religious music would prepare 'the hearts of the spectators for the important lesson they were about to receive'. Jeremy Bentham, *The Works of Jeremy Bentham*, ed. John Bowring, New York: Russell & Russell, 1962, Vol. i, p.549.

was apprehended. On being asked by the chaplain of Newgate how he could venture on such a deed at such a time, he very frankly replied that executions were the best harvest he and his associates had.[6]

Witnesses before the 1819 Select Committee on Capital Punishment expressed similar opinions. The Reverend Horace Cotton, ordinary at Newgate, gave evidence. From his experience with public executions at Newgate, he testified that they made little impression on the public. 'They appear to come to it,' he said, 'as a spectacle and go away thinking no more about it.'[7] Moreover, he added, public executions tended to excite further crimes. Executions did not take place without some extraordinary case or some very peculiar crime occurring shortly afterwards.[8] Also examined by the Select Committee was a keeper at Newgate Prison who felt that executions in public hardly had 'any moral effect, or make any advantageous impression'.[9]

Public executions continued, untarnished and inviolate from these sporadic, lonely voices of condemnation and dissent. The anomalous punishment of hanging for burglary, forgery, issuing base coins and lesser crimes had by 1836 been abolished; the sentence of death was restricted almost entirely to murder. As a result, conservatives and reactionaries, as well as a number of liberals, decided they had gone far enough in reforming criminal laws. Murder was a heinous crime which still deserved death. Many liberals and almost all radicals, on the other hand, considered the reform of criminal law an unfinished business as long as capital punishment still existed. Conservatives and reactionaries still firmly believed in the deterrent power of public hangings. Radicals also wished to retain public executions, fearing their alteration to private executions would abort the total reform of capital punishment. All shades of political and social opinion, however, agreed that the English people would never accept private executions.

The opposition of both the conservatives and radicals to the abolition of public executions became apparent and was manifested on the occasions when alterations of public executions were suggested. Dr Stephen Lushington, an opponent of civil disabilities of Jews and a proponent of the secret ballot, was examined as a witness by the Criminal Law Committee of 1836. When asked what advantage could be gained by the substitution of private executions for public ones, he replied, 'I doubt the possibility of that being done in this country, or the advantage of it, could it be done.'[10]

When George Grote, the historian and philosophic radical, suggested an alteration of public executions he ran head-on into opposition from Lord John Russell and Sir Robert Peel. In a debate on capital punishment in the House of Commons on 19 May 1837 Grote said that 'if the punishment of death is to be retained, it would be better that it should be inflicted in private, as public executions are never attended with beneficial results'.[11] The reaction was a monolith of opposition. Lord John Russell, the Home Secretary and government spokesman on matters relating to criminal law, admitted that some revolting experiences had happened at public executions, but these were not irreparable. The Home Secretary 'hoped that after what had occurred, means would be taken to prevent a repetition of them'.* Sir Robert Peel agreed that such spectacles never produced pleasant effects, but he warned, 'It could be a dangerous principle to permit executions to take place in private.'[12]

One of the most compelling but unheralded speeches made against public executions was given by Henry Rich on 16 February 1841, in the first attempt to introduce a Bill in Parliament to abolish public executions.† Despite his eloquent

---

* *Hansard*, Vol. xxxviii (1837), col.924. Lord John Russell referred to the hanging of James Greenacre, executed on 2 May 1837. Greenacre had murdered his mistress, dismembered her body and distributed it over different parts of London. 'The case made a great sensation, and there were upwards to 16,000 spectators at the execution. The houses fronting Newgate charged three guineas for a station at the windows . . . Two sovereigns were given for a seat on the roofs of some of the houses.' Henry Mayhew and John Binny, *The Criminal Prisons of London and Scenes of Prison Life*, London: Griffin, Bohn, 1862, p.609.

† *Hansard*, loc. cit. Henry Rich was described as a reformer whose 'efforts will ever be in support of that steady, firm and progressive Reform which best preserves all of our institutions by keeping them in harmony with the advanced education and morality of our countrymen'.

pleading, the Bill was rejected outright by almost total opposition and even at one point in his speech by mocking laughter. Aware that a proposal to alter public executions had never before been discussed in Parliament except by Grote's suggestion in May 1837, Rich was anxious to dispel any misapprehensions or misrepresentations about his proposed Bill. His sole desire, he informed the Members, was to do away with a pernicious, barbarous practice.

Unprompted and unsupported by any special interest, section or party, Rich came before the House. He did not even connect his Bill with the closely related question of abolition of the death penalty. He merely sought a 'formal reverent and sufficiently public and authentic method of conducting the execution of criminals'[13] to replace the present exhibitions. Rich denied he sought secret executions; he wished to eliminate the kind of publicity which pandered to the coarse and the morbid. He wanted executions conducted before an appropriate number of witnesses to give assurance that an execution had been performed, and he advocated additional authentication of that fact, to be officially certified by authorities, witnessed by friends of the criminal and reported fully in the press.[14]

Rich was very anxious to obtain Sir Robert Peel's support; he apparently had some notion that Peel would be sympathetic.[15] Mindful that in 1837 Peel had dismissed Grote's suggestion of substituting private for public execution as a 'most dangerous principle', Rich was extravagant in his attempts to dispel that assertion. He protested, also, the other often-repeated assertion that public executions instilled a salutary horror. Experience showed that public executions hardened where they were meant to reform, and consequently, Rich claimed, they encouraged rather than diminished crime. Now impassioned, Rich pleaded eloquently:

We had got rid of the practice, although not the law for hanging in chains, on cart and coffin processions to Tyburn; we had got rid of the practice, though not the law, for drawing on hurdles . . .

Charles R. Dodd, *Dodd's Parliamentary Companion*, Whittaker & Co., 1847, p.227.

Mutilating, torturing, burning are now abolished; all these are passed away and are remembered now only to be repudiated. Nothing so easy as to repudiate the abuses of former days; nothing more difficult than to acknowledge and root out those of our own ... Conscientious men who could denounce the rack and in the same breath declare Charles II's head would not be safe on his shoulders should the living entrails of regicides, like Harrison's, not be torn out and burnt before his dying face ... This generation passes away, and another arises. Liberal supporters of the House of Hanover, could heartily denounce those enormities inflicted on the regicides, and yet in 1745 could find no security without planting the heads of the wretched Jacobite rebels on the Temple Bar. And now all honourable Gentlemen can fully perceive these barbarous errors of their predecessors. Even later still honourable Gentlemen have seen their contemporaries defend the whipping of women in prison, the pillory, the practice of hanging in chains, and the driving of stakes through the bodies of suicides ... And what, pray, is the inference of all of this? ... That we have at length arrived at perfection? The only way of viewing this gradual abandonment of terror is that it has been abandoned in its extreme vigour – if each succeeding generation confirming by experience and by further mitigation, the mitigation of its predecessors – then surely the only fair, rational and common sense deduction is, that the terror, this exhibition of terror is erroneous not in degree, but in principle and application.[16]

Rich's proposal was doomed from the start. His confidence in the support of Sir Robert Peel, then the Leader of the opposition, was misplaced. As Rich rose to speak, Peel was walking down the floor to leave the chamber; he returned and resumed his seat with a flourish to a rising chorus of 'great laughter'.[17]

'There was no hope of the bill which the honourable Member asked leave to introduce ever passing into law,' General Johnson stated with finality, 'because there was too much good sense, both in this and in the other House of Parliament to permit parties to be privately put to death'.[18] That was the tenor of all the speeches in debate – only one member, George Strickland, who had seconded the motion, supported Rich. William Ewart also felt bound to oppose the Bill because it could, if passed, prolong capital punishments. Whence, he rhetorically asked, came the rack, the torture and the inquisition which Rich had deplored so fervently in his speech? 'From private executions,'[19] Ewart answered – and implicit in his question was the inference that these would return should private executions be reimposed. Fox Maule astutely observed that Rich had against him 'not only those who were in favour of continuing public executions, but also those who were against their further existence'.[20]

Observing that the preponderent sentiment of the House was in opposition to his Bill, and being unwilling to pursue the matter against the general opinion, Rich capitulated. But he reserved the right – which he never exercised – to move at a future date for a committee upon the subject of public executions. Then he withdrew his motion.[21] It was a stunning, crushing defeat.

On 7 August 1844 the Mayor of Nottingham wrote to Sir James Graham, the Home Secretary in Peel's cabinet, to inform him of a most calamitous occurrence. An hysterical mob had stampeded after the execution of William Saville, crushing many people underfoot in a rush to escape the scene.[22] Estimating the death-toll at twelve, the number of injured great, with sixteen hospitalized and an indeterminate number believed to be elsewhere in town still unreported, the Mayor expressed the opinion that the area in front of the County Gaol in Nottingham was unfit for public executions.[23]

The Under-Sheriff of Nottingham, Mr Enfield, was requested to investigate the causes of the disaster. In reporting his findings to Sir James Graham on 14 August 1844 the Under-Sheriff suggested that a change in the place of the executions would meet the strong objections raised against them continuing before the County Gaol. Mr Enfield thought the executions should take place in the Debtor's Yard, about eighty feet above the adjoining part of town and open to view only from distant streets and meadows beyond. 'There is a strong impression that the assembly of a dense mass of spectators on the occasion of an execution has an injurious effect,'[24] he reported. The proposed new site, should it be deemed public enough, would offer a solution; it would permit viewing the execution from a distance and from different points without 'attracting together at one spot a dense and sometimes disorderly body of spectators'.[25]

The proposed change in the place of execution was submitted to the Magistrates of Nottingham when they met at Shire Hall on 17 August to consider the report. Their unanimous resolution, which was sent to Sir James Graham, was irresolute. On one hand they favoured the different location for executions for reasons of public safety; on the other hand, they were uncertain whether the new site would be sufficiently public.

That it appears to the Magistrates assembled that the South Side of the prison would be a more convenient place of execution in future, as being attended with little or no risk to the populace assembled, there being no more points of observation; but at the nearest point it appears that the Spectators would not be enabled to recognize the identity of the Criminal, the magistrates doubt that could be considered a sufficiently public execution.[26]

Official and authoritative guidelines for conditions deemed necessary for an execution to be considered sufficiently public were contained in a memorandum from Sir James Graham to the Nottingham magistrates. 'The principal object of capital punishment,' he wrote, 'is the terror of the example.'[27] No place, said the Home Secretary, could be considered fit for the purpose of demonstrating that purpose unless a large multitude of spectators could assemble sufficiently near the scaffold to recognize the criminal. And some of the bystanders should be able to hear any word of warning the criminal might wish to address them preserving as well the didactic nature of public executions. The proper place rested with the High Sheriff. 'But my opinion being asked,' he continued, 'I must say that I agree with the Magistrates in doubting whether the place proposed is sufficiently public.'[28]

On 2 July 1845 Monckton Milnes rose to speak in the House of Commons. Five years earlier he had gone to Courvoisier's execution with Thackeray for the professed purpose of seeing for himself how mobs behaved at an execution. The effect of the scene had as great an impact on him as on Thackeray, but the impression remained longer with Milnes;

his resolve to do something about public executions was firmer and deeper. Now his object was to denounce public executions and to confer on judges the authority to appoint at their discretion places for the execution of criminals within the walls of prisons.* The sanctity of publicity, which was so jealously guarded, Milnes thought, would be preserved if the execution within the prison walls admitted properly authorized persons, including reporters, who would ensure true publicity. He cited the successful American experience with the practices he proposed which 'had been adopted in Pennsylvania, and since then in all Northern States of the Union'.[29]

While Milnes had the floor, a Member received recognition from the Speaker for a motion to count the House. With only thirty-two Members present, the House adjourned.† Milnes's self-styled 'pioneering' effort ended; he never again made an effort to abolish public executions.

The hanging of Moses Hatto on 24 March 1854 – the first execution before the new County Gaol in Aylesbury – resulted in a petition from inhabitants in and around Aylesbury to the House of Lords requesting the abolition of public executions. There was nothing sensational about this hanging: the crowd was not particularly large and it responded with little

* *Hansard*, Vol. LXXXI (1845), cols.1411–14. In his Presidential Address to the Social Science Congress in 1873, Milnes, now Lord Houghton, referred to his 'pioneer' effort to substitute private for public executions. Lord Houghton claimed he had urged on Sir James Graham the wisdom of acceding to private executions. T. W. Reid, *The Life, Letters and Friendships of Richard Monckton Milnes, First Lord Houghton*, Cassell & Co., 1890, p.280.

† ibid. The Anti-Corn Law League newspaper of 5 July 1845 stated that 'Mr Monckton Milnes had made an important motion respecting the present mode of executing criminals ... There were present to listen to and to support him all those leading members of the House of Commons who are identified with the Anti-Corn Law League.' Quite inexplicably included as supporters of abolishing public executions were Richard Cobden and John Bright, the two inveterate opponents of private executions. The tone of the article and the inclusion of leading members of the House of Commons identified with Anti-Corn Law League as supporters would indicate sentiment in the League for the motion. See J. T. Mills, *Bright and the Quakers*, Vol. II, Methuen, 1935, pp.161–2.

excitement at the sight of the wretched man's appearance on the scaffold.[30] But any execution in Aylesbury, regardless of the scene it engendered, would have been reprehensible to a minority of interested and vocal residents. Since 1845, there had been an Aylesbury Committee on Capital Punishment organized by its radical–Whig Member of Parliament, George Nugent Grenville,[31] who was a criminal-law reformer and abolitionist. In addition, the Archdeacon Bickersteth, the spiritual leader of Aylesbury, was an outspoken critic of public-execution spectacles.

The petition was presented to the Bishop of Oxford, who presented it to the House of Lords.* He announced that he would raise a precedent in regard to public executions rather than make a motion to abolish them as recommended by the petitioners. A motion to change the mode of carrying out executions was quite unnecessary, he claimed, and therefore there was no need for new legislation. The time and place of executing the last sentence of the law rested with the Crown. He cited the order given in the case of Doyle and Barry that execution should be at Bethnal Green, an unusual place.[32] The legality of the arrangement was then questioned by the Lord Mayor and the sheriffs, and they appealed to the government. The judges, including Lord Chief Justice Mansfield, unanimously agreed that the decision rested with the Crown to appoint the place of executions.[33] Their decision also defined the conditions to which executions must adhere: 'That they were to take place in the presence of sufficient witnesses, to prevent the possibility of any suspicion of undue torture or of the sentence not being carried out.'[34] The Bishop of Oxford announced that he simply would ask Her Majesty's Government on the basis of an established precedent to consider the propriety of changing the practice of execution in England.

* *Hansard*, Vol. cxxxiii (1854), col.305. Samuel Wilberforce (1805–73) became Bishop of Oxford in 1845. The son of William Wilberforce, he made his mark as an influential debater in the House of Lords. Although he for the most part concerned himself with ecclesiastical matters, he took an interest in the laws of charitable trusts, the prevention of cruelty to women and children, and national education. *Dictionary of National Biography*, Vol. xxi, Oxford University Press, 1959–60, p.205.

The time for change had arrived. The Lord Bishop reminded the House of Lords that moralists had condemned and written against public executions for one hundred years; that they had argued that public executions tended to every possible effect except add to the awfulness of the sentence and to deter others from crime. He chided the Members that in other countries men's progress was reflected in legislative progress as well; the American states were tending in the direction of humane, progressive legislation, and the New England states had altogether adopted the system of executing criminals within their prisons. It had been stated that 'the people of England would not bear to have executions within walls of the prison',[35] said the Bishop of Oxford, and he believed that that was about the best argument against it. But the Bishop was not pessimistic; he had great faith in the good sense and right moral feeling of his fellow countrymen.

The Earl of Aberdeen, then Prime Minister, was not per-suaded by the Lord Bishop's arguments. He responded negatively and declared that private executions would be ex-ceedingly dangerous to the public peace. Those who were most conversant with criminal jurisprudence throughout the country and had the greatest insight into the masses 'are not in favour of secret executions,' he said.[36] Lord Brougham wondered 'whether it would be better to forego the death punishment altogether than to undergo the periodical recurrence of such scenes'.[37]

In reply to the Bishop of Oxford's reference to the precedent established by the Doyle and Barry execution in 1769, Lord Chief Justice Campbell informed him that a judge at a trial had the residual power to order an execution in any part of the country; it was not even unusual that the execution should be ordered to take place where the murder was com-mitted. Lord Campbell affirmed that it was the common law of England that punishments should take place in public and only an Act of Parliament could alter such a practice. It was the Lord Chief Justice's legal opinion that neither the judge nor the Queen could order executions within prison walls. 'And those who would order it,' he warned, 'must take care that they themselves did not incur the penalties which would attend such a contravention of the law.'*

The Bishop of Oxford deferred to the legal opinion of the Lord Chief Justice, but he was anxious to impress on the assembled Members of the House of Lords that he believed the continuation of capital punishment was essential to the highest principles of justice. He sought the abolition of public executions because he felt the present system of capital punishment was threatened by the continuation of public executions. Further gruesome executions, the Bishop of Oxford continued, would make men recoil from inflicting the death penalty. The debate ended, and the problem of public executions was again shunted aside for several years.[38]

Two years later, while public excitement and interest ballooned with the conviction and impending execution of Dr William Palmer, concern was growing in some quarters that homicidal women were escaping the death penalty because of a distaste to execute women publicly. Rising in the House of Lords on 9 May 1856, to shouts of 'Hear! Hear!', the Bishop of Oxford moved for the appointment of a select committee on the present mode of carrying capital punishment into effect.[39]

He retraced much of the ground he had covered when he had brought the matter of public executions before the House of Lords in 1854. He assured them that he was not espousing private executions which were both reprehensible and intolerable to Englishmen; he praised the great moralist Fielding, whose hostile opinion of public execution was based on his experiences as police magistrate, and he repeated the familiar arguments about the great evils which had arisen from the present system of public executions.[40] He spoke of the American system of executing criminals before prescribed witnesses; this system, he pointed out, could correct the grosser conditions of public executions and still retain enough of the former public nature. 'In America, where the English

* *Hansard*, Vol. cxxxiii (1854), col.312. Lord Campbell was quite liberal in matters of criminal-law reform; he had voted in the House of Commons in 1837 to abolish capital punishment in all cases except murder.

THE LIFE AND TRIAL OF PALMER;

Oh listen unto William Palmer
  Who dies in anguish sore bewail.
Now guilty they at last have found me
  and sent me back to Stafford Jail
Every one appears against me,
  Every person does me hate,
What excitement is impending
  On guilty William Palmers fate,

CHORUS.

My trial causes great excitement,
  In town and country everywhere.
Now guilty found is William Palmer,
  Of Rugeley town in Staffordshire,

Many years I was a sportsman,
  Many wondrous deeds I've done
Many a race I have attended
  Many a thousand lost and won,
They say I poisoned my wifes mother
  And took away her precious life
And slew poor Cook and my own brother,
  And poisoned my own lawful wife

Everything looks black against me
  That I really can't confess
The very thoughts that does oppress me
  Causes me pain and distress
Now the Jury did convict me
  And prove I did commit the deed
And sentenced on William Palmer
  To Stafford I was sent with speed

In Rugely I was once respected
  A gentleman lived at my case
With noblemen I was connected
  And sporting men of all degrees
Although a doctor no one knew me
  To do anything amiss
Now every one strives to undo me
  I never thought I'd come to this

My poor old mother now at Rugeley
  My awful end must now bewail
To know her son must die with scorn
  a felons death in stafford jail
Every charge alleged against me
  I have strongly it denied
Twelve long days my trial lasted
  and now I am condemd to die

Dreadful is my situation
  Before the awful bar I stand
I might have filled a noble station
  Unfortunate unhappy man
Infants yet unborn will mention
  When to manhood they appear
The name of Doctor William Palmer
  Of Rugeley Town in Staffordshire

Will no one sympathise with Palmer
  who every charge did strong deny
You are all aware I am found guilty
  For by a Jury I've been tried
My situation makes me tremble
  I am borne down with grief and care
all conversation is of Palmer
  Of Rugeley town in Staffordshire

'The Life and Trial of Palmer.' Broadside from 'Murders – Broadsides and Ballads'. While most criminals had only their executions commemorated by broadsides, a notorious figure like Palmer had wide attention given to every stage of his case.

system at first prevailed, there had been substituted for it a mode of carrying executions before prescribed witnesses,' and the Bishop emphasized very reassuringly, '. . . with a sufficient showing of the man who was to suffer, and sufficient provision for their knowing that he actually suffered death.'[41] There had been much prejudice against the system at first, the Bishop told the Lords, but he was recently assured by an eminent citizen of the United States that 'there was not a single person present in America who would return to the old system of conducting executions'.[42]

Taking a leaf from the arguments of the criminal-law-reformers, the Bishop of Oxford applied their principle that the more punishment was a certainty, the greater would be the deterrent. 'There could be no greater evil in legislation,' he postulated, 'than to have severe penalties of the law fitfully carried out.'[43] If the last penalty of the law is a brutal spectacle, he warned, there will be increasing difficulty in imposing the death penalty. This was already becoming evident, he said. Every year there was increasing resistance to carrying into effect the last sentence of the law in cases in which it ought to be carried out. He was alarmed that there had been recently very few executions of women, even for the highest offences.* He could hardly conceive of a stronger case for the forfeiture of life than that of a woman who escaped the gallows for murder of a five-year-old boy. Should evasions of punishing such guilty persons persist from a dread of public executions, serious consequences could occur.

The very foundation of civil society rested upon the declaration that it was God's institution, and our right to punish was based on the same foundation. The civil government bore the sword on God's behalf.[44]

* Lord St Leonards was disturbed about this problem too. During the debate on 6 June 1856, on the punishment by death of women, he declared himself in favour of executing women in private – he was outraged by two women who had been pardoned for the murders of their illegitimate children. 'If the sole reason were any supposed feeling as to the indecency of executing women in public,' he stated, '. . . it would be better to execute women in private than to let it be understood that they were not to be executed at all.' *Hansard*, Vol. CXLII (1856), cols. 1055–6.

Lord Campbell, the Lord Chief Justice, was pliant; he agreed with the Bishop of Oxford about the evils of public executions that had been described by Fielding 'and another novelist not inferior to him, Mr Charles Dickens'.[45] He was still beset by doubts and uncertainty about what would result should public executions be abolished and how the public would respond to the change. 'Very great evils might arise from private executions and there was a strong feeling against them,' he said.[46] He recalled that when Mr Rich brought forth a proposal to substitute private for public executions, he 'incurred great obloquy'.[47] The Lord Chief Justice, however, was willing to concede that since then there had been a great change in public feeling and he was aware that private executions had been introduced in America with good effect.

One member interjected the problem of what to do with persons convicted of high treason. The imposition of private executions, generally, was untenable to Lord Redesdale, and private executions for political offences would be utterly reprehensible. Another Member revealed his apprehension that private executions would give rise to all forms of distortions and suspicions. Lord Lansdowne recalled, as a school-boy, hearing again and again the indestructable rumour that Dr Dodd was seen walking the streets of London ten and even twenty years after he had been supposedly executed.[48] Viscount Dungannon admitted that public executions were deplorable exhibitions which hardened and calloused the vulgar mind, but he was unwilling to abolish public executions because the public must know and accept the fact that the sentence of death had really been imposed. 'A middle course between the absolutely public execution and an execution conducted altogether in a private, secret manner'[49] must be found, he insisted. Despite objections and reservations expressed, the motion was voted upon affirmatively and the committee was named. The Select Committee of the House of Lords met on 27 May and the Bishop of Oxford was appointed its chairman.

While the Lords' Committee on Capital Punishment was meeting, the focus on capital punishment shifted to the House of Commons. There William Ewart attempted to introduce a motion which would pledge the House to look into the matter of capital punishment. Ewart was piqued with the developments in the House of Lords; he felt the need to demean efforts made to press for the abolition of public executions; he was quite concerned about the inroads the House of Lords' Committee might make into the efforts for total abolition of capital punishment. 'But what remedies have been proposed?' he asked disparagingly. 'A right reverend prelate has lately suggested the consideration of a new mode of conducting executions.'[50] He dismissed the proposed alteration as a numbers game; instead of the execution being viewed by the public, it will be viewed by a deputation on its behalf. The facilities of modern times, the march of technological progress, he asserted, mitigated against conducting any executions under conditions which might be described as private. 'Even now,' he said, 'special trains are announced in the newspapers as about to run to and from Stafford [where William Palmer was to be executed] to enable the public to witness the last moments of an expected victim.'[51] Even if the public was excluded, the press could not be; many millions would read the accounts rather than a few thousand witnessing it, and reading about executions would become as public as seeing them. The abolition of public executions would not resolve the problems they created; the evils will have been veiled, not removed.[52]

The Home Secretary was wary of being drawn into a discussion about public executions; he had made no statement concerning them since the controversy created by the vague concession he made about their possible alteration in 1849. 'I need not touch on public executions,' he said, 'since they do not enter into the question whether or not the punishment of death ought to be retained.'[53] Thus, Sir George Grey was unwilling to commit the government to a consideration of any policy change. Nor was he willing to accept the abolitionists' contention that the myriad problems of public execution could only be resolved by the abolition of capital punishment itself.

The possibility of capital-punishment abolition had grown more remote. In taking up the matter of the many petitions to abolish the death penalty, Sir George Grey gave little serious attention to them, viewing them as the handiwork of a small, dedicated group without any mandate to speak for a greater proportion of the population. He thought it strange that a great many petitions were presented for abolishing capital punishment and none against it. A strong inference might be drawn, he felt, that public opinion ran strongly in one direction, and that the general desire of the country was for the abolition of capital punishment. 'That inference,' Grey stated to cheers from many Members, 'cannot be drawn in this instance.'[54] Of his suspicions of the petition campaign waged by abolitionist societies, he commented, 'There are a number of persons who devote their time and their exertions to procure the abolition of the punishment of death. They get up petitions on the subject. Many of the petitions are almost stereotyped in the same terms.'[55]

Ewart's motion that a select committee should be appointed to review the laws relating to capital punishment was defeated by a margin of ninety-four votes. The government had defeated one measure in the House of Commons, and now had to contend with the related issue in the House of Lords.

The first witness examined by the Lords' Committee on Capital Punishment was Archdeacon Bickersteth of Aylesbury, a churchman who had opposed public executions since the first one he saw in 1841. He favoured private executions provided they were conducted before competent witnesses and the body of each victim was exhibited in a coffin before the gaol. The salutary effect of public executions, he thought, would be better served 'by the still corpse close at hand' rather than by 'the dangling body in the distance'.[56] He advised placing the body with friends and relatives as conclusive proof that the sentence had been carried out. But Lord Redesdale was uncertain that public display of the body would silence the deep suspicions of the public. Did the Archdeacon really believe that it 'would satisfy the public mind in so many instances that the sentence had been carried into effect'?[57]

There was great preoccupation, not only about where to dispose of an executed criminal's body, but also about what kind of appropriate ceremonies would be permitted him. In reply to the question of whether he thought a body should be buried in its own parish and with the usual ceremonies, Arch-deacon Bickersteth said it depended on the state in which the prisoner died. 'A difference might be made between the case of a man dying impenitent and without confession.'[58]

Lord Bruce was sceptical; he could not conceive that if executions were private, even though the corpse were after-wards exhibited, people would not believe that a man of edu-cation had been permitted to die an equally painful death. 'Just recall,' he said, 'the case of the Duc de Praslin, condemned to death for the murder of his wife; he had in some manner been enabled to poison himself.'[59] Detective Inspectors Thornton and Sanders, in a written statement submitted to the Lords' Committee, gave credence and substance to Lord Bruce's scepticism: 'Up to this time the public thinks that the Duke de Praslin is still alive and in the United States; that a corpse was put in his cell, and he was allowed to escape to avoid dying on the scaffold.'[60]

The testimony of the second witness, Colonel John Le Couteur, Viscomte of the Isle of Jersey, indicated that Jersey may have been the first place in Great Britain that received official sanction from the Home Office to execute criminals in a quasi-private manner. Le Couteur had requested the Home Secretary to permit the Isle of Jersey to hang prisoners within the walls of the prison; he had made application for the change because he believed the publicity of an execution made it a spectacle devoid of any solemnity. He felt that if the execu-tion could take place before officials and prisoners it would be sufficiently public. When pressed by the Bishop of St David's, Le Couteur admitted he could not recall whether he had actually asked the Secretary of State if executions might be conducted this way. Actually, between the time of the Home Secretary's approval and Le Couteur's testimony before the Lords' Select Committee, no one had been hanged in Jersey either publicly or privately. Nevertheless, from the testimony the sanctity of public executions had been dented.

LORD REDESDALE: After all, the correspondence amounted only to this: you asked to be allowed to hang elsewhere than on Gallows Hill, but still that the execution should be public.

LE COUTEUR: It was to be within the walls of the prison.

LORD SOMERHILL: Did you say that you expressed the opinion to the Secretary of State, that if the prisoners could be present, that would be sufficient?

LE COUTEUR: I know I expressed that to the Prison Board. Whether I expressed it to the Secretary of State, I am not sure.

BISHOP OF ST DAVID'S: The Secretary of State would have a power in Jersey to regulate the mode of execution, which he would not have in England, would not he?

LE COUTEUR: To this extent: since the formation of the Prison Board, an Order in Council has provided that the Secretary of State shall have the power to confirm bye-Laws made by the Prison Board.[61]

A manifestation of concern that the public would regard private executions as class legislation was revealed by the repetitious questions regarding the possible reaction of the mass of people. Lord Bruce asked Mr Henry Barber, governor of Winchester Gaol for seven years and Bridewell for twenty-four years before that, whether the common people would ever believe 'a prisoner of a superior class was actually executed without members of the lower classes present to see it'?[62]

Two police officials, with long experience in police work, testified in favour of private hangings. The police officials had consistently opposed abolishing capital punishment, feeling that abolition would increase crimes of violence and jeopardize the safety of policemen. Public executions, however, were opposed by many police officials as they caused mob gatherings that spawned crime and violence. The Earl of Shaftesbury examined Adam Sparry, an inspector of the reserve in the City of London police, who had been present at sixteen executions in eighteen years. Asked whether he had ever discussed the matter of private executions with his fellow officers, Sparry replied, 'They are of the opinion that it would be much better they should take place within precincts of the gaol.'[63]

Charles H. Hodgson, Superintendent of the City of London police, the other police official examined who opposed public hangings, said he had no objection to returning the body to relatives, unless retaining it prevented the family from making a public exhibition. The Earl of Shaftesbury expressed some anxiety that public funerals of executed criminals would transform them into unruly mobs reminiscent of public executions.

Cases sometimes occur in which a great criminal has the sympathies of those vast assemblages which you have been describing; would not there be a great hazard, if the bodies of such criminals, were given up to the relatives, that there would be a kind of a public funeral attended by those mobs, with funeral harangues over the grave?[64]

The Reverend John Clay, chaplain at Preston House of Correction for thirty-five years, favoured retaining the bodies, and burying them under sombre grave-stones with short, didactic inscriptions carved on them. These, he thought, 'would have ten times more effect upon evil-doers as find their way into a gaol than the sight of a public execution'.[65]

John Haynes, former Superintendent of the Metropolitan police, was the only witness who favoured public executions. He was confident that they prevented crime; it was inconceivable that anyone, however calloused, could witness an execution and not consider its effect. 'No one likes to be hung like a dog,' he commented. The public attitude against private executions, he believed, was fixed and permanent, but under further questioning he modified his own opinion.

Speaking individually, I am decidedly of the opinion that it would be much better that executions should take place privately, but I am perfectly satisfied that it would not satisfy the public, and when I speak of the public, I speak of the large mass of the middle class as well as the lower class. In this last case, I do not believe nine tenths of the population would have been satisfied that Palmer had been executed if it had been done in private.[66]

The experiences of several foreign countries in private executions were sought after. The Bishop of Oxford had carefully selected foreign witnesses with a favourable point of view of private execution. Frederick de Katte, attaché at the Prussian legation, was such a witness. He described the procedures by which private executions had been conducted during the last ten or twelve years in his country; official witnesses, including the judge, the solicitor of the Crown, the magistrates and a

deputation were required to attend the decapitation of criminals by hatchet; others, judged to have a particular interest
in the execution, such as physicians, attorneys, psychologists
and phrenologists, were admitted into the prison to witness the
execution by application for tickets from the criminal court.[67]

The question of whether people – particularly the lower
classes – accepted the fact of private executions was again
touched on. The Bishop of Oxford wondered if there had
been difficulty in persuading people of the reality of executions
since the change. 'No; as far as I know,' the Prussian attaché
replied, 'it has never been doubted by the people.'[68] Viscount
Dungannon was interested in how the fact of an execution
was communicated to the public; he asked whether reporters
of newspapers were admitted. As far as de Katte knew, they
were not; he was certain, however, that full information concerning the execution was published officially afterwards in the
newspapers by the criminal court. Information was sought
about what accommodation was given the lower classes at
Prussian executions.

LORD BRUCE: And none of the lower classes have a right to be
admitted?
DE KATTE: No. Admission are given by the Criminal Court to
such persons they see fit.[69]

Intense interest was shown by the Lords' Committee on
Capital Punishment in the American method of executing privately. The questioning of J. P. Kennedy, formerly the
Secretary of the Navy in President Fillmore's cabinet, was
more searching than that of any other witness. Kennedy told
the Lords that private executions were introduced out of
necessity in many of the states about twelve years previously;
and he assured the Lords that 'the practice is now extending
over the Union'.[70] The Lord Privy Seal, the Earl of Harrowby,
wondered whether there had been any demonstration of popular feeling about the new method of executing criminals; he
pursued this line of questioning:

LORD PRIVY SEAL: You never find that questions are raised in
the public papers subsequently as to the fact of such a person
having been executed?

KENNEDY: No. I never heard of a doubt of that kind.
LORD BRUCE: In those executions which take place within the prison-yard, are any persons permitted to come there by right?
KENNEDY: It is a matter requiring the permission of the Sheriff . . . and he is very careful not to bring in persons except those of intelligence and character to witness the execution.
LORD BRUCE: None are admitted of the lowest class?
KENNEDY: No.[71]

Admitted as evidence in the Committee's Report were eight letters from police officials and prison authorities; their opinion preponderantly favoured private executions, only one letter favouring public. R. H. Rider, governor of the County Gaol, Carlisle, was most decidedly in favour of private executions. 'Depend on it, my lord,' he wrote with absolute assurance, 'if criminals were executed within Prison walls, and seen no more by the public after trial and sentence, it would strike terror and dismay in the wicked.'[72] Captain Mayne, Chief Constable of the Shropshire Constabulary, was ambivalent, but he concluded that public executions were 'a show rather than an awful punishment'.[73] Chief Constable M'Hardy from Essex denied that neither direct nor indirect benefit was derived from public hangings, and he never heard an opinion to the contrary 'from any person who may have had an opportunity of judging'.[74]

After receiving the evidence, the Lords' Committee on Capital Punishment issued its Report on 7 July 1856. The Report summarized the prevailing purport of the evidence: the sight of capital executions had no deterring effect; the present system of executions glorified the criminal, cast him in a martyr's role and lightened the terrors of death; other countries including Prussia and the United States executed criminals within prison walls without injurious consequences and with the approval of strong public opinion.[75]

The Committee Report recommended that henceforth executions should take place within the prison walls or in some other comparatively private location. A certain number of unspecified official witnesses must attend each execution and sign a deposition that they had witnessed it. The selection of additional witnesses was left to the discretion of local authorities to admit whom they saw fit to be present. The tolling of a bell would inform those outside the prison wall that an execution was taking place; at the moment of execution the bell would cease tolling and a black flag would simultaneously be hoisted.[76]

Radicals and abolitionists incisively condemned the Report. Charles Phillips thought the joint Report and the evidence on which it was founded was a cogent argument for total abolition of capital punishment. Noting that the Committee had not made any provision for the role of the press in reporting executions, Phillips warned, 'We dare not exclude the press, and every incident which now thrills the land with pity or with horror, will be made just as public as if enacted on a platform.' Reiterated as a radical–abolitionist litany that the English character will never accept private executions, regardless of the modifications given them, Phillips predicted that 'private blood-shedding' would make the public recoil from them instinctively.[77] And Henry Mayhew warned that private executions were retrogressive and that the concession of entrusting government with the power to put men to death secretly was too perilous to grant. Once government had such authority, all that was needed was the right of trying in secret 'in order to carry us politically back to the times of the old Bastille'.*

Conservative opinion as well was added to the voices of disapproval. *The Times* was concerned about preserving the cherished nature of the English system of government which the House of Lords' Committee on Capital Punishment was attempting to undermine; publicity was one of the bulwarks

---

* Henry Mayhew, 'On Capital Punishment', *Three Papers on Capital Punishment*, London: Society for Promoting the Amendment of the Law, 1856, p.55. Englishmen, whether radical, liberal or conservative, shared an abiding dread of the power of the executive. John Stuart Mill spoke in 1859 for majority opinion when he warned that 'those who have the executive in their hands easily work any institutions to the purposes of despotism'. John Stuart Mill, *Essays on Politics and Culture*, ed. Gertrude Himmelfarb, New York: Doubleday & Co., 1962, p.141. There was ample evidence in nineteenth-century Europe of the absolutism from which England was spared and against which it had to be vigilant.

of English freedom which had to be jealously guarded. More-over, the common people would never accept private execu-tions, because publicity was their only guarantee for fairness; deprive them of that and they would lose confidence in the impartiality of the law and respect for the law would be endangered.[78]

So despite the Committee's recommendation, the possibi-lity of abolishing public executions remained remote. The antagonism of the Lord Chief Justice and the Home Secretary to private executions arrayed governmental and judicial oppo-sition in an almost irresistible force. Although the possibility of some movement for change was dim in 1856, it was less so than it had been just two years earlier. Another step towards progress had been taken: public executions had been con-demned by a committee of the House of Lords, and additional authoritative testimony had been added to the growing body of literature and opinion against them.

6

THE ROYAL COMMISSION, 1864–6: THE REFORM OF PUBLIC EXECUTIONS PUSHED FORWARD

ON 23 February 1864, just twenty-four hours after the 'Five Pirates' had been cut down from the gallows and their bodies placed in five lime-filled graves within Newgate Prison, John Hibbert indignantly protested against 'that disgusting display which had just taken place in the heart of London'.* He entreated his fellow Members of Parliament to legislate public hangings out of existence along with the gibbet, the rack, the stake and other relics of the past.

To the hallowed names of Romilly and Mackintosh, whose reforming zeal led to the progressive dismantling of the Draconian code in the first third of the nineteenth century, Hibbert added the names of opponents of public executions: he mentioned Rich's courageous effort in 1841 to abolish public executions; he invoked the prestigious Charles Dickens, whose famous letters to *The Times* in 1849 following the executions of the Mannings made such an impact on the public at that time; he reminded his fellow Members of the House of Commons that in 1856 a committee of the House of Lords under the chairmanship of the Bishop of Oxford had recommended private executions because of the prepondering weight of evidence given against public executions.

Hibbert hastened to assure those Members who still had serious doubts about executions within prison walls that

---

* *Hansard*, Vol. CLXXIII (1864), cols.942–4. John T. Hibbert (1824–1908) was a barrister and liberal M.P. and a magistrate. He served as President of the Local Government Board from 1872 to 1874 and from 1880 to 1883; he also held posts in the Home Office, Admiralty and Treasury. Gordon Rose, *The Struggle for Penal Reform: The Howard League and its Predecessors,* London: Stevens & Sons, 1961, p.17.

many American states and the Australian colonies executed their criminals inside prisons without suspicion or protest. Mr Henry Adams, the American Ambassador, had just written him, Hibbert informed the chamber, to report the complete acceptance and satisfaction of private-execution arrangements by the American public. Hibbert urged Parliament to take up again the problem of public executions, and he inquired of Sir George Grey, the Home Secretary, whether the government was now prepared to take the lead in legislating private executions.

The government, in the person of Sir George Grey, its able and articulate spokesman on criminal matters, had no such intention. Stating that the primary function of government was to protect its citizens from those who would destroy them with impunity, Sir George Grey insisted that the government would not abrogate that duty because of criticisms from misguided and misinformed sentimentalists. He conceded the occasional inconveniences caused by public executions, but he thought their alleged injurious effects were exaggerated. 'We must put up with these inconveniences,' he said firmly, 'in order to carry out what we feel necessary for the public good.'[1]

The repeated charge that executions were becoming more brutal and the crowds larger and less manageable irked the Home Secretary. He warned the Members of the House against acting imprudently because of these allegations. The crowds had become larger simply because executions were less frequent, he explained. And as for the recommendation for private executions made by the Lords' Committee on Capital Punishment, he cautioned the House of Commons not to attach too much weight to the Committee's Report. 'No committee ever came to a positive decision on a subject on less clear and inconclusive grounds,' he declared.[2]

Those wishing to abolish public executions, the Home Secretary continued, were caught up in a web of contradictions of their own making. He flatly affirmed that the critics of the present system of executing criminals – despite outward appearance – were actually in agreement with the official policy of publicity. All of the critics' proposals for reforms contained elements of publicity, he contended. He urged

Parliament to consider the reformers' suggestions and to note that publicity was an important aspect of each. The Lords' Committee on Capital Punishment would compel jurors and witnesses to attend executions; recommendations had been made that the bodies of executed criminals should be exposed to public view; a hoisted black flag and the loud tolling of bells was considered an effective way of informing the public that an execution was concurrently taking place. But, Sir George claimed, all these expedients – the witnesses, exposed bodies and tolling bells – were self-defeating; they would lure crowds to the gaol where unseemly scramblings for places at executions would occur. The Home Secretary concluded his defence of public hangings by repeating the old rubric that 'private executions would be thoroughly abhorrent to the public'.[3]

Others in Parliament were not quite so satisfied with the public arrangements for executions. Lord Henry Lennox had gone to the execution of the 'Five Pirates' and he expressed the opinion that the whole lamentable affair was without any saving grace whatsoever. He wondered whether the Home Secretary, with his undoubted power in the matter of criminal punishment, could not inveigh upon the authorities at Newgate to change the day of execution from Monday to another day. 'We live in a country where the Sabbath is respected,' he said, 'but what would the Honourable members say when I told you that on Sunday from 11 A.M. the place in front of Newgate Gaol was surging to and fro with the scum of our population?'[4] He hoped the authorities throughout the nation would adopt the policy of never announcing the day of an execution in advance; the day of an execution was never announced in Warwick. Such a procedure would discourage railroad boards from profiting by the misery of others and they would cease to run pleasure excursions to executions. 'It is high time,' Lord Lennox stated vehemently, 'the Home Secretary should interfere in this matter.'[5]

Hibbert had not had too much hope for his motion to abolish public executions, but he did hope that it might induce Sir George Grey to make inquiries into execution-practice in other countries. Also, he wished to arouse debate and to keep pressure on individual members and on the government about this recurrent problem. Despite Hibbert's failure to obtain one concession from the government, he was satisfied with the course of the debate and the many expressions of dissatisfaction expressed by a number of the Members. Expressing his conviction that a change of opinion in England concerning private executions was only a matter of time, Hibbert withdrew his motion.[6]

The debates and agitation about capital punishment and public executions which sporadically had been heard and felt in the chambers of both Houses of Parliament, in press and journal, and in meetings throughout the nation, reached a climax in 1864 with the appointment of the Royal Commission on Capital Punishment. As so often in the past, it was William Ewart – he introduced the motion which led to the formation of the Royal Commission – who played an important role in another landmark in English criminal-law history.

In calling for the appointment of a Select Committee of the House of Commons to look into the need to retain the death penalty, Ewart went over the many arguments he had used so often: he said progress was against the retention of capital punishment; he claimed the chances of escaping conviction were greater in capital crimes than in other criminal cases. And he asked: 'Supposing an aversion to inflict capital punishment goes on increasing, what remedies are proposed?'[7] Private executions were not the solution; they were totally unacceptable. Moreover, Ewart insisted, private executions were an admission that executions had always been shameful, ineffectual, brutal and useless. Sir George Grey, unwilling to accept a select committee, agreed to Charles Neate's amendment, which requested appointing a royal commission, and which also broadened the scope of its inquiry to include public executions as well.[8]

The debate of 3 May 1864, which had led to the formation of the Royal Commission on Capital Punishment, caused the abolitionist, Alfred Dymond, to be optimistic. He enthusiastically anticipated the support William Ewart could expect in the cabinet and in Parliament. His was an act of self-delusion and wishful thinking. Earl Russell, the Foreign Secretary in

Palmerston's cabinet, and undoubtedly the most influential member of the government after Palmerston, was claimed by Dymond as a supporter of abolition 'whilst other members of the Cabinet are presumed to be favourable to extensive alterations in the existing law'.[9] Earl Russell had as long ago as 1837 declared he was opposed to further diminution of capital-punishment laws, and the other cabinet members exhibited little zeal for abolition.

Dymond exulted over the 3 May debate; he thought it had brought forward a remarkable unanimity between men of the most adverse and varied shades of political opinion. William Ewart, George Denman, Charles Neate, John Bright, Sir Francis Crossley and John Hibbert were identified by Dymond as independent liberals and as supporters of abolition. They were, in fact, very divided in the debate. Ewart, Denman, Neate and Bright were thorough abolitionists; Hibbert assiduously worked to end public executions; Sir Francis Crossley used reactionary language in the debate in support of capital punishment, claiming it had a 'wholesome effect on the imagination and feelings of mankind'.[10] Such conservatives as Lord Henry Lennox and Mitford, whom Dymond described as 'worthy coadjutors to the independent liberals',[11] were not totally reliable. Lord Henry Lennox was not 'on that occasion to advocate abolishing capital punishment';[12] and in the same debate, Mitford advocated retention of capital punishment 'until they devise some secondary punishment which would have some deterring effect'.[13]

The important ministers and the influential coalition in Parliament behind Ewart's efforts to abolish capital punishment were the stuff on which dreams and reforms are made. Dymond did not even share a thorough commitment on the issue with such ideologues as Ewart and Bright. Although he was appalled by the suggestion of private executions, he wondered 'whether the gross evils attendant upon public hangings do not outweigh the objections that may be urged against a private performance of the hateful tragedy'.[14]

Although the Lords' Committee on Capital Punishment of 1856 included such influential members as the Lord Privy Seal and the Lord Chief Justice, that Committee did not have the substance of the Royal Commission on Capital Punishment of 1864. Unlike the Lords' Committee, the Royal Commission had the obvious and energetic support of the government. The Royal Commission had at its disposal a worldwide network of ambassadors and colonial officials furnishing it with requested information about capital-punishment laws and execution practices.* Thus, from dispatches circulated through the Foreign Office and Colonial Office, comprehensive accounts of criminal laws and execution practices were compiled about countries of Europe, North and South America and the Australian colonies.

The Royal Commission on Capital Punishment was enhanced by the appointment of experienced and distinguished political figures to it. In addition to its chairman, the sixth Duke of Richmond, who became leader of the Conservative Party in the House of Lords in 1868, there were other aspiring Members of Parliament: Lord Stanley became Foreign Secretary in the Derby government; George Ward Hunt was made Chancellor of the Exchequer under Disraeli and Gathorne Hardy was Home Secretary in 1867 in Lord Derby's cabinet. Knowledge of legal and criminal law was supplied by Stephen Lushington, Judge of the High Court of Admiralty, Thomas O'Hagan, Attorney-General of Ireland, and James Moncrieff, Advocate of Scotland. John Bright, the leading radical of the period, was a member, as was William Ewart, the foremost criminal-law reformer of the second half of the nineteenth century. Of the lesser luminaries, Charles Neate was one of the more distinguished Members of Parliament.

From the start, the Royal Commission was hopelessly divided. Four of the twelve Commissioners – Lushington, Bright, Neate and Ewart – were irrevocably committed to

---

* Sir George Grey requested Lord Russell, the Foreign Secretary, to furnish the Royal Commission with information about the 'various laws of various countries with regard to offences punishable with death'. Edward Cardwell, the Secretary of State for the Colonial Office, was asked to obtain information from the Australian colonies concerning 'the effect produced upon the Public by the execution of criminals within the Walls of the Gaol where such a course was pursued'. Public Record Office, Home Office, *Commissions of Inquiry*, 1850–1868, 73, No. 3, pp. 231–5.

abolition of the death penalty; Bright and Ewart were active members of the Committee for the Abolition of Capital Punishment. The majority of the remaining Commissioners favoured abolishing public executions. By the logic of their position, the four abolitionists were cast in the role of the minority, attempting to thwart the majority's decision to reform public executions.

Between 29 November 1864 and 25 March 1865 the Royal Commission on Capital Punishment held fifteen hearings. During that time, thirty well-qualified and often eminent men – including a former and current Home Secretary, judges, prison governors, police officials and clergymen – gave extensive testimony. Their evidence and the information gathered in the index created a voluminous Report of 723 pages. The Report is a comprehensive compendium of criminal history, criminology, penal practices and criminal law, as well as a prime source of social history.

The judges who appeared before the commissioners, as expected, were quite conservative, and they tenaciously supported capital punishment. As for public executions, they were indecisive and had differing opinions. Lord Cranworth, a baron of the Court of Exchequer, was inconsistent about what should be done with public executions. He thought the criminal class would be more deterred by seeing an execution than by reading about it; he also believed private executions would be more suitable in a modern state. His major concern was a fear that disgust with public executions might dispose many people towards the abolition of capital punishment entirely. He could not quite understand all the evils, about which some people complained, in public executions, but he did believe 'they do excite great disgust in the minds of many people'.[15] Sir George Bramwell, also a baron of the Court of Exchequer, fully shared his colleague's view that great precaution must be taken, should private executions be adopted, that they would not be 'secret'.[16]

Another baron of the Court of Exchequer, Sir Samuel Martin, urged retention of both capital punishment and public executions. He thought murder a crime committed exclusively by the lower classes, and hardly ever by a person of the middle classes. Fear and terror were the only ways to suppress lower-class crime: they would know that if they murdered they would be punished by death on the public gallows.[17]

The thrust of the questions put to Sir Samuel Martin by William Ewart and Charles Neate was to undermine his argument favouring capital punishment. In reply to Ewart's question of whether women and children should be permitted to attend executions, Sir Samuel expressed uncertainty, but in regard to certain cases in court he knew women and children were excluded. He thought that might be done at executions. Noting the irony, Neate asked, 'If women are to be hung, ought they to see what it is?'[18]

Gathorne Hardy, opposed to abolition of capital punishment and favourable to private executions, sought to lead Sir Samuel Martin to these conclusions. For the most obvious reasons of implanting fear as a possible condition of the abolition of the death penalty, he asked Sir Samuel whether he believed there would be the likelihood of a lynch law if capital punishment was abolished.[19]

This verbal fencing between commissioners and witnesses could bring forth cutting, sardonic responses, particularly when the witness advocated an opposing view. Henry Avery, Clerk of Arraigns at the Central Criminal Court, and deputy Clerk of Assize for the Home Circuit Court, saw capital punishment as a necessity; he advocated executions within prison walls, with the proper safeguards to convince the public, including listing the names of all persons present at the execution and publishing them in the *Gazette* and newspapers. John Bright asked archly, 'In the same way as the game certificates are?'[20]

When examining Lord Wensleydale, a retired jurist, the Duke of Richmond received a most unexpected reply. Expecting a negative answer, he had asked Lord Wensleydale whether he thought there were better substitutes for capital punishment. 'I think there are punishments which are capable of producing a much greater effect,' Lord Wensleydale said, 'but they are punishments which the public would not endure, as cutting off a man's members, depriving him of his eyesight, cutting off his limbs . . .'[21]

The impetus for reforming public executions was given considerable encouragement by the testimonies of Spencer Walpole, Home Secretary in 1852 and 1858, and by Sir George Grey, the incumbent Home Secretary. The principle of publicity and terror of public hangings, so long and tenaciously defended by succeeding home secretaries, particularly within the last twenty-five years, was given a jarring disavowal by Walpole: 'One of the great objects of public executions is supposed to be the deterring effect of the example which it would have on others; but the effect of a public execution would be the reverse of that.'[22] Concern was expressed to Walpole by the Duke of Richmond about the public acceptance of private executions, and the absolute necessity of making the public know an execution had taken place. In essence he wanted to know what assurances could be given the public if executions were done privately. Walpole cited the American practice of publishing the report of the coroner's inquest upon the body of the executed criminal; this, he thought, was not only a means of informing the public about an execution, but an added security, reassuring them that an execution had been carried out and dispelling any lingering suspicions of state sadism. As an additional safeguard, Walpole recommended that the press should be permitted to witness and report upon executions under regulations and restrictions prescribed by law, urging, 'You must legislate for it and it would require careful legislation.'[23]

The testimony given by Sir George Grey was both crucial and dramatic, and a complete reversal of his previous consistent declarations. Now he openly advocated private executions, in marked contrast to the timorous suggestion he made in 1849 that possible alteration of public executions should be considered. In 1849 he had made an ignominious retreat into silence following the harsh treatment he received after his vague concessions to consider private executions; now there was indication of an entirely new climate of opinion, and he was aware of it. 'I think,' he said, 'there is a growing feeling in favour.'[24] A slow, evolving pace leading to reform suited his philosophy and temperament. 'Gradual changes,' he believed, 'are much easier than violent ones.'[25] – this in reply to

Ewart's jibe that Sir Robert Peel had justified the death penalty for the theft of five shillings from a dwelling-house.

The new decade of the 1860s had brought with it new conditions and a change in the moral attitudes and conduct of the lower classes, and this resulted in reduced tensions and fears. In particular, the anxiety of the upper classes was diminished and their morbid dread of the sullen, criminal masses subsided.* Ewart attributed the change in the lower classes to the moral agencies which had been at work with the people and had such a great influence upon the population, so much so that Sir George Grey was able to announce to the House of Commons, 'I think there has been a diminution in crime generally.'† The decrease in crime and the new moral tone evident in the country combined to create an awareness that public executions had become a growing source of embarrassment and a superfluous anachronism. This growing self-consciousness prompted Grey to do something immediately to temporize conditions at executions. He informed the House that the execution day at Newgate would be moved from Monday to Wednesday. Sunday gave people the chance to collect all day and night and he hoped the change would reduce the size of crowds.[26]

The information which most profoundly influenced Sir George Grey, and obviously the leaders of the government,

* Steven Marcus has come to the same conclusion: 'That life was degraded and often bestial; drink, violence, early and promiscuous sexuality and disease were the counterparts of poverty, endless labor, and a life whose vision of futurity was at best cheerless. In such a context, the typical values, and indeed Victorianism itself, take on new meaning. It is not usual nowadays to regard such values as chastity, propriety, modesty, even rigid prudery as positive moral values, but it is difficult to doubt that in the situation of the urban lower social classes they operated with positive force. The discipline and self-restraint which the exercise of such virtues required could not but be a giant step towards the humanization of a class of persons who had been traditionally regarded as almost of another species.' *The Other Victorians*, New York: Bantam Books, 1967, p. 147.

† *Parliamentary Papers*, 'Report of the Royal Commission on Capital Punishment', Vol. XXI, 1866, p.213. Recent scholarship has corroborated this reduction of crime during the course of the century. See J. J. Tobias, *Crime and Industrial Society in the 19th Century*, New York: Schocken Books, 1967.

THE ILLUSTRATED
POLICE NEWS,
LAW-COURTS AND CRIMINAL RECORD.

LONDON, SATURDAY, FEBRUARY 20, 1864.

[PRICE, ONE PENNY.

The 'Five Pirates' from *The Illustrated Police News*, 20 February 1864. The 'Five Pirates' were executed on 23 February 1864 for their involvement in the mutiny on the Flowery Land.

Franz Müller, a German, was executed on 14 November 1864, convicted for the 'Railway Train Murder'.

were the accounts of execution practices in America and in the Australian colonies. English insularity and the traditional feeling of the uniqueness and superiority of English institutions conditioned the authorities to overlook Europe for insights and ideas for reform; instead they turned to America and Australia where the people, institutions, laws and traditions all had their origins in their English past. That the former American colonies and Australian colonies could evolve innovatory methods with the acceptance and approval of the inhabitants was encouraging and reassuring for the English. 'The letters which I have, as to America, state that a certain number of persons are required to be present,' Sir George Grey stated, 'and that the regulations there existing (and I believe the same in the case of Australia) completely satisfy the public the executions take place.'[27]

The information forwarded to Grey by the Foreign and Colonial Offices described very defined, involved procedures for executions in America and Australia. These procedures were developed to destroy any doubt that the law had not been carried out to the fullest extent and to dispel any suspicion of torture committed in the act of executing. Pennsylvania, which adopted private executions in 1834, made mandatory the presence of panels of juries, sheriffs, deputies and medical staffs at all executions; all official persons had to sign certified public returns. This basic system, with some variations and modifications, soon spread to the other states of the north-east.[28]

Similar innovations in executing privately were introduced in the Australian colonies of South Australia, New South Wales, Tasmania and Queensland. In South Australia 'An Act to Regulate the Execution of Criminals' was passed in 1858. It provided that criminals should be taken to the gaol-yard in Adelaide, and there hanged before the sheriff, the gaoler, other prison officers and a medical officer. Although Justices of the Peace, ministers and police officers were entitled to attend the execution, other adult witnesses could be admitted only by the discretion of the sheriff. Scrupulous adherence to procedure in establishing and publicizing an execution was followed. A coroner's and juror's inquest officially investigated and certified that the sentence of execution had been duly performed; the certificate and declaration were forwarded to the Master of the Supreme Court, recorded and published three separate times in the *South Australian Government Gazette*.*

Australian officials testified that the new system was not only acceptable to the people, but that it went far to correct practices which had become repellent to a changing society. Sir George Bowen, Governor of Queensland, wrote that he had arrived in Australia with complete acquiescence to the practice of executing as established in England, but that after sufficient experience his former opinion changed considerably. The altered system got rid of the demoralizing consequences of mobs gathered around the gallows. He described a recent execution at Brisbane in explicit detail to illustrate how much more awesome and fearful were private executions. He asked whether such a scene described in minute detail in all public journals would not be more likely to produce a deterrent effect than a public execution recently described in London newspapers

when a convict named Wright, executed in front of Horsemonger-lane Gaol was received by the multitude with enthusiastic cheers, and stood bowing on the scaffold like a popular actor on the stage in acknowledgment of the applause with which he was greeted.[29]

Additional support for private executions came from John West, editor of the *Sydney Morning Herald*. He thought the Act enforcing the execution of criminals within prison walls met with the almost universal approval of the people of Sydney, with the possible exception of a small number of habitual frequenters of executions. West's further qualifications about private executions, and his own anti-capital-punishment bias, were very acceptable to the minority of abolitionists on the

---

* *Parliamentary Papers*, Report of the Capital Punishment Commission, Vol. XXI, 1866, appendix, p.585. An amendment was added to the Act of 1861; it permitted the Aborigine to be executed publicly where the crime was committed; the amendment was added because the Aborigine could not accept the fact of death by execution of one of his own unless witnessed by his own people.

Royal Commission. The questions he raised were disquietingly pertinent. West wondered whether publicity was more important in ratio to population density; whether in the more tumultuous, explosive atmosphere of major urban centres the lack of publicity about executions might find conditions rife for the proliferation of rumours ugly enough to incite riotous acts. He challenged the Commissioners to consider the relative social conditions and population factors of England and Australia and to determine whether Australian practices and experiences were relevant or practicable in England. 'The objection to the public execution of criminals lies very near to the objection to capital punishment in any form'[30] was a judgement Ewart, Bright, Neate and Lushington shared with West.

Two leading members of the Society for the Abolition of Capital Punishment, William Tallack and Thomas Beggs, and two abolitionist Members of Parliament, George Denman and Lord Hobart, appeared before the Royal Commission. Paradoxically, they gave authoritative support for abolition of public executions despite their well-known aversion to capital punishment. The dilemma of the abolitionists continued; they were unable to condemn capital punishment without also condemning public executions. But by concentrating on the latter, they obscured and jeopardized their prime aim of total abolition.

Beggs, who was chairman of the Society for the Abolition of Capital Punishment, was placed in a quandary. As a sensitive, enlightened person he was placed in the unconscionable position of condemning capital punishment, while ignoring frightful public executions – which he was unable to do. Attempting to illustrate the futility of executions and to document their pervasive danger, Beggs described the execution of a John Jones in Nottingham in 1842. Jones, an exemplary prisoner, praised by the chaplain, visited by the Bishop of Lincoln, fawned over by pious, benevolent Nottingham ladies, had a sympathetic crowd to see him hanged for the murder of an unworthy, faithless girl-friend. A man told his son, 'I wish you were ready to die as he is.'[31] Beggs didactically commented, 'He was raised into a hero or saint, and made almost an

JACK KETCH'S LEVEE

OR, THE

GREAT SENSATION SCENE AT NEWGATE.

BY AN EX OFFICIAL.

CONTAINING AN ACCOUNT OF

THE BARBAROUS CUSTOMS OF THE OLDEN TIMES:

TRIALS BY BATTLE; DEATH PUNISHMENT OF THE INNOCENT;

200 Crimes Punishable by Death reduced to 1

Showing also that the Gallows is no Corrective but a fearful Promoter of Crime.

PRICE 1d.]   PUBLISHED BY C. ELLIOT, SHOE LANE.   [PRICE 1d.

'Jack Ketch's Levee or, the Great Sensation Scene at Newgate', published by C. Elliot, London, 1863. This pamphlet, purportedly written by an ex-official of Newgate Prison, claimed that the gallows were a 'fearful promoter of crime' and urged the abolition of public hanging.

object of envy among his class.'[32] The obvious conclusion to those unwilling to relinquish death penalties was that private executions would have deprived Jones of this undue attention.

But Beggs struggled to counteract the notion that private executions were the method to resolve public executions. He insisted that private executions were neither acceptable to the working class nor feasible. The criminal would still be an object of interest; the press would cater to the insatiable craving for sensation with obnoxious anecdotes about the criminal, lurid tales about the crime and explicitly vivid details about the execution. Beggs contended that newspaper accounts of executions were far more pernicious in effect than the evil which resulted from large congregated masses of people at the actual scene. The demoralizing influence of public executions, thought Beggs, resulted far more from newspaper reporting of the last days of the criminal than the events around the gallows. To which the chairman of the Royal Commission, the Duke of Richmond, asked:

CHAIRMAN: Am I to understand you to think that publicity should not be given to the trial and sentence of the prisoner?
BEGGS: I think that after the sentence is passed the criminal should be as much secluded from the world as possible . . . And I fear that private executions would surround the matter with an air of mystery that would only make these inquiries a subject of still greater anxiety amongst the multitude outside.[33]

Beggs continued his attack on private executions. The masses would never accept them; they would give rise to ugly rumours and distortions. 'It was, I remember, gravely asserted in a newspaper some years ago that Fauntleroy had not been executed and that most improbable statement was credited by many.'[34] The inference was that if such a suspicion could become so entrenched when thousands saw that execution, what credibility could private executions have?

Beggs raised the spectre of increased class-hatred caused by private executions. The lower classes would see private executions as discriminatory, as class legislation; such executions would arouse bitter opposition among them, even violence. Beggs was certain of their opposition; he knew the working classes. Mingling with the poor, he had often heard them claim that the rich were favoured at their expense, 'even amongst the more intelligent and educated of the working class'.[35]

The testimony of William Tallack was more denunciatory of public executions than of capital punishment. According to Tallack, now the first Secretary of the Howard Association, public executions did not deter and did not shock and frighten people from committing crimes. They had a morbid and compulsive effect on viewers; people were driven by irresistible desire to attain the notoriety and practise the same reckless bravado on the gallows. Exploiting the still fresh episode of the execution of Müller, Tallack reminded the Commissioners of the 'crop of homicidal murders' following that execution. And as illustration, he recalled the case of the murderer confessing to the police, 'I stabbed him and I will do it again if he tells lies about me. I will be hung for him as Müller for Briggs,' and of the soldier, arrested for attempted murder of a prostitute, saying, 'I will be hung for her. I don't mind swinging for such a — as her.'*

George Denman, the radical M.P., attempted to extricate the public-execution issue from the abolition of capital punishment, but only succeeded in merging the two hopelessly. Gathorne Hardy forced Denman to agree that public executions influenced people to murder compulsively and to invite their own self-destruction.[36] Lord Hobart, the other abolitionist M.P. called to give evidence to the Royal Commission, was equally unsuccessful in separating the two issues. Although admittedly scandalized by public executions, he preferred to classify them as minor evils in what he termed 'the social arrangements of the country',[37] and in the scale of the overall objections to capital punishment 'a less weighty reason against the retention of capital punishment'.[38]

Governors of prisons, and others in the prison service, were

---

* ibid., p.174. The abolitionists were not above embroidering testimony to make it conform to their ends. The anonymous author of *Analysis and Review of the Blue Book of the Royal Commission on Capital Punishment* quoted Tallack as having said, 'I will be hung for her. I don't mind swinging with Müller for such as her.' London: Committee for the Abolition of Capital Punishment, 1866, p.12.

unanimously in favour of private executions; even those who, like Henry Cartwright, governor of Gloucester County Prison, favoured total abolition were prepared to accept private executions as an alternative. Asked by the Duke of Richmond whether he thought executions should be private or public, Cartwright responded unhesitatingly: 'In private, decidedly as being more deterrent ... for greater solemnity, and ... more humane to the criminal himself.'[39] Colonel Henry Stace, the former governor of Oxford Gaol and an opponent of capital punishment, resigned from his post rather than officiate at an execution. He informed the Commissioners of his deep revulsion of public executions, so much so that during his four-year tenure at Oxford Gaol he did not allow any executions to be carried out there.[40] Immediately after his resignation, an execution occurred before Oxford Gaol.

Prison chaplains tended generally to be opposed to public executions. Even the Reverend Davis, ordinary at Newgate for twenty years, a man full of vindictive hatred for murderers, advocated private executions. He admitted to the Commissioners that his conversion to private executions was of a recent origin, stemming from the assurances given him by an American judge that the experiments in executing criminals in private there proved 'beneficial'.[41] He was also influenced by the solid middle-class Manchester jury's memorial to the Home Secretary beseeching him to abolish public executions.[42] His conversion to private executions was still too recent and superficial to disguise his deep aversions to criminals and his wish to have them repent their wicked sins publicly.

When Reverend Davis stated that the taking of human life required a punishment of equal dimension, John Bright inquired sharply whether he really believed that reverence for human life was not impaired by hanging a man before 100,000 people. Reverend Davis replied, 'I do not think that the reverence for human life is injured by public executions.'[43]

Both Bright and Charles Neate attempted to shape Reverend Davis's responses to their purposes. Reverend Davis testified that new sheriffs occasionally fainted, and that even he had been ill for three days following his first execution; Neate tried to get Davis to agree to the contention that prison officials would no longer cooperate in executing criminals. While guiding, or at least trying to guide, Reverend Davis to admit the possibility of the non-deterrence of capital punishment, John Bright managed to highlight the non-deterrent quality of public executions. Bright's own line of questioning indicted the punishment rather than the law as the agent in inciting the maladjusted to violence:

BRIGHT: Do you recollect a young man by the name of Wicks being hanged at Newgate?
REVEREND DAVIS: Yes.
BRIGHT: He shot his master in Drury-lane.
DAVIS: He did.
BRIGHT: Do you recollect the fact that he had been only a short time before to see an execution?
DAVIS: Yes.
BRIGHT: And that the same morning he ran as hard as he could to see another person hanged?
DAVIS: Yes, he was a great execution seer.
BRIGHT: Do you recollect the statement which he made after he had seen it, that he snapped his fingers and said, 'It is nothing; it is only a kick!' And then he went home and shot his master.[44]

The Reverend John Jessop had no such ambivalence about public executions. To Lord Stanley's inquiry whether private executions, similar to the practice followed in some American states, would remove the evils of public executions, he responded unhesitatingly, 'Most decidedly.'[45] In addition to moral objections, he felt public executions had no utilitarian purpose; they were contrary to the primary purpose of good government which was to educate and elevate the most ignorant and depraved classes. And they were ineffectual in making any salutary impression on the criminal class; criminals in prison were often heard to say, 'Well, so-and-so is to be hanged tomorrow; I wish I were outside; I could go in for a good swag.'[46]

The abolitionists on the Royal Commission tried to counteract the trend of the testimony when it gave priority to the abolition of public executions, particularly when sympathetic witnesses appeared, and leading statements could be made for their benign approval. The Reverend Lord Sidney Godolphin

Osborne, who proclaimed his reforming and anti-capital-punishment opinions in numerous letters to *The Times*,[47] was asked hypothetically whether he favoured public or private executions. He naturally had admitted he would, under such a circumstance, opt for private executions. He had a singular disgust of the notorious scum at executions 'whose foul language, obscene songs and drunken jollity pollute the air'.[48] Ewart moved directly for an affirmative response against private executions:

A few days ago at Durham when a prisoner was executed a dreadful scene occurred by the breaking of the rope and hanging the man by another rope; it seems to have been altogether a terrible scene. Do you think that such scenes would be endured by people supposing that the execution was a private one; do you not think that popular discontent would be so manifested that it scarcely allow of such scenes being permitted?[49]

Police officials expressed a wide range of ideas and attitudes about how best to suppress crime and deal with criminals. Police Inspector Kittle told William Ewart that public executions provided a great moral lesson and exercised a 'deterring influence on the commission of crime';[50] but at another point in his testimony the police inspector stated in contradiction, 'I do not think witnessing an execution excites fear'.[51] He was indifferent to whether executions were public or private. And Inspector Richard Tanner of the metropolitan detective force, a rigid believer in capital punishment, was equally indecisive and contradictory. Presumably opposed to public executions – he never saw an execution because he had 'no such morbid taste'[52] – he was indifferent to whether public executions were reformed.

Unlike Kittle and Tanner, Hilary Nissen, the Sheriff of the City of London, was adamant in his rejection of public executions, and even somewhat uncertain about continuing the death penalty.* He also had some advanced insights into the

* ibid., p.222. Hilary Nissen, during his shrievalty in 1864, witnessed officially more executions in London than any sheriff in England and Wales during that quarter of a century. William Tallack, *A General Review of the Subject of Capital Punishment*, London: Society for the Abolition of Capital Punishment, 1866, p.8.

social and environmental conditions predetermining anti-social acts, arguing that men who spent a lifetime in misery with drunken wives and starving children would not hesitate to take a life because death held no terror for them.[53] The sight of a man on the gallows did not brutalize and harden; the misery of the working classes had already made them insensate. People approved the display of state sadism which offered the destruction of a human being for their enjoyment. Nissen could not possibly conceive of public executions having any effect on masses of people so conditioned and so empty of compassion.

Four very eminent lawyers appeared before the Royal Commission to be examined, and they had widely divergent opinions about the death penalty and public executions. Émile Chedieu of France urged a gradual abolition of capital punishment, but would still wish to retain public executions in France in the meanwhile; Sir James Fitzjames Stephens, the noted criminal-law historian, strongly advocated keeping capital punishment and public executions. Leone Levi, Professor of Common Law at King's College, London, a barrister with a doctor's degree in economics, supported total abolition; John Humphrey Parry, the serjeant-at-law who defended the Mannings and Müller in their murder trials, would accept private executions if capital punishment were continued.

The experiences of the French Revolution and the Revolution of 1848 influenced Chedieu's consideration about implementing private executions in France; he was fearful that the security of the individual would be jeopardized by private executions during great social eruptions. According to Chedieu, there were factors which moderated the conditions of executions in France so that public ones there never even approximated those in England. The French never announced the date and times of executions beforehand; consequently the numbers at executions never exceeded 4,000, a small and controllable crowd by English standards.[54]

Their views being so well publicized and opposed to one another, it was inevitable that William Ewart and Sir James Stephens would clash. 'Is it not better,' Ewart asked Stephens, with some obvious pique, 'to give your population a horror of the crime than a horror of the punishment?'[55]

Expressing middle-class self-consciousness, Serjeant Parry claimed that no gentleman, except from pure eccentricity, attended executions, and certainly no respectable one would ever go. And yet, he did not see why the ladies and gentlemen of respectable society should not attend executions if they were didactic, as claimed. Despite his anti-capital-punishment preference, he gave rather emphatic endorsement to private executions. Disagreeing with the opinion of Charles Neate, that the public would recoil in repugnance from private executions, Parry insisted that the successful American experience belied that assertion. Private executions would be as acceptable in England as they were in America, if equal care were taken to have a coroner's inquest after each execution as in New England.[56]

Professor Levi introduced psychological insights to show the non-deterrent effect of capital punishment. He suggested that suicidal tendencies diminished the effectiveness of posing death as a threat and a punishment. He cited the statistics that in 1857 only thirteen criminals died on the gallows, whereas in that same year 1,349 people killed themselves.[57]

Two physicians with a specialized interest in mental illness contributed additional testimony about the psychological factors in crime. Dr Thomas Harrington Tuke, a member of the Royal College of Physicians, interested in the study and treatment of nervous disorders, testified that suicide succeeded homicide often enough to demonstrate a strong relationship between the two. Despite this observation linking drives of self-destruction with the destruction of others, he gave a tentative, qualified approval to the continuation of capital punishment.[58] Dr William Charles Hood, visitor in lunacy with a two-year appointment from the Lord Chancellor, opposed capital punishment, although not too forcefully.

Execution practices of nations in Europe, South America, American states and Australian colonies filled 245 pages of the Report of the Royal Commission on Capital Punishment. Two of the six questions circulated through the foreign offices in 1864 inquired about methods of execution, and whether the executions were private or public. The information was to be forwarded to Earl Russell, the Foreign Secretary, who would in turn furnish the information to the Capital Punishment Commission. The majority of the countries canvassed, which included France, Belgium, Holland, Austria, Spain, Russia, Denmark, Sweden and most of the Swiss cantons, still executed in public; they used a variety of methods, including, in addition to hanging, the guillotine, sword, axe, garrotte and firing-squad.

There was, however, a reforming trend abroad. Almost concurrently with the hearings of the Royal Commission, the governments of several European states discontinued capital punishment. The Grand Council of Berne as recently as 22 February 1864 – just three months before the first session of the Royal Commission – legislated private executions. A proposal to abolish capital punishment was defeated by the opposition of the Württemberg government, Upper Chamber and Maires de Communes after passing through the Chamber by the majority of fifty-six to twenty-seven.* Previously the German states of Prussia, Saxony, Brunswick and Bavaria had made execution private, and the states of Oldenburg and Anhalt had abolished capital punishment as did the Swiss cantons of Neuchâtel and Freiberg. The reform impetus had also reached the South American countries of Colombia and Venezuela which abolished capital punishment in 1863 and 1864, and in the United States death penalties had been abolished in Michigan, Rhode Island and Wisconsin in the previous decade.

The majority of the members of the Royal Commission determined from the evidence given them 'a great preponderance of opinion' against public executions; and accordingly, the Report of the Capital Punishment Commission, issued on

---

* The English Ambassador in Stuttgart forwarded this information to Earl Russell, the Foreign Secretary, on 25 February 1865. 'My Lord,' it read, 'a proposal for the abolition of Capital Punishment was brought before the Chamber of Deputies last week, after the excitement of pretty extensive agitation throughout the country in its favour, chiefly promoted by the religious party.' Parliamentary Papers, Report of the Capital Punishment Commission, Vol. XXI, 1866, appendix, p.568.

8 January 1866, recommended passing an Act to end public executions. The Commissioners felt it impossible to resist such weight of authority.[59] Unlike the Report in 1856 of the House of Lords Committee on Capital Punishment, the Royal Commission gave no specific details about how an execution should be conducted other than a broad recommendation that the executions should be carried out within the precincts of the prison 'under such regulations as may be considered necessary to prevent abuse and to satisfy the public that the law had been complied with'.[60]

William Ewart, John Bright, Dr Lushington and Charles Neate, joined by James Moncrieff, the Advocate of Scotland, voted against the majority. Instead, Ewart substituted a minority clause which stated that 'capital punishment might safely and with advantage to the community be at once abolished'.[61] Bright, Neate and Lushington signed the minority Report. Thomas O'Hagan, the Attorney-General for Ireland, declared himself in principle in favour of the minority Report because 'the weight of evidence and reason was in favour of the abolition of Capital Punishment but he doubted whether public opinion was ripe for such a change'.[62]

Ostensibly, William Ewart and his three allies on the Commission dissented from the majority recommendation because they thought private executions would cease to be the 'great moral lesson' and therefore would lack any reason for continuance. Moreover, they were convinced that public suspicion would never allow private executions.[63] *The Times* was not entirely correct in stating that 'Bright and his friends did not object to private executions but were opposed to executions of any kind whatsoever'.[64] The abolitionists were opposed to private executions because they were apprehensive that private executions would abort the abolition of capital punishment, their ultimate concern.

As expected, *The Times* rejected the majority clause of the Royal Commission in respect to private executions. The newspaper retained its faith in the efficacy of public executions; it thought that men not frightened by the prospect of death would be frightened by the prospect of dying in public on the gallows.[65]

As expected, also, the abolitionists denounced the majority recommendation favouring private executions. The general opinion of the abolitionist critics of the Report was that the evidence given to the Royal Commission had been an irresistible weight of authority in favour of abolition of capital punishment and not private executions.[66]

Of the critical writings against the recommendations of the Royal Commission, Humphrey Woolrych was the most analytical and detailed. Woolrych, a serjeant-at-law, biographer and writer on criminal law, surveyed minutely the testimony and index of the Report, and came to the conclusion that the preponderance of opinion favoured abolition of the death penalty. Woolrych was vexed that the influence of America and Australia should be so decisive.

Really . . . when nearly the whole of the continent of Europe follow the natural instinct of holding up to all within reach the terrible example which awaits a deadly crime, it seems strange that we should adopt the views of the American people or the more youthful colony of Australia – views which may suit the genius of these nations very well, but may not by any means be in accordance with those entertained in this old Kingdom.[67]

He did not understand the subtle and peculiar influence of Australian and American execution reforms.

Xenophobic, insular Englishmen were more likely to accept practices from nations which had originated from England than from the alien Europeans. The peculiar and ambivalent relationships of England towards the American states and her Australian colonies were of the kind that age and experience feel over youth. There was both a paternalistic superiority and a vague sense of being threatened by youth and vigour. The Commissioners had seen the need to reform public executions, a need long overdue, they had sought assurances that private executions were feasible, and they were impressed and discomfited to learn that America and Australia had evolved successful execution practices which removed the ugly public blemishes which still persisted so prominently and notoriously in Victorian England.

The *Temple Bar*, less polemical and propagandistic than the abolitionist critics of the Report of the Capital Punishment

Commission, felt that the balance of evidence was decidedly in favour of abolition of public executions. Perceptively pinpointing the dilemma of the abolitionists, the author of a *Temple Bar* article observed that the evidence given by Thomas Beggs to the Commissioners, though in support of the abolition of capital punishment, 'bears more powerfully upon the proposed step of making executions private instead of public'.[68] The same observation could have been made for all the abolitionists who gave evidence before the Royal Commission.

Mr Justice O'Hagan declared that the weight of evidence and reason was in favour of the abolition of capital punishment, but that public opinion was not yet ripe for such a change. This statement brought into focus the fact that the majority of the English people accepted the indispensibility of capital punishment. It has taken almost one hundred years to abolish capital punishment since Justice O'Hagan doubted the public acceptance of it, and its public acceptability remains today very much in doubt.* Reason and evidence – and perhaps this was what was underlying Justice O'Hagan's observation about public opinion – have nothing to do with the public acceptance of a humane reform like the abolition of capital punishment when the raw nerve of fear is touched. Enlightened and informed reformers became in the public eye well-meaning theorists, or even worse, crackpots urging virtual license for desperate, maniacal killers.

* The experimental abolition of capital punishment, introduced for a five-year period in England in 1965, is still so controversial that 'Tories who see the return of the Hangman as a useful electoral issue have fed and watered the latest grisly growth in punitive emotion'. 'Hanging or Rotting Alive', *New Statesman*, Vol. LXXVII, 14 March 1969, p.345.

7

THE END OF PUBLIC HANGINGS

AGAINST the background of the Royal Commission for Capital Punishment meeting and considering evidence – much of it critical both of public executions and of the death penalty – fears induced by disorders continued and even intensified. Robberies with violence in London became such an endemic problem that Parliament enacted the Garrotters Act in 1863. Judges were given the power by the Act of giving as many as fifty lashes of the whip to persons convicted of either committing or attempting violence in the act of robbery.* A judge in 1866 had twelve young men flogged in addition to the prison sentences he meted out to them.

Added to sporadic crime-waves and the inevitable reactions by the authorities in the form of repressive punishments were the Fenian disturbances in Ireland and England, which outraged public opinion and raised apprehensions. The large numbers of Irish who swarmed into the major urban centres, where problems multiplied in proportion to the swelling populations, became subjects of deepening concern. The Fenian insurrectionary violence culminated in the murder of a Manchester constable. Three Fenians, Allen, Larkin and Gould, were convicted of the crime.[1]

They were the first Fenians hanged in Great Britain, and their executions 'excited more public interest than any execution within the memory of living man'.[2] Massive precautions were taken by the authorities against violent protest and a possible rescue-attempt. On the day of execution, 23 Novem-

---

* Gordon Rose, *The Struggle for Penal Reform: The Howard League and its Predecessors*, London: Stevens & Sons, 1961, p.207. Garrotting was an attack on a robbery victim by which the attacker left the victim half or wholly strangled by means of a rope or scarf drawn around the neck from the back.

ber 1867, the government and the Manchester municipal
authorities took extraordinary precautions. They posted an
artillery detachment, troops of the 72nd Highlanders and
2,500 special constables in strategic positions, all poised to
crush any attempt to save the doomed men. Despite the expected violence, the mob of 12,000 was 'more quiet and
orderly than usual'.[3]

Fenian-induced alarm reached a climax in January 1868.
During that month, in the expectation of raging disturbances,
London and the provinces braced themselves. Five thousand
men filled the London Guildhall to be sworn in as special
constables; in St Martin's Parish, several hundred were made
auxiliary constables; 1,272 residents of the Covent Garden
district received warrants, staves and instructions in how to
deal with Fenian marauders. The middle class was not alone
in its fear and hatred of the Irish. Scores of workmen volun-
teered as special constables in Southwark, and a large number
of workmen ringed the Chatham dockyard to forestall Fenian
sabotage there. The swearing-in of auxiliary constables spread
throughout all parts of England.[4]

The ever-widening anxiety from real and imagined Fenian
disorders and the periodic outbursts of crime did not restrain
efforts to abolish public executions. In fact attempts at abolition proceeded at a quicker rate and at more frequent inter-
vals. The persistent John Hibbert introduced on 25 February
1865 the Capital Punishments Within Gaols Bill, the first such
Bill ever to receive a first reading.[5] Because Parliament had
not yet received the Report of the Royal Capital Punishment
Commission, Hibbert withdrew his Bill with regrets. At the
same time, he admonished the House that if he were to retain
his seat in the next Parliament, he would reintroduce the Bill.[6]

With release of the Report of the Royal Capital Punishment Commission on 8 January 1866 John Hibbert, as he had
promised, reintroduced another Capital Punishments Within
Gaols Bill on 6 March 1866. He felt obliged to bring in a Bill
because there was no observable disposition by the government to do so. Hibbert recognized the obstacles which still lay
ahead, and sombrely pleaded for support. He appeared to be
directly appealing to the abolitionists, the major obstructionists

to private executions. While genuflecting to past abolitionist heroes, he also commended William Ewart for continuing
the reform of the penal code begun under Romilly and
Mackintosh.

Hibbert etched in the dismal, often retrogressive, history of
cruel, vengeful punishments of the past.

In the year 1754 the country was not satisfied hanging a man outside the gaol, but required him to be publicly carted from Newgate
to Tyburn. There he was hung in chains, and after the body was
cut down, and was dissected. A few years later Parliament required
that the execution should follow sentence within forty-eight hours.
A few years later, again, the culprit was allowed nothing but
bread and water.[7]

The reformer now had cause for optimism; he discerned a
change in attitudes and a marked diminution in cruelty and
sadism. He claimed the support of the press in London and
throughout the provinces; even *The Times*, he said, had seen
reason to change its views. Hibbert was happy to report that
there was a growing disinclination to continue brutalizing
punishment throughout the world. Public executions were no
longer conducted in Prussia, Bavaria, Saxony, Hanover,
Brunswick, the states of New York, Pennsylvania, Massachu-
setts, Maine or the Australian colonies.

Hibbert was meticulous with constant and repetitious assurances to the House that executions within the prison walls
would not signal the return of covert, secret strangulation. The
presence of sheriffs, gaolers, magistrates, the press, a coroner's inquest and a jury's certification of death were guarantees to the public of the certainty of execution and the absence
of privately inflicted torture. He was convinced that the solemnity and formality of private executions would inspire more
fear, and as a consequence they would be more deterring than
public executions.

Sir George Grey replied that he had no opposition to
Hibbert's bill. He stated that when he announced the intention of the government to advise

Her Majesty to issue a Royal Commission to consider the question
of capital punishments, I assented to the proposal to offer for the

consideration of the Commission whether these punishments should be conducted in private or as present.[8]

Praising the Royal Commission Report as very valuable, Grey singled out the information obtained by the government about executions in the Australian colonies as having produced a great impression on him. He urged Hibbert, however, not to press for a second reading of his Bill because Horatio Waddington, the Assistant Secretary of the Home Department, and one of the Royal Commissioners on the Capital Punishment Commission, was framing a Bill to contain the recommendations of the Royal Commission which would include, also, Hibbert's proposals.[9]

The abolitionists were determined to oppose every effort to end public executions. Charles Gilpin, the leading abolitionist spokesman after Ewart and Bright, was convinced that enlightened opinion asked for, and would obtain, by an almost inexorable determination, complete abolition, and not settle for what he contemptuously termed 'concealment'. Ewart was equally condemning; he accused those advocating private executions of a complicit willingness to prolong capital punishment even after its public example, its only justification, had been totally discredited by withdrawing it from public view.[10] Complying with Grey's request, Hibbert once again withdrew his Bill.

A Bill which embodied the recommendations of the Royal Commission on Capital Punishment was introduced in the House of Lords as the Law of Capital Punishment Amendment Bill on 23 March 1866.[11] There it received the authoritative endorsement of Lord Cranworth, the Lord Chancellor in Earl Russell's second cabinet. Broader than the previous bills introduced by John Hibbert, which had dealt solely with executions within prison walls, this proposed law followed the recommendations of the Royal Commission and contained a conglomerate mixture of parts. These amended the laws of murder, gave greater protection to new-born babies and provided for other reforms in addition to providing for executions within prisons. Such a cumbersome Bill, which covered too many facets of criminal law and punishments, was bound to please very few. Its two separate parts, the one dealing with definitions of murder and the other with private executions, would have to be separated, so that the adherents of each might be able to select one part rather than accept both or reject the entire bill.

At the second reading of the Law of Capital Punishment Amendment Bill, on 1 May 1866, there was a spirited, prolonged debate. Lord Cranworth confessed that when he was first asked to consider changing the mode of executions he had had great doubts about it; he now gave it his entire support. He believed the superfluity of enormous crowds at disgusting scenes of executions far outweighed the merits of the occasional criminal who might be deterred by seeing a hanging. Tweaking the sensibilities of his fellow lords, he reminded them that the American states and many European countries had surpassed them in carrying out more reasonable forms of executions. Cranworth thought the theoretical objections against private executions the height of absurdity; as to their ushering in torture and bribery of authorities by the rich, 'that notion might have prevailed 300 or 400 years ago', he said.*

The conviction persisted that the sight of a public execution left an indelible image of horror which all the cumulative evidence to the contrary could neither undermine nor even bring into question. The Earl of Malmesbury dogmatically laid down as fundamental fact that only fear of public disgrace worked on the human mind, haunting it with a lasting sense of dread:

There is a great difference between a public execution and a private one . . . I remember that sixty years ago, in the part of the country where I lived, two men were hung for the murder of their father. That execution made the greatest impression upon the people of the neighbourhood, and the tradition of it has passed down to this day.[12]

Lord Malmesbury inverted the usual argument of the retentionists who claimed that the continuation of public execution spectacles would result in complete abolition. Instead he pre-

* *Hansard*, Vol. CLXXXIII, col.235. The *Spectator* did not think the objection theoretical and absurd; it warned the peers 'not to be led away by the anomolies of the present system to substitute torture for death'. Vol. XXXIX, 5 May 1866, p.483.

dicted the abolition of death penalties would follow the introduction of private executions. This argument also contradicted
the abolitionists' pervasive fear that private executions would
perpetuate capital punishment. Urging rejection of the clause
in the Bill which would permit executing behind prison walls,
he pleaded, 'We must not give way to the natural sentiments
which civilization prompts.'[13]

Lord de Ros believed with the Earl of Malmesbury that
public executions held a peculiar fascination and fear in the
minds of viewers. He had heard that during the Peninsular
War there was an extraordinary contrast between the effects
of public and private executions. Public executions, he insisted, resulted in better discipline in the British Army, while
frequent private executions in the French armies did not discourage the rampant desertions there. Although the Duke of
Wellington executed only thirteen of his soldiers, he made a
greater display of them than did the French who had executed
250. The English mustered all the troops, marched the culprit
before them, and when he was dead paraded the troops past
his body. French executions were done in comparative privacy.
'Fewer executions were necessary in the British Army,' commented Lord de Ros didactically.[14]

The Earl of Shaftesbury, who had been a member of the
House of Lords Select Committee on Capital Punishment a
decade before, thought, on the whole, that executions within
prisons would be an excellent substitute for the current practices. He held to his position of ten years ago, as though
the evidence on American and Australian execution practices
had not been disseminated by government and press, and
pressed earnestly for the admission at executions of two or
three from the lower classes 'so that no relic of suspicion
should exist among the people as to the reality of every
execution'.[15]

So many amendments were tacked to the Law of Capital
Punishment Amendment Bill that there was considerable difficulty in framing the numerous additions into an enlarged
measure. Thus action on it was delayed until 15 June 1866,
when it was debated on its recommitment to Committee in the
House of Lords. At that time Lord St Leonard, a staunch

proponent of public executions, sought to strike out Clause 13, which would authorize hangings within prisons. In a rambling speech he raised almost all of the objections which had ever been levelled against private executions. If the military executed a man before his own regiment as an exemplary punishment, civilians ought likewise to be hanged in public as an example for others.

'To be hanged like a dog' had a deterrent effect, for the boldest man shuddered at it; and if they resorted to private executions, in his opinion they would deprive capital punishments of their deterrent quality ... All proceedings involving life and liberty should be conducted in public, and it was only in accordance with it that the punishments should also be carried out in public ... It was only by public executions that the great mass of the people could be induced to believe that the law had taken effect in such cases should a man of influence be unfortunately condemned.*

He moved to omit from the Bill Clause 13.

In reply, the Lord Chancellor rhetorically asked why flogging was not conducted in public as was hanging. Was it not, he mused, that flogging was considered revolting to popular feeling whereas hanging a man in public was considered not objectionable but beneficial?[16]

Another peer who wished to have private executions was Lord Dunsany, not because of the inconsistent, paradoxical application of punishments ridiculed by the Lord Chancellor, but because of the hideous nature of these punishments. The public needed to be shielded from them. He described the excruciating anguish suffered by men on the gallows; often a merciful death did not come to a man until he had hung for fifteen, even twenty minutes. He attributed much of the suffering to the gross ineptness of the executioners; he could recall only one skilful executioner in all of England. As a result, criminals died from suffocation, from dislocation of the neck, and even sometimes from apoplexy caused by the unnatural flow of blood to the brain. Lord Dunsany's solution was to

* *Hansard*, Vol. CLXXXIV (1866), cols.451–2. *The Times* rebuked Lord St Leonard, writing that he 'hardly did justice to his own case, dwelling almost exclusively on the impression to be made on by-standers'. 15 June 1866, p.6.

have private executions; then 'they would be more solemn and decorous'.*

The Earl of Malmesbury questioned the suitability of the House of Lords as a body to discuss and pass judgement as to the effect of public executions upon the lower classes. The Lords, he thought, were the worst judges to consider how the lower classes would react. Their lordships were, after all, highly educated men: they possessed refined feelings and minds; they naturally were shocked at the sight of public executions; such scenes would naturally revolt them. How, then, could they be able to determine the effect produced by public executions upon the minds of uneducated persons? As explanation of his question, he recounted how his servant attended an execution and 'the effect on him was so great that he was unfitted for work for three or four days'.[17] As for opposition to public executions on the grounds that they demoralized people who reacted obscenely to them, Lord Malmesbury refuted that contention.

An objection was raised that the people indulged in obscene language at these executions, but the same thing occurred at great public spectacles such as the funeral of the late Lord Palmerston, and at Her Majesty's Coronation. Those people were obscene not because of what was taking place, but because it was their habit to be obscene.[18]

The Bishop of Oxford disagreed with Malmesbury's opinion that the Lords were unable to understand the minds and needs of the lower classes. On the contrary, he asserted, people of breeding and education were eminently qualified by

* *Hansard*, Vol. CLXXXIV (1866), col.453. A twentieth-century crusader for abolition of capital punishment in England commented that until public executions were abolished in England there was no pretence that death was instantaneous. However, he claimed that after executions were conducted in private, the authorities attempted to withhold the nature of the reality of hanging from the public. He asserted that a secret Home Office memorandum, dated 10 January 1925, was circulated to all prison governors; it read: 'Any reference to the manner in which an execution has been carried out should be confined to as few words as possible, e.g., "it was carried out expeditiously and without a hitch".' Roy E. Calvert, *Executions*, London: National Council for the Abolition of the Death Penalty, 1926, p.4.

careful application to study these matters, to develop insights about these things and to judge the influence public executions had on the mass of people. As for the Earl's assertion that private executions must of necessity lead to the abolition of capital punishment, he could not allow that to go unchallenged. Those who supported executions within prison walls were right in the view that the tendency would be in the opposite direction, because public executions hardened people to death on the gallows and hence the deterring influence was diminished. Unless this erosion of the effectiveness of executions was not soon put an end to, capital punishments would soon become obsolete, he warned.[19]

With the approval of Clause 13 of the Law of Capital Punishment Amendment Bill, the Lords proceeded to debate other clauses and amendments. The Duke of Marlborough, who had voted against Clause 13, sought to amend Clause 14, which provided for the compulsory attendance of all designated officials at executions. Marlborough's amendment would empower the visiting justices to admit as many spectators at executions as the prison could safely accommodate. In effect, much of the purpose of execution inside prisons would have been negated by this amendment. Lord Teynham's amendment also sought to enlarge the numbers permitted at executions; it would make the presence of the press mandatory.[20] The Lord Chancellor intervened requesting that the discretion of admitting persons to executions should remain with the sheriffs and visiting justices.[21] The proposed amendments were rejected. In addition to the approval of Clause 14 by the House of Lords, Clause 15, providing for a surgeon's certification of death following each execution as well as a declaration to that effect signed by a sheriff, was also approved.

Clause 16 of the Law of Capital Punishment Amendment Bill directed the setting up of a coroner's inquest to ascertain and establish all the circumstances of death by execution. Earl Nelson believed a much more salutary effect could be achieved if the coroner's jury were summoned from the district where the crime had been committed because the jury would report back to their respective neighbourhoods the eyewitness account that the crime had been punished by death.[22] But he

withdrew his amendment after the Lord Chancellor had expressed his opinion that it would add needless difficulty.[23]
After its third reading, the Law of Capital Punishment
Amendment Bill was sent to the House of Commons on
13 July 1866.

On 20 July William Ewart asked the Home Secretary,
Spencer Walpole, what course the government intended to
pursue with regard to this Bill. Walpole replied the government had decided not to continue with the Bill for the remainder of the session of Parliament; he was of the opinion
that the Bill varied considerably from the recommendations
of the Royal Commission on Capital Punishment and had become encumbered with too many diverse matters.[24] It was
withdrawn on 30 July.

On 14 February of the following year the government introduced two Bills derived from the defunct Law of Capital
Punishment Amendment Bill. These were the Murder Law
Amendment Bill and the Capital Punishment Within Prisons
Bill. In presenting the latter, Walpole pointed out that it
followed the recommendations of the Royal Commission on
Capital Punishment in regard to execution inside the precincts
of prisons. The main question, he thought, was the propriety
with which executions would be carried out. In this respect he
thought the Bill provided adequate securities. Provisions were
made for the presence at each execution of all prison officials;
visiting justices would have the authority to admit friends
and relatives of the convicted criminal; there would be the
certification of death by the prison surgeon and a coroner's
inquest would be convened. 'With all these securities,' Walpole stated confidently, 'it seems to me that the community
may feel confident as to the way in which the execution is
carried into effect.'[25]

The radicals kept up their opposition to private executions,
and their two leading spokesmen, William Ewart and Charles
Gilpin, spoke contemptuously of carrying out the death
penalty in private. Ewart predicted that there would be
greater excitement and interest in private executions than previously, and that the condemned criminal would become a
greater hero to the public than heretofore.[26] Gilpin claimed

that there was popular discontent and disgust with the legislature; the public was bitterly disappointed with the House for discussing the propriety of putting men and women to death, regardless of whether it was private or public.[27]

Two prominent voices were raised in support of the Bill: Sir George Grey, the still influential former Whig Home Secretary who had recently been converted to the acceptance of private executions, and the liberal John Hibbert, its persistent champion. Grey attributed his conversion to the reported success of private executions in the Australian colonies. 'That argument,' he said, referring to the Australian experience, 'weighed with me in favour of private executions.'[28] Hibbert was willing to guarantee to all doubters the greater efficacy of private executions as a deterrent.[29] Despite the apparent support of the government, however, the Capital Punishment Within Prisons Bill was withdrawn.

Gathorne Hardy became the Home Secretary in May 1867, when Walpole resigned,* and it was he who introduced the Capital Punishment Within Prisons Bill again in the new session of Parliament, on 26 November 1867; its companion legislation, the Murder Law Amendment Bill, was abandoned. The new Home Secretary admitted defeat of any legislation relating to laws concerning murder because of the entangled maze of definitions relating to degrees of murder. As a consequence, private executions were going to be considered

* Gathorne Hardy had gone with a group of Members of Parliament to the Home Office on 13 March 1864 to make one last plea for the life of a convicted murderer. As he was leaving the Home Office Sir George Grey, then the Home Secretary, said prophetically to him, 'You will soon be here in my place, and gladly shall I give it up!' The rest of Hardy's comments on that occasion reveal that even before he had become a member of the Royal Commission for Capital Punishment he had already decided against abolition of the death penalty and further definitions of degrees of murder. Hardy wrote: 'He [Grey] had been much wrought upon, and his nerves were unstrung . . . In some hands that prerogative must remain, or humanity will be outraged by the letter of the law . . . Definitions of murder will not do. Extenuating circumstances are the refuge of faint-hearted jurors or men set against capital punishment.' A. E. S. Gathorne-Hardy, ed., *Gathorne Hardy, First Earl of Cranbrook: A Memoir*, Vol. I, Longman & Co., 1910, pp.162–3.

separately from any other measure relating to reform of the criminal law. Capital-punishment law reform was a dead issue.

In the short debate following the first reading of the Capital Punishment Within Prisons Bill, a reactionary and a radical both gave notice that they would make an effort to impede the progress of it. Mr Bazeley, the reactionary, contemptuously excoriated the 'philanthropists' who were inured to any experience, totally unrealistic and irreversibly doctrinaire; he hoped that after Manchester – referring to the murder there of Constable Brett by the three Fenians – some change would take place in their minds.[30] He declared that when the Capital Punishment Within Prisons Bill was brought forward for its second reading he would move that it should be read that day six months later. The radical Serjeant Gaselee gave notice that he also would move to postpone the second reading for a six-month period.[31]

A crucial and prolonged debate on the second reading of the Bill began on 5 March 1868, when it was taken up again. Gathorne Hardy, who had been a very active member of the Royal Commission, and whose proclivities on behalf of private executions were most evident, reminded the House, particularly with the opposition in mind, that the Capital Punishment Within Prisons Bill was similar to the one introduced by the late government and by Sir George Grey, 'who as a witness before the Commission supported its principle'.[32]

Hardy dashed any hope for immediate capital-punishment law reform; he stated bluntly that capital punishment was the law, and there was no object to be gained by its repeal. Assuming the continuation of capital punishments, he said his aim was to show that executions could be carried out with greater effect when they were conducted privately. Experience bore this out, and as confirmation he cited the overwhelmingly favourable evidence given by American and Australian authorities. The government had already been moving in certain parts of the country to add an element of privacy to public executions; screens had been erected on scaffolds so that as the drop fell the criminal disappeared. 'Everything of interest to the crowd,' he said, 'is out of sight.'[33]

Then Hardy turned the thrust of his arguments against the hesitant, the reactionaries and the traditionalists, who still had reservations about private executions. His intent was to assure them beyond any reasonable doubt that private executions were effective deterrents not designed to pamper the criminal classes, but to suppress their murderous instincts by a more fearful, awe-inspiring, silent death. He continued by indicating that public executions had become a species of amusement; they had no longer a desirable effect on the criminal classes; the executions had become vulgar and objectionable.

The Home Secretary all but promised that the new mode of executions would remedy these defects, and restore that needed quality of deterrence again to the death penalty.

How impressive and how deterrent would be the scene when the criminal was removed from the Court on sentence of death being pronounced ... and the people feel that although he has been removed from their sight, he will be subjected to a punishment which will be extremely painful, and the mystery and indefiniteness attending the punishment serves only to increase its terrors in their eyes.[34]

Serjeant Gaselee, in opposition, warned the House against private executions because of their inherent dangers. A private hanging of the Fenians in Manchester, he thought, would have been accepted with absolute scepticism. The Dublin friends of the executed men would have added more injustices to their present disaffections; they would have clamoured against government-inflicted torture of their countrymen.

Gaselee was opposed to the death penalty, but he was also against private executions. He cautioned the government on establishing the example of 'private assassination' in an 'age of assassination'.[35] He contended that the disgusting scenes like those at Müller's execution were unknown except in London. And he foresaw Calcraft's clumsy roughness as an executioner becoming more pronounced when executions would be hidden from public gaze behind prison walls.

The opinion was prevalent in some quarters that if a rich man were condemned to death, he would be able to procure a substitute as in

China. [*laughter*] He viewed this as a poor man's question, for the poor man had a right to be hung in public. If innocent he had a right to appear before the people and declare his innocence, or if guilty to acknowledge his crime, and warn others by his example.[36]

For these reasons he offered an amendment to the proposal 'that the Bill should now be read a second time'; he proposed to leave out the word 'now', and at the end of the question to add the words 'upon this day six months'. The question was put 'that the word "now" should stand part of the question'.[37]

Sir George Bowyer seconded the motion. He had attended two executions and mingled with the crowds during the night in order to observe everything. Because he was not ensconced in a window seat, remote from the common people, his experiences and impressions were very vivid, and what he saw confirmed his preconceptions. He could vouch for the accuracy of the hideous accounts of executions appearing in newspapers. Unless anyone was willing to see executions under the conditions he experienced, no real impression could be formed about how the spectators reacted 'when they saw the dreadful spectacle of a man in full vigour about to be put to death'.[38] He said that it was rumoured that any man possessing £1000 might escape hanging, even after sentence had been pronounced. He claimed having once seen instructions for counsel to draw a bill in Chancery on the assumption that Fauntleroy was alive; and he repeated the persistent story that the Quaker Tawell had escaped death on the gallows and that a stuffed figure had been strung up in his stead.[39] Then the House divided; Gaselee's amendment was defeated by 181 votes to twenty-five.*

---

* *Divisions: Session 1867–1868*, pp.11–12. Benjamin Disraeli, the Prime Minister, and William E. Gladstone, leader of the opposition, voted for the immediate second reading of the Bill; both opposed further changes in capital-punishment laws, but were willing to abolish public executions. Unexpectedly, George Denman, whom Alfred Dymond called a loyal supporter of abolition, and John Bright, also voted for the immediate reading of the Bill. Other abolitionists like Charles Gilpin and Charles Neate voted with reactionaries like Charles Newdegate for a postponement of the Bill. The small vote for postponement and the defection of votes by Denman and Bright and others indicated some in-

The debate resumed at once and continued into the evening. In an attempt to minimize the overwhelming defeat of Gaselee's motion, Charles Gilpin boasted that he could have taken more Members into the lobby with him in support of the motion had he felt the motion and vote were that crucial. He reminded the Members that only a short fifteen years before almost one hundred Members of the House of Commons had voted for immediate abolition. He anticipated the end of capital punishment as a result of private executions because 'three quarters of the arguments in favour of capital punishment would fall to the ground'.[40] Gilpin had it on the good authority of Richard Cobden who had once written that 'if hanging be acknowledged to be so unclean a thing that it is no longer to be tolerated in the broad sunlight, the English people will have none of it'.[41]

One who saw the Capital Punishment Within Prisons Bill as another step in the vicious course of legislation which eroded the certainty and force of law was Charles Newdegate, a critic both of the abolitionists and those advocating private executions. He presented a petition from 3,000 residents of Birmingham protesting the remissions granted to criminals by the Home Secretary after sentence had been pronounced in court. Newdegate thought the mollifying of criminals made the people feel uncertain about punishment as an expression of the law; people, instead, believed punishment had become vengeance imposed maliciously on victims by government. Newdegate believed there was an inherent danger in private executions, which were open to all kinds of interpretations and rumours. The scandal of the Duc de Praslin's suicide in his cell while awaiting the guillotine – it was widely believed the government had concurred in permitting it – was one of the main factors causing the downfall of Louis Philippe. There was grave suspicion about the quality of justice in France as a result of the nobleman's death, and the implicit danger to English institutions was quite obvious to Newdegate.[42]

Influential support for private executions came from Scotland. Mr M'Laren produced a copy of the 1854 petition in

---

decision among the ranks of the abolitionists. Their solid front of unity was cracking.

support of the principle of private executions which the Town Council of Edinburgh had passed unanimously. He also reminded the House that similar petitions were adopted in 1865 and 1866 by the Edinburgh Town Council. Although M'Laren preferred the total abolition of capital punishments, he was prepared to support the Capital Punishment Within Prisons Bill because it improved the present method of execution.[43] He hoped the provisions of the bill would include Scotland, and he received the assurance of the Lord Advocate that steps would be taken to comply with his wish.

The abolitionists were still hopeful for their reform and very active in opposing the drift towards private executions.* On the motion of 21 April 1868, for going into Committee on the Capital Punishment Within Prisons Bill, Charles Gilpin moved instead to amend the Bill to read 'that in the opinion of this House, it is expedient, instead of carrying out the punishment of death within prisons, that Capital Punishment be abolished'.[44] As long as the death penalty was irrevocable, and judges and juries were fallible, there must be a risk that the wrong life was sacrificed. Gilpin was positive that the abolition of capital punishment would result in greater sanctity for human life and would sharply reduce the number of murders.

Mr Gregory asked the House to reject Gilpin's resolution. He recalled that eight very eminent members of the Royal Commission for Capital Punishment had favoured the continuation of capital punishment against a minority of four who had voted to abolish it. 'Of that four,' he said, 'they had already made their minds up, having been members of the Society for the Abolition of Capital Punishment.'[45] Gregory

* Abolitionist expectation, which had been ebbing, may have been raised by the news that the Saxon Second Chamber had opposed the abolition of capital punishment by a majority of two thirds. Joseph Irving, *The Annals of Our Time, 1837–1868*, Macmillan & Co., 1869, p.673. Besides, abolition of the death penalty still remained a creed of radicalism. J. Passmore Edwards promised in his election address in 1868 the abolition of the purchase system in the army, games laws and religious tests for entrance into universities, and added, 'I would abolish the death penalty.' Simon Maccoby, ed., *The English Radical Tradition, 1763–1914*, London: Nichols Kaye Ltd., 1952, pp.177–8.

wished to retain public executions; they taught incipient criminals a long and hard lesson; it was inconceivable, he thought,
that a man could depart from that evil gathering around the
gallows without a barrier coming between indulgence and his
brutal instincts. But he thought the time had arrived when
public executions ought to be abolished, because they were no
longer in accordance with the spirit of the age.[46]

An irate Charles Neate accused the government of under-
mining the work of the Royal Commission by abandoning the
important parts of its recommendations, particularly its object of providing a better definition of murder, with which the
late government had grappled. He grumbled – amid rising cries
of 'Divide!' – that the present Capital Punishment Within
Prisons Bill only dealt with the smaller issue investigated by
the Royal Commission.[47]

With cries of 'Divide!' still resounding, John Stuart Mill
rose in order ruefully to announce that he would be unable
to support the abolition of capital punishment. He said that
it was always a matter of regret

when on any subject he found himself in opposition to those who
are called – sometimes in the way of honour, and sometimes in
what is intended for ridicule – philanthropists.[48]

Because of their exertions, he continued, revolting punishments had vanished and death was inflicted only for murder.
Mill felt, however, that the deprivation of a demonstrably unworthy life was more impressive and appropriate, and less
cruel, than the suggested life imprisonment. And he was glad
that the mania for paring down punishment had come none
too soon.* In his opinion there was a need to strengthen
punishments, and he suggested flogging as being particularly
fitted for cases of brutality.

The House then divided, and Gilpin's amendment to abolish capital punishment was defeated by the one-sided vote of
127 to twenty-three.† Expressing surprise and pleasure at the

---

* *Hansard*, Vol. cxci (1868), col.1,045. Mill once contributed to that
mania as an abolitionist in the 1840s. Philip Collins, *Dickens and Crime*,
Macmillan & Co., 1962, p.248.

† In addition to John Stuart Mill, Disraeli and Gladstone both voted

China statues of the Mannings. The case of Maria and Frederick Manning attracted considerable attention. Almost 2,500,000 broadsheets of their execution were sold.

THE ILLUSTRATED
POLICE NEWS,
LAW COURTS AND WEEKLY RECORD.

THE EXECUTION OF BARRETT.

FATAL STRUGGLE WITH AN EXCISEMAN

MURDER & ATTEMPTED SUICIDE AT SALFORD

'The Execution of Barrett' from *The Illustrated Police News*, 30 May 1868. Michael Barrett was hanged outside Newgate on 27 May 1868, the last public execution in Britain.

amendment's decisive defeat and concluding that all of
Gilpin's supporters must have been in the House for the
vote, *The Times* pointed out that former abolitionists now
gave tacit acquiescence to the need for retaining the death
penalty.*

The Bill was then considered in Committee, where its
clauses were debated. George Denman, who was one of the
foremost of the abolitionists voting against Gaselee's motion
to postpone the Bill, believed private executions would
guarantee the coming of abolition. Reflecting the ambivalence
of many supporters of abolition, Denman reasoned that if
death penalties were to be retained for the immediate future,
it would be far better if executions were carried out within the
prisons and 'thus avoid the horrible and disgusting scenes'.[49]
Private executions would condition public opinion to the
realization that there was neither inherent need nor safety in
putting a person out of the world before throngs of people;
they would eventually accept the confining of a criminal in
prison where he could do no harm. 'It will not be long,' he
confidently predicted, 'before public opinion will declare that
a secret act of assassination within the gaol is not necessary
nor expedient.'[50]

Radicals moved a number of disabling clauses to destroy
the Bill; they were all unsuccessful. Charles Neate attempted
to amend Clause 4 to broaden the list of official spectators required to attend executions. If the House agreed to deprive
executions of their public character, he suggested, they should
be solemnly performed. Towards this end, he recommended that
the High Sheriff, not just the sheriff, the foreman of the jury

---

against abolition. Advanced liberals like Bright, Denman, Samuel
Gurney, George Hadfield and Charles Neate voted for abolition. *Divisions: Session 1867–1868*, p.51. Mill, writing about his speech against
the abolition of capital punishment, said he was opposed to what he
regarded as the position of advanced liberal opinion. Mill, *Autobiography*,
New American Library, 1964, p.200.

* *The Times* attributed to Mill a large measure of responsibility for
the defeat of the amendment with his 'remarkable speech'. It also
believed the House reflected the opposition in the country to changing
the law, particularly after two recent murders – the Todmorden murder,
and the McGee murder in Canada. 22 April 1868, p.6.

and at least three Grand Jurors must be present at each execution. The derisive shouts with which Neate's suggestions
were greeted made it known that his opponents were aware of
the intent to destroy the purpose of the Bill. Facetiously, he
proposed New Palace Yard as a suitable place for executions
and four o'clock in the afternoon as a most appropriate
time.[51]

Continuing in this sardonic manner, Neate offered additional suggestions for improvements of executions. Science, he
thought, could be exploited to devise better methods of executions. It was well known, he said, that the dislocation of the
neck did not produce instantaneous death; he offered the
garrotte as a more 'merciful' substitute punishment.* Or life
might be taken by administering carbonic acid. Even suicide,
he thought, might provide a more amenable alternative to the
gallows. Then Neate made a motion for an additional clause
in the Bill: 'Her Majesty or her successor may, by the advice
of the Privy Council, prescribe any other mode of execution in
lieu of hanging.'[52]

This clause, as well as his other motion to make mandatory
the presence of the High Sheriff and others, was defeated.
Other motions made by opponents of private executions were
made and met a similar fate. Lowther moved to permit relatives of the condemned prisoner into the prison to view his
execution. Alderman Lusk's amendment would have permitted
as many of the public into the prison as space would allow.
Alderman Lawrence's motion to insert the phrase 'so many
reporters of the public press' was defeated by forty-six votes
to twenty-four.† All of the other clauses were approved, in-

* Neate knew well how tortured was death by the garrotte. An
account of a public execution in Spain described how the iron collar
enclosed the neck causing strangulation by turns of a powerful screw until
'the face of the dead man was slightly convulsed, the mouth open, the
eyeballs turned into their sockets from the wrench'. *Parliamentary
Papers*, Report from the Select Committee of the House of Lords,
Vol. VII, 1856, appendix, p.47.

† Alderman Lusk's amendment received the support of those radicals
who had consistently supported abolition of capital punishment; Bright,
Denman, Hadfield, Neate and Lawrence voted for it; Disraeli voted
against it.

cluding Clause 5 which provided for a surgeon's certification of death and a declaration to that effect signed by the sheriff, and Clause 6 which established a coroner's inquest to be held after each execution.[53]

In the spring of 1868 a Fenian, in reprisal for the hanging of three Fenians in Manchester on 23 November the previous year, shot the Duke of Edinburgh while he was at a public picnic during an Australian tour.[54] Despite this attempt to kill Queen Victoria's second son, the House was undeterred in its resolution to accept the Capital Punishment Within Prisons Bill; by now public executions were deemed so non-deterrent that even the attempted assassination of royalty could not resurrect the old faith in its deterrent quality. That the House was shocked by the assassination-attempt was expressed in the address to the Queen conveying its 'indignation . . . of the atrocious attempt to assassinate His Royal Highness the Duke of Edinburgh'.[55] The resolution for the address to the Queen was voted on Monday 27 April 1868; the Capital Punishment Within Prisons Bill received its third reading on Tuesday 28 April 1868.

Two days later the Bill was introduced in the House of Lords by the Duke of Richmond. Before it came up for its second reading there, *The Times* finally capitulated. It accepted the inevitability and the desirability of private executions. Expressing the wish that the Capital Punishment Within Prisons Bill would receive the fullest consideration in the House of Lords, it declared:

If we could put an end to the disgusting scenes now incident to the infliction of capital punishment without making it exemplary, it would be most desirable.[56]

While the Capital Punishment Within Prisons Bill moved through both Houses, the *Morning Herald* was reflecting public apprehension over the rash of recent murders. It deplored the tidings of bloodshed which came from all quarters – from Bristol, Dover, Durham, Sydenham, Todmorden and London – as a 'mania for murder which seems to be insatiable'.[57] A wave of murder, the newspaper warned, would soon engulf the world. It reminded its readers of the assassination of D'Arcy

McGee in Canada,* and the attempt on the life of the Duke of Edinburgh in Australia. Revealing a consistent view of capital punishment, it stated:

It may be said that the prevalence of crime proves the inutility of capital punishment. But the fact that passionate men commit murder is no proof that hanging is other wise than deterrent.†

There was no corresponding dread of a pervading 'mania' and a 'rising tide of blood' in the House of Lords; none, at least, which carried over to the consideration of the second reading of the Bill on 7 May 1868. Accepting the need to discontinue an outdated execution-system, the Lords proceeded to pass the Bill with dispatch. A crime-wave, both threatened and real Fenian violence, a sensational assassination and another attempted one did not harden the Lords' resolve to crush murders with exemplary and brutal lessons of the public gallows; the dependence on them had passed. Capital punishment would continue, as almost everyone thought it should, but its unseemly punishment would be private.

On introducing the Bill for its second reading, the Duke of Richmond said it embodied the recommendation of the Royal Commission on Capital Punishment.[58] Lord Cranworth, the Lord Chancellor, gave his influential and official approval to the Bill: he hoped private executions 'would put a stop to the saturnalia which occurred on the occasion of every execution in the Metropolis'.[59] And Lord Houghton, who as Monckton Milnes had attended the hanging of the Mannings in 1849 with Dickens, gave the Bill his support. He expressed a personal

* Thomas D'Arcy McGee, who had been a Fenian and revolutionary in 1848, became a leading Irish-Canadian statesman and eloquent spokesman for confederation and Canadian patriotism. As a member of the Dominion Parliament, he denounced the threatened Fenian invasion, and supported the prosecution of disloyal Irishmen. He was shot by a Fenian assassin on 7 April 1868, in Ottawa. *Dictionary of National Biography*; Vol. XII, Oxford University Press, 1959–60, pp.529–30.

† *Morning Herald*, 4 May 1868, p.11. Nineteen years previously the *Morning Herald* had offered an almost identical argument against abolition of the death penalty. Conceding then that there was a good argument for abolition, the newspaper still insisted on some 'strong deterring cause to prevent the man from evil passions'. ibid., 14 November 1849, p.4.

satisfaction that private executions were likely to become law, because he had kept the subject of the evil consequences of public executions before the House of Commons on several occasions.[60]

The third reading of the Bill moved through the House of Lords with just one minor delay, and even that had no element of hostility towards the proposed change in carrying out the death penalty. Lord Ravensworth felt it would be beneficial for all prisoners to be required to view any execution within their prison. He made a motion for a new clause, but was unwilling to force a division. The Duke of Richmond refused to endorse such an addition to the Bill, considering forced attendance at executions of both tried and untried prisoners a gross violation of the principle which presumed every man innocent until proven guilty. The clause was rejected and the Capital Punishment Bill received its third reading on 11 May 1868, and was sent to the Queen for her assent.

Private executions were no longer considered dangerous and inimical to the public nature of English law and justice. The ease with which the Bill passed the conservative House of Lords exposed the weaknesses of all the arguments which had been used to impede the reform of public hangings; it had become neither controversial nor debatable. Outside of Parliament the Bill was also received with approval. The *Annual Register* considered the Bill brought in by the government an important and practical reform in the administration of justice:

The execution of capital sentences in public had for sometime past been strongly condemned by public opinion on account of the scandalous and revolting scenes with which these spectacles were attended, the lawlessness and brutality of the crowds which they brought together, and the tendency of the exhibition rather to degrade and harden the minds of the spectators than to reduce any ameliorating or deterrent effect.[61]

The *Annual Register* attributed the successful passage of the Bill to the investigation of the subject by the Royal Commission on Capital Punishment. Its Report, thought the journal, confirmed the prevailing impression of the public, and induced the government to abolish public executions.[62]

While the Capital Punishment Within Prisons Bill was being considered in the House of Commons, an attempt was made on 13 December 1867, to abet the escape of the Fenian prisoners, Burke and Casey, from Clerkenwell Prison. A barrel of explosives, placed at the base of the wall of the prison, killed six persons outright; six died later from wounds and 120 were wounded by the explosion. A contemporary observer wrote, 'Outrage created such a feeling in the Metropolis that it became dangerous to be known as in the slightest degree associated with members of the Fenian brotherhood.'[63] The government offered a 300-shilling reward for information leading to the capture of those responsible for the explosion. This act hardened all groups against any further reform of the death penalty.

Michael Barrett and James O'Neil were arrested in Glasgow on 8 January 1868 for unlawful use of firearms. They were identified as Fenians and brought to London in custody. Eye-witnesses identified them as the men responsible for the Clerkenwell explosion, and Barrett was distinctly identified as the man responsible for firing the barrel of explosives.[64]

The twenty-seven-year-old Irish stevedore claimed throughout his trial that he had been elsewhere during the Clerkenwell explosion. Despite a verdict of 'guilty' rendered by the jury, his execution was postponed until 26 May to allow for an extra-judicial inquiry to investigate his contention that he had not been in the vicinity of Clerkenwell at the time of the crime. *The Times* believed that Barrett really had two trials. 'It is rare in the history of our criminal jurisprudence,' the newspaper stated, 'that Government allows a sort of special commission to inquire into the validity of a jury's verdict and the judge's approval.'[65]

Just three days before the Capital Punishment Within Prisons Bill received the Royal Assent on 29 May 1868 Barrett's execution, the last public execution in England, took place.* The barriers went up for an execution for the last time

* On Monday 25 May 1868, the day before Barrett's execution, John Bright made one last appeal on behalf of the condemned Fenian. *The Times*, in a rather conciliatory tone, saw no impropriety in Bright's public question to Gathorne Hardy, the Home Secretary, concerning the

on Monday 25 May, and that night small groups of sightseers assembled for their final opportunity to witness a hanging in Great Britain.

There were the usual catcalls, comic choruses and mock hymns; these continued until two o'clock in the morning when the alcohol-induced gaiety began to fade. But during that night there were very few lights in the windows opposite Newgate and no sounds from the rooms overlooking the gallows where on previous occasions wealthy revellers made a night of it with drinking and feasting.[66] Down below, among the crowds of people there were few cries of distress, for there was less maltreatment and robbery than usually accompanied public hangings.

The arrival of the scaffold stirred the crowd with interest. Through the dawn people streamed into the area before Newgate, a great proportion of them young women and children who joined many thieves and prostitutes, the latter two groups drawn there by the opportunities for plying their trades. By seven o'clock that morning the mob had grown immense.

When the first peal of the great bell of St Sepulchre's began its dirge-like tolling, a great roar arose from the crowd, and repeated and insistent shouts of 'Hats off!' came from the spectators, like a chorus of cheers from a football stadium.

The whole dense, bareheaded mass stood white and ghastly looking in the morning sun, and the pressure on the barriers increased so that the girls and women in the front ranks began to struggle to get free.[67]

The muscular, prepossessing Barrett mounted the steps of the scaffold with firmness. There was a burst of cheers immediately followed by hisses, but he paid no attention to either. He was very attentive to what the priest was saying to him, and then he began to pray fervently. Calcraft put the cap over Barrett's face and adjusted the rope around his neck with

---

scheduled execution of Barrett. The newspaper respected Bright's concern for Barrett because of the faint suspicion he had been unjustly condemned; the newspaper 'was glad Mr Bright was able to elicit from Mr Hardy such strong opinions that the prisoner Barrett has been rightly convicted'. *The Times*, 26 May 1868, p.5.

THE GROANS
OF THE
GALLOWS,
Or the Past and Present
LIFE OF
WILLIAM CALCRAFT,

THE LIVING
Hangman of Newgate.

" The Cross shall displace the Gibbet,
and all will be accomplished."   Victor Hugo.

ENTERED AT STATIONERS' HALL.

'The Groans of the Gallows, Or the Past and Present Life of William Calcraft, the Living Hangman of Newgate.' Colop, London, 1846. William Calcraft, executioner from 1829 until 1874, received much attention from the popular press. This particular pamphlet was critical of the hangman and his profession.

even more haste and roughness than usual.* The bolt was drawn, and the drop fell with a loud boom and echo. Barrett died without a struggle.

With the fall of the drop, the crowd began to disperse, but a still sizeable number of people milled about waiting for the body to be cut down. When nine o'clock came, they became impatient, and several of the more vociferous began to shout tauntingly, 'Come on body-snatcher! Take away the man you killed!'[68] Calcraft appeared, still very apprehensive, and hastily cut down the body to the chorus of jeers and curses which continued until the hangman and his assistant retreated with the body through Debtors' Door into Newgate Gaol and out of sight. There was nothing more to be seen and the crowd broke up.†

The newspapers breathed a sigh of relief that Barrett's was the last public execution. The *Daily News* commented that the event demonstrated the expediency of the recent change in the law. It described the crowd at Barrett's hanging as 'an incarnation of evil persons with perverted sympathies',[69] which was unable to show either pity for the criminal or horror for the crime. 'The bastard pride in his animal courage and the brutal delight that he died game made the law and its ministers seem to them to be the real murderers, and Barrett to be a martyred man.'[70]

The reporter from *The Times* thought that no one could look on the scene of Barrett's hanging, even with all its exceptional quietness, without gratitude that this was to be the last public execution. 'Most assuredly,' he wrote, indicating his own relief of self-deliverance,

* Calcraft had received many abusive and threatening anonymous letters, and he was panic-stricken that in that mass of people stood an assassin waiting for the propitious moment to shoot him. H. W. Bleackley, *The Hangmen of England*, Chapman & Hall, 1929, p.223.

† *The Times*, 27 May 1868, p.6. By all the news accounts, the behaviour of the crowd was comparatively good. The *Morning Star* thought the crowd quite docile; 'It was a crowd that might have been waiting for a coronation, Lord Mayor's show or any public procession'. 27 May 1868, p.5. *The Times* thought there was very little to distinguish the last execution from others which preceded it except the crowd was possibly bigger and better behaved. 27 May 1868, p.6.

the sight of public executions to those who have to witness them is as disgusting as it must be demoralizing, even to all the hordes of thieves and prostitutes it draws together.[71]

The new Capital Punishment Amendment Act of 1868[72] provided that each execution would henceforth be carried out within the walls of the prison in which the condemned person was confined at the time.* The sheriff charged with the execution, the gaoler, chaplain and prison surgeon were required to attend the execution. Attendance was optional for Justices of the Peace for counties, boroughs and other jurisdictions to which the prison belonged, but the admission of relatives of the prisoner and other persons was left to the discretion of the sheriff or visiting justices of the prison.† These provisions, which allowed officials to view executions, were designed to avoid the stigma of 'secret executions' with all the associated connotations.

Additional guarantees that the executions within prison

* A writer of capital-punishment history reported that when Roger Casement was to be sentenced to death in 1917 for treason, it was asserted then that he must be executed in public as the Act abolishing public executions did not apply to treason. 'In any case,' the writer stated, 'the Act of 1887 authorized sheriffs to execute any death sentence in a prison under their jurisdiction.' John Laurence, *A History of Capital Punishment*, New York: Citadel Press, 1963, p.26.

† Newspapermen, who were not specifically cited by the Act to attend executions within prisons, were deemed by the authorities as suitable and proper persons to view executions. Their presence continued to rankle the abolitionists, who had predicted that newspaper accounts of private executions would not correct the evils of public executions. Frederic Hill was such an unhappy reformer; he wrote, 'but the brutalizing effect of an execution is but diminished not banished. The cheap newspapers carry the account of the final scene of disgrace and pain far and wide, and it is eagerly read by all who are eagerly attracted by baneful excitement.' Frederic Hill, *An Autobiography of Fifty Years in Times of Reform*, ed. Constance Hill, London: R. Bentley & Son, 1894, p.286. Executions were witnessed by the press for another twenty years after the enactment of the Capital Punishment Amendment Act. The exclusion of the press occurred because the Home Office considered newspaper accounts of executions harmful to the morals of the public. Sheriffs were warned that the Official Secrets Act prohibited them from giving information about executions to outsiders. Bleackley, op. cit., p.281.

walls would not inflict unusual punishments, like some medie-
val inquisition, were written into the Act. The body of the
deceased criminal had to be examined immediately after the
execution by the surgeon and a declaration ascertaining
the fact of death had to be signed by the sheriff, gaoler and
chaplain of the prison. Within twenty-four hours following the
execution, a coroner's inquest was to be held on the body, and
it was to be buried within the walls of the prison where the
execution took place.

Some flexibility was also contained in the Act; its purposes
were to allow for a re-examination of the rules and regulations
governing executions with a view, particularly, to eliminating
any possible abuses which might develop in the act of execution. Periodic inspections of executions were to be made by
officials of the Home Office, and the principal secretaries of
state were charged with the responsibility for framing new
rules and regulations which then had to be laid before Parliament. Revisions of executions were also to be concerned with
how to make them more solemn, should there be such a need,
and how better to make known to the public outside the prison
walls the fact that an execution was taking place, should such
a change be deemed necessary.

Concern was manifested about the falsification of the facts
of executions, and appropriate penalties were designed to discourage such an offence. For persons who wilfully and know-
ingly signed any false declaration or certificate, prison terms
not exceeding two years were provided. Stringent regulations
about informing the public of the fact of death by execution
were reinforced by the exhibition of every certificate, declaration and coroner's report on or near the principal entrance to
the prison where the execution occurred. The Act was brought
to conform to the changes in terminology for officials in Scotland and Ireland, changing, for example, the Chief Secretary
to the Lord Lieutenant in Ireland, and the High Sheriff to the
Lord Provost in Scotland, among other modifications.

William Ewart and his abolitionist supporters had opposed
private executions because they thought that if public executions were still insisted upon then capital punishment could
not continue.[73] Paradoxically, the advocates of abolishing the

death penalty were largely responsible for the Capital Punishment Within Prisons Bill of 1868 despite their antipathy to this reform. Every agitation made by abolitionist societies, every utterance made in abomination of public executions, every argument made to show how capital punishment defeated the principle of deterrence, every memorial to the Home Secretary and every petition to Parliament which they inspired helped to prepare the government and the authorities to accept private executions. The very language and arguments made against capital punishment were often the very language and arguments against public executions. And it was the end of public executions which Parliament and the public were finally ready to accept, not the abolition of the death penalty.*

The abolition of public executions was not just a minor reform which came into being by default to block progress on a much broader one. Like the capital-punishment-abolition movement, the abolition of public executions was a linear descendent of a long line of criminal reforms in the administration of justice initiated by Sir Samuel Romilly, Beccaria and Bentham. It was part of that even older humanitarian movement which grew to abhor iniquities in justice and brutality in punishment.

The reform of public executions was an independent movement and not just a subordinate part of a larger movement. It had as propagandists some of the greatest figures in English literature in Henry Fielding and Charles Dickens. It had two

* Not only was the abolition of capital punishment not forthcoming, but even the relatively less controversial changes in the definition of murder were defeated in 1872, 1874, 1876, 1877 and 1878. Revision by a distinguished Royal Commission of all indictable offences, including several types of homicide, failed to become law when introduced in 1879–80; even simple division into two degrees of murder also failed in 1881. Bills for total abolition of capital punishment were presented without success in 1869, 1872, 1873 and 1881. Rose, op. cit., pp.27–9. Little progress was made during the remainder of the nineteenth century towards the abolition of capital punishment. 'Indeed,' a recent study of the abolition of capital punishment concluded, 'no real steps towards this goal were taken until well into the twentieth century.' Elizabeth Tuttle, *The Crusade Against Capital Punishment*, London: Stevens & Sons Ltd, 1961, p.26.

of the nineteenth century's outstanding polemicists and pamphleteers in Edward Gibbon Wakefield and George Jacob Holyoake. Public executions were condemned by influential newspapers and journals. A history of important legislative committees, from the Select Committee of the House of Commons in 1819 to the prestigious Royal Commission in 1864, cast doubts about the efficacy of public executions. It had individual champions in Parliament such as Thomas Fowell Buxton, George Grote, Henry Rich, Monckton Milnes, the Bishop of Oxford and John Hibbert.

Public opinion had at last crystallized against a form of punishment which had come to be considered anachronistic and barbaric, not in keeping with the spirit of an age exemplified by the Crystal Palace and by the technological advancement demonstrated by the laying of the Atlantic under-water cable.

On the morning of 13 August 1868 Thomas Wells, aged eighteen, was hanged. On the following day *The Times* wrote:

This was the first execution under the new Act requiring execution to be inflicted within the prison walls ... at the moment of the drop there were very few, if any, strangers in the vicinity of the prison, and the town of Maidstone presented quite its usual appearance, presenting a marked extraordinary contrast to that which it exhibited on the occasion of a public execution.[74]

As the drop fell, young Thomas Wells's last two or three convulsive struggles were at least concealed from a morbidly curious mob. Although public executions were over, it was apparent that the crusade against capital punishment would continue.*

* Writing about the Wells execution, the *Morning Advertiser* said, 'When we turn ... to the account of calm and apparently satisfactory manner in which the culprit met his doom we cannot but think ... the system yesterday is an act of mercy to the man who is the wretched hero of the day ... We are not reconciled to capital punishment by the fact that it was yesterday carried out in the least offensive manner of which it is capable.' 14 August 1868, p.4. The *Morning Star* wrote, 'The first private execution is over, and a criminal has been put to death without the traditional scaffold and crowd ... and the citizens shall be freed from the odious accompaniment of an execution.' But the newspaper also complained that 'new and ghastly elements are introduced ... the

An overdue reform had at last been put into effect. A degrading spectacle had now become legend. Henceforth, the Act of 1868 relegated the Roman-circus atmosphere of public executions to the past. Gone would be the drunk, becauched, debased crowds; no longer would there be the condemned man's 'dying words' and 'confessions'; never again would seats be sold at windows overlooking the gallows. Future generations would be spared scenes that dulled sensibilities. Another landmark in the more humane treatment of criminals was reached, while, correspondingly, a new deference and, concern for the opinions and feelings of the mass of people were being manifested.

---

want of ceremony . . . the little courtyard, the saw-pit, the rude instrument of strangulation, the handful of spectators . . . No, the English people cannot long tolerate the spectacle of criminals put to death in a private pit.' 15 August 1868, p.4.

REFERENCES

CHAPTER 1 THE LESSON OF THE GALLOWS

1. Leon Radzinowicz, *A History of English Criminal Law and its Administration from 1750*, Vol. I *The Movement for Reform*, London: Stevens & Sons, 1948, pp.206–7.
2. ibid., p.165.
3. ibid., p.216.
4. Charles Phillips, *Vacation Thoughts on Capital Punishment*, London: W. and F. G. Cash, 1856, p.54.
5. W. L. Burn, *The Age of Equipoise: A Study of the Mid-Victorian Generation*, New York: W. W. Norton & Co., 1964, p.54.
6. *Morning Star*, 23 February 1864, p.2.
7. John Laurence, *A History of Capital Punishment*, New York: Citadel Press, 1963, p. 171.
8. Rev. J. Charles Cox, *Three Centuries of Derbyshire Annals*, Vol. II, London and Derby: Bemrose & Sons, 1890, pp.41–2.
9. Thomas Mozley, *Reminiscences Chiefly of Oriel College and the Oxford Movement*, 2nd edn, Vol. I, Longman & Co., 1882, pp.191–2.
10. Laurence, op. cit., pp.42–3.
11. Horace W. Bleackley, *The Hangmen of England*, Chapman & Hall, 1929, pp. 98–9.
12. *The Newgate Calendar, or Malefactors' Bloody Register*, London: Capricorn Books, 1961, p.94.
13. Radzinowicz, op. cit., Vol. I, p.201.
14. Bleackley, op. cit., p.80.
15. G. T. Crook and John L. Rayner, eds., *The Complete Newgate Calendar*, London: Navarre Society 1926, pp.327–8. See also Radzinowicz, op. cit., Vol. 1, p.204, and Bleackley, op. cit., pp. 142–3.
16. *The Times*, 29 November 1824, p.5.
17. *Morning Herald*, 2 December 1824, p.4.
18. *Annual Register*, 1824, p.163.
19. Bleackley, op. cit., p.184.
20. Laurence, op. cit., p.184.
21. William M. Thackeray, 'Going to See a Man Hanged', *Fraser's Magazine*, Vol. XX, August 1840, p.150.
22. Philip Collins, *Dickens and Crime*, Macmillan & Co., 1962, pp.24–5.

23. Thackeray, loc. cit.

24. Collins, op. cit., pp. 235–6.

25. British Museum, *Murders* (*A Collection of Broadsides Containing Accounts in Prose and Verse of Murders and Executions*), London and Edinburgh, 1794–1860 and 1830–55, p.176. Hereafter referred to as British Museum, *Murders*.

26. *Daily News*, 14 November 1849, p.5.

27. *The Times*, 14 November 1849, p.5.

28. Collins, op. cit., pp.234–6.

29. John Forster, *The Life of Charles Dickens*, Vol. ii, Chapman & Hall, 1873, p.447.

30. Bleackley, op. cit., p.222.

31. See *Morning Post*, 14 November 1864, and *Morning Star*, 15 November 1864.

32. *The Times*, 16 November 1864, p.10.

33. *Morning Herald*, 23 February 1864, p.4.

34. ibid.

35. *Morning Star*, 23 February 1864, p.2.

36. ibid.

37. ibid.

38. *Morning Herald*, 15 November 1864, p.5.

39. ibid. 23 February 1864, p.5.

40. ibid.

41. ibid.

42. ibid.

43. *The Times*, 23 February 1864, p.5.

44. ibid.

45. *Daily News*, 23 February 1864, p.5.

46. *Morning Herald*, 23 February 1864, p.5.

47. *Parliamentary Papers*, Report of the Capital Punishment Commission, Vol. vii, 1866, p.225.

48. *The Times*, 23 February 1864, p.5.

49. *Parliamentary Papers*, Report from the Select Committee of the House of Lords, Vol. vii, 1856, p.23.

50. *Hansard*, Vol. lxxiii (1864), col.951.

51. George J. Holyoake, 'Public Lessons of the Hangman', London: Farrah, 1864, pp.2–3.

52. British Museum, *Murders*, p.52.

53. See G. D. H. Cole and Raymond Postgate, *The British Common People: 1746–1946*, Methuen, 1961, pp.354–5.

54. Radzinowicz, op. cit., Vol. i, pp.206–7.

55. Alfred H. Dymond, *The Law on Trial, or Personal Recollections of the Death Penalty, and its Opponents,* London: Society for the Abolition of Capital Punishment, 1865, pp.160–63.

56. William N. Molesworth, *The History of England from the Year 1830*, Vol. iii, Chapman & Hall, 1874, p.76.

57. Charles Hindley, *The History of the Catnach Press*, London: C. Hindley the Younger, 1886, pp.65–8.
58. ibid.
59. ibid.
60. British Museum, *Murders*, p.82.
61. ibid., p.72.

CHAPTER 2   THE 'BLOODY CODE'

1. Charles Phillips, *Vacation Thoughts on Capital Punishment*, London: W. and F. G. Cash, 1856, p.4.
2. Basil Montagu, *The Opinions of Different Authors Upon the Punishment of Death*, Vol. III, Longman, Hurst, Rees & Orme, 1809, p.213.
3. See Llewellyn Woodward, *The Age of Reform: 1815–1870*, Oxford University Press, 1962, p.1.
4. J. H. Plumb, *England in the Eighteenth Century: 1714–1815*, Penguin Books Ltd., 1959, p.20.
5. George Ollyfe, *An Essay Humbly Offer'd for an Act of Parliament to Prevent Capital Crimes, and the Loss of Many Lives and to Promote a Desirable Improvement and Blessing in the Nation*, London: J. Downing, 1731, pp.8–9.
6. ibid.
7. Anonymous, *Hanging Not Punishment Enough for Murtherers, Highway Men and House Breakers, Offer'd to the Consideration of the Two Houses of Parliament*, London, 1701, p.4.
8. ibid.
9. Thomas More, 'Utopia', *Ideal Commonwealths*, ed. Henry Morley, New York, Colonial Press, 1901, p.10.
10. J. Spedding, R. L. Ellis and D. D. Heath, eds., *The Works of Francis Bacon*, Vol. VII, Longman & Co., 1874, p.315.
11. Marvin E. Wolfgang, 'Cesare Bonesana Beccaria', *The Encyclopedia of Philosophy*, ed. Paul Edwards, Vol. I, New York: Macmillan, 1967, p.267.
12. Harry E. Barnes, 'Cesare Bonesana Beccaria, Marchese di Beccaria', *Encyclopedia of the Social Sciences*, ed. Edwin R. A. Seligman, Vol. II, New York: Macmillan, 1954, pp.488–9.
13. Cesare Bonesana Beccaria, *An Essay on Crimes and Punishments*, Philadelphia: Philip H. Nicklin, 1819, p.93.
14. *Dictionary of National Biography*, Oxford University Press, 1959–60, p.278. Henceforth this will be referred to as *D.N.B.*
15. Samuel Romilly, *Observations on the Criminal Law of England as it Relates to the Capital Punishments, and on the Mode in Which it is Administered*, London: McCreery, 1810, p.10.
16. ibid.
17. *Hansard*, Vol. XVI (1810), col.769.
18. Basil Montagu, ed., *Debates in the Year 1810, Upon Sir Samuel*

Romilly's Bills for Abolishing the Punishment of Death for Stealing to the Amount of Forty Shillings in a Dwelling House, for Stealing to the Amount of Five Shillings Privately in a Shop, and for Stealing on Navigable Rivers, London: Society for the Diffusion of Knowledge Respecting the Punishment of Death and the Improvement of Prison Discipline, 1810, p.17.

19. Coleman Phillipson, *Three Criminal Law Reformers: Beccaria, Bentham, Romilly,* J. M. Dent & Sons, 1923, p.265.

20. Oakes, op. cit., p.219.

21. Radzinowicz, *A History of English Criminal Law and its Administration from 1750,* Vol. i, p.512.

22. Montagu, *Opinions of Different Authors Upon the Punishment of Death,* Vol. iii, p.273.

23. ibid., p.272.

24. ibid., p.266

25. ibid.

26. Samuel Romilly, *Memoirs of the Life of Sir Samuel Romilly, Written by Himself,* edited by his sons, Vol. ii, J. Murray, 1840, pp.177–8.

27. *Hansard,* Vol. xix (1811), appendix cxii.

28. ibid., appendix lxxiv.

29. ibid., appendix cx.

30. Radzinowicz, op. cit., Vol. i, p.527.

31. Norman Gash, *Mr Secretary Peel: The Life of Sir Robert Peel to 1830,* Cambridge, Mass.: Harvard University Press, 1961, p.487.

32. Radzinowicz, op. cit., Vol. i, p.352.

33. David E. Owen, *English Philanthropy, 1660–1960,* Cambridge, Mass.: Harvard University Press, 1964, p.99, quoting Sarah Trimmer, *The Oeconomy of Charity,* Vol. ii, London, 1801, p.45.

34. *Hansard,* Vol. xix (1811), appendix lxxxvii.

35. ibid., Vol. xxxix (1819), col. 862.

36. See Raymond J. Cowherd, *The Politics of English Dissent: The Religious Aspects of Liberal and Humanitarian Reform Movements from 1815 to 1848,* New York: New York University Press, 1956, pp. 52 and 62.

37. Gordon Rose, *The Struggle for Penal Reform: The Howard League and its Predecessors,* London: Stevens & Sons, 1961, p.2.

38. Gash, op. cit., p.487. Peel served as Home Secretary from 1822 to 1827 and again from 1828 to 1830.

39. John W. Croker, *The Croker Papers. The Correspondence and Diaries of the Late Right Honourable J. W. Croker,* ed. L. J. Jennings, Vol. i, J. Murray, 1885, p.170.

40. Gash, op. cit., p.478.

41. Élie Halévy, *The Growth of Philosophic Radicalism,* Boston: Beacon Press, 1955, p.509.

42. *Hansard,* Vol. xxiii (1830), cols.1179–80.

43. Gash, op. cit., pp.482–3.

44. Alfred H. Dymond, *The Law on Trial, or Personal Recollections of the Death Penalty and its Opponents*, London: Society for the Abolition of Capital Punishment, 1865, p.27.

45. Sydney Smith, *The Works of the Rev. Sydney Smith*, Longman & Co., 1869, p.670.

46. J. E. T. Rogers, ed., *Bright's Speeches on Questions of Public Policy*, Macmillan & Co., 1869, p.160.

47. Radzinowicz, op. cit., Vol. iv, p.303.

48. W. A. Munford, *William Ewart, M.P., 1788–1869*, Grafton p.68.

49. Dymond, op. cit., p.57.

50. ibid.

51. *Hansard*, Vol. xxxviii (1837), col.922.

52. Harriet Martineau, *The History of England During the Thirty Years' Peace, 1816–1846*, Vol. ii, London: Charles Knight, 1849, p.419.

53. *Hansard*, loc. cit.

54. ibid. Vol. lii (1840), col.920.

55. ibid.

56. ibid., col.935.

57. ibid., col.928.

58. Taylor, *Selections from the Writings of J. Sydney Taylor*, pp.426–7.

59. ibid., p.430.

60. ibid.

61. C. C. F. Greville, *The Greville Memoirs: Second Part: A Journal of the Reign of Queen Victoria, 1837–1852*, ed. H. Reeve, Vol. i, Longman, Green, 1885, p.284.

62. *Hansard*, Vol. civ (1849), col. 1063.

63. ibid.

64. Broughton, *Recollections of a Long Life*, Vol. v, J. Murray, 1911, p.273.

65. *Hansard*, Vol. civ (1849), cols.1071–2.

66. Edwin Hodder, *The Life and Work of the Seventh Earl of Shaftesbury*, Vol. ii, Cassell & Co., 1886, p.281.

67. *Hansard*, loc. cit.

68. *Eclectic Review*, Vol. xci (1849), p.107.

69. *Hansard*, Vol. cxii (1850), col.1258.

70. ibid., col. 1259.

71. ibid., col.1278.

72. *The Times*, 20 November 1849, p.4.

73. *Eclectic Review*, Vol. xcii (1850), p.850.

74. ibid.

75. *The Times*, 23 April 1850, p.5.

CHAPTER 3 STIRRINGS FOR REFORM: SOCIETIES, PAMPHLETS AND JOURNALS

1. A. V. Dicey, *Lectures on the Relation between Law and Public Opinion*

in England During the Nineteenth Century, 2nd edn, Macmillan & Co., 1914, pp.9 and 10.

2. Auguste Jorns, *The Quakers as Pioneers in Social Work*, p. 179.

3. William Tallack, *A General Review of the Subject of Capital Punishment*, London: Society for the Abolition of Capital Punishment, 1866, p.2.

4. ibid., p.3.

5. ibid., p.4.

6. Dymond, *The Law on Trial, or Personal Recollections of the Death Penalty and its Opponents*, p.258.

7. ibid., p.90.

8. ibid., p.290.

9. ibid.

10. *The Times*, 10 June 1856, p.12.

11. ibid., 22 November 1856, p.12.

12. ibid., 22 January 1856, p.5.

13. Rose, *The Struggle for Penal Reform*, p.26.

14. ibid., p.17.

15. B. Rodgers, 'The Social Science Association, 1857–1886', Vol. xx, p.288.

16. ibid.

17. ibid., p.283.

18. ibid., p.289.

19. Dymond, op. cit., introduction.

20. *The Times*, 3 May 1868, p.11.

21. ibid.

22. Edward Gibbon Wakefield, *Facts Relating to the Punishment of Death in the Metropolis*, London, 1832, p.177.

23. ibid., pp.182–3.

24. ibid., p.179.

25. Edward Gibbon Wakefield, *Terrorstruck Town*, London: Steill, 1833, p.13.

26. Edward Gibbon Wakefield, *The Hangman and the Judge, or a Letter from Jack Ketch to Mr Justice Alderson*, London: Effingham Wilson, 1833, p.12.

27. ibid.

28. ibid., p.4.

29. ibid., p.5.

30. Wakefield, *Terrorstruck Town*, p.10.

31. ibid., p.8.

32. ibid.

33. ibid., p.9.

34. George Jacob Holyoake, *Sixty Years of an Agitator's Life*, Vol. ii, Unwin, 1893, pp.117–18.

35. ibid., p.118.

36. ibid.

37. ibid.
38. ibid.
39. ibid.
40. Holyoake, 'Public Lessons of the Hangman', pp.6–7.
41. ibid., p.8.
42. See Walter E. Houghton, ed., *The Wellesley Index to Victorian Periodicals, 1824–1900*, Vol. I, Toronto: University of Toronto Press, 1966, Routledge & Kegan Paul, 1966, and William Frederick Poole, ed., *Poole's Index to Periodical Literature, 1802–81*, Vols. I and II, Gloucester, Mass.: Peter Smith, 1963.
43. M. H. Spielmann, *The History of Punch*, Cassell & Co., 1895, p.2.
44. Collins, *Dickens and Crime*, p.242.
45. ibid.
46. R. E. Williams, ed., *A Century of Punch Cartoons*, New York: Simon & Schuster, 1955, p.xiii.
47. *Punch*, Vol. XVII, 13 November 1849, p.210.
48. ibid.
49. Spielmann, op. cit., p.73.
50. *Eclectic Review*, Vol. XXI, August 1848, p.394.
51. The articles and books 'amongst the writers who present themselves for review' were Oscar, King of Sweden, *On Punishment and Prisons*, London: A. May, 1842; the Reverend Henry Christmas, 'Capital Punishments Unnecessary in a Christian State', London: Smith, Elder & Co., 1846; Russell and Cruikshank, *Reports of Speeches Delivered Before the Town Council of Edinburgh*, Edinburgh: Oliphant, 1845; Charles Dickens, 'Letters on Capital Punishment', *Daily News*, 1846; Walter Scott, President and Theological Tutor in Disdale College, Bradford, Yorkshire, *The Punishment of Death – Scriptural, Moral and Salutary*, London: Simpkins & Co., 1846; Thomas Cooper, the Chartist, *Two Orations Against Taking Away Human Life Under Any Circumstance*, London: Chapman Bros., 1846; Lord Nugent, M.P., 'Crime and Punishment', *The People's Journal*, Vol. LXXXVIII, August 1848, pp.393–4.
52. *Eclectic Review*, Vol. XXIII, January 1850, p.37.
53. ibid., p.38.
54. ibid.
55. W. M. Thackeray, *Fraser's Magazine*, Vol. XX, July 1840, p.150.
56. ibid.
57. ibid.
58. ibid.
59. James F. Stephens, 'Capital Punishment', *Fraser's Magazine*, Vol. LXIX, June 1864, p.753.
60. 'Hanging, Public or Private?', *Spectator*, Vol. XXII, 24 November 1849, pp.111–12.
61. ibid.

62. ibid.

63. ibid.

64. ibid.

65. 'The Five Executions', *Spectator*, Vol. XXXVII, 27 February 1864, p.87.

66. ibid.

67. Henry Rogers, 'On Public Executions', p.104.

68. ibid., p.106.

69. ibid., p.111.

70. ibid., p.112.

71. ibid.

72. 'Now!', *All the Year Round*, Vol. XX, 8 August 1868, pp.223–5.

73. ibid.

74. ibid.

CHAPTER 4   CONTROVERSY OVER PUNISHMENTS: THE PRESS AND PUBLIC OPINION

1. James H. Wellard, 'The State of Reading Among the Working Classes of England During the First Half of the Nineteenth Century', *The Library Quarterly*, Vol. V, 1935, p.97.

2. D. C. Somervell, *English Thought in the Nineteenth Century*, p.56.

3. *Morning Advertiser*, 19 May 1837, p.6.

4. J. S. Taylor, *Selections from the Writings of John Sydney Taylor*, p. xxxii.

5. *Morning Post*, 17 February 1841, p.5.

6. Georgina Hogarth, ed., *The Letters of Charles Dickens, 1833–1870*, Chapman & Hall, 1909, pp.140–41.

7. P. Collins, *Dickens and Crime*, p.227.

8. Charles Dickens, *Miscellaneous Papers*, p.33.

9. ibid., p.50.

10. ibid., pp.50-51

11. Louis Blom-Cooper, *The Law as Literature*, p.283.

12. ibid.

13. G. E. Bryant and G. P. Baker, *A Quaker Journal: Being a Diary and Reminiscences of William Lucas, 1804–1861*, Vol. I, Hutchinson & Co., 1933, p.436.

14. *The Times*, 14 November 1849, p.4.

15. ibid.

16. Walter Dexter, ed., *The Letters of Charles Dickens, 1845–1847*, Vol. II, London: Nonesuch Press, 1938, p.185.

17. ibid.

18. *The Times*, 14 November 1849, p.3.

19. ibid. 19 November 1849, p.5.

20. ibid.

21. ibid., 20 November 1849, p.5.

22. ibid.
23. ibid.
24. ibid.
25. ibid., 21 November 1849, p.3.
26. ibid.
27. ibid.
28. ibid., 24 November 1849, p.5.
29. ibid.
30. Dexter, op. cit., p.186.
31. ibid., p.195.
32. Collins, op. cit., p.17.
33. ibid.
34. *The Times*, 12 July 1850, pp.4–5.
35. ibid., 20 February 1854, p.11.
36. *Hansard*, Vol. CXLII (1856), col.452.
37. ibid., col.1239.
38. *The Times*, 11 June 1856, p.5.
39. *Parliamentary Papers*, Report from the Select Committee of the House of Lords Appointed to take into Consideration the Present Mode of Carrying into Effect Capital Punishments, Vol. VII, July 1856, p.5.
40. *The Times*, 17 July 1856, p.8.
41. ibid.
42. ibid.
43. ibid., 17 July 1856, p.6.
44. ibid., 13 January 1864, p.5.
45. ibid.
46. ibid.
47. *Morning Herald*, 23 February 1864, pp.4–5.
48. ibid.
49. *Morning Star*, 24 February 1864, p.4.
50. ibid.
51. *Morning Post*, 23 February 1864, p.5.
52. ibid.
53. *The Times*, 4 May 1864, p.9.
54. ibid.
55. *Morning Post*, 4 May 1864, p.9.
56. *The Times*, 4 May 1864, p.4.
57. ibid.
58. ibid., 1 August 1864, p.11.
59. ibid., 2 August 1864, p.6.
60. ibid.
61. ibid.
62. ibid.
63. *Daily News*, 15 November 1864, p.5.
64. Dexter, op. cit., Vol. III, p.402.

65. Herman Ausubel, *John Bright, Victorian Reformer*, New York: John Wiley & Sons, 1966, p.82.
66. *Morning Star*, 16 November 1864, pp.4–5.
67. *Morning Herald*, 21 November 1864, p.6.

CHAPTER 5   ATTEMPTS IN PARLIAMENT TO ABOLISH
PUBLIC EXECUTIONS: 1841–56

1. Henry Fielding, *An Enquiry into the Causes of the Late Increase of Robbers, With Some Proposals for Remedying this Growing Evil*, London, 1751, p.122.
2. ibid., p.121.
3. ibid., p.122.
4. ibid.
5. ibid., p.124.
6. *Hansard*, Vol. xxxix (1819), col.821.
7. *Parliamentary Papers*, Report from the Select Committee appointed to consider of so much of criminal law as relates to capital punishments in felonies, Vol. viii, 1819, p.63.
8. ibid.
9. ibid., p.68.
10. *Parliamentary Papers*, Second Report from His Majesty's Commissioners on Criminal Law, Vol. xxxvi, 1836, p.56.
11. *Hansard*, Vol. xxxviii, 1837, col.923.
12. ibid., col.925.
13. ibid., Vol. lvi (1841), cols.647–66.
14. ibid.
15. *The Times*, 17 February 1841, p.4.
16. *Hansard*, loc. cit.
17. *The Times*, 17 February 1841, p.4.
18. *Hansard*, Vol. lvi (1841), col.666.
19. ibid., col.667.
20. ibid., col.668.
21. ibid., col.670.
22. Public Record Office, Home Office 45, No. 05681.
23. ibid.
24. ibid.
25. ibid.
26. ibid.
27. ibid.
28. ibid.
29. *Hansard*, Vol. lxxxi (1845), cols.1411–14.
30. *The Times*, 25 March 1854, p.9.
31. Charles Dickens, *Miscellaneous Papers*, ed. Bertram Waldron Matz, Chapman & Hall, 1908, p.39.
32. *Hansard*, Vol. cxxxiii, cols.310–12.

33. ibid.
34. ibid.
35. ibid., col.308.
36. ibid., col.310.
37. ibid., col.312.
38. ibid., col.318.
39. ibid., Vol. cxlii (1856), col.247.
40. ibid.
41. ibid.
42. ibid.
43. ibid.
44. ibid.
45. ibid., col.250.
46. ibid., col.251.
47. ibid.
48. ibid., cols.251–2.
49. ibid., cols.252–3.
50. ibid., cols.1239–42.
51. ibid.
52. ibid.
53. ibid., col.1256.
54. ibid., col.1257.
55. ibid.
56. *Parliamentary Papers*, Report from the Select Committee of the House of Lords, Vol. vii, 1856, p.5.
57. ibid., p.8.
58. ibid., p.9.
59. ibid., p.12.
60. ibid., appendix, p.45.
61. ibid., pp.16–17.
62. ibid., p.23.
63. ibid., pp.30–31.
64. ibid.
65. ibid., p.34.
66. ibid.
67. ibid., pp.38–9.
68. ibid., p.40.
69. ibid.
70. ibid., pp.40–41.
71. ibid.
72. ibid., appendix, p.45.
73. ibid.
74. ibid., p.47.
75. ibid., appendix, p.48.

76. ibid., p.v.
77. Charles Phillips, *Vacation Thoughts on Capital Punishment*, London W. and F. G. Cash, 1856, p.63.
78. *The Times*, 17 July 1856, p.8.

CHAPTER 6 THE ROYAL COMMISSION, 1864–6: THE REFORM OF PUBLIC EXECUTIONS PUSHED FORWARD

1. *The Times*, 24 February 1864, p.4.
2. ibid.
3. ibid.
4. ibid.
5. ibid.
6. *Hansard*, Vol. CLXXII (1864), col.255.
7. ibid., Vol. CLXXIV (1864), cols.2063–4.
8. ibid., col.2092.
9. Alfred H. Dymond, *The Law on Trial, or Personal Recollections of the Death Penalty and its Opponents*, London: Society for the Abolition of Capital Punishment, 1865, p.298.
10. *Hansard*, Vol. CLXXIV (1864), col.2114.
11. Dymond, loc. cit.
12. *Hansard*, Vol. CLXXIV (1864), col.2070.
13. ibid., col.2071.
14. Dymond, op. cit., pp.311–12.
15. *Parliamentary Papers*, Report of the Capital Punishment Commission, Vol. XXI, 1866, p.14.
16. ibid.
17. ibid., p.45.
18. ibid.
19. ibid., p.245.
20. ibid.
21. ibid., p.49.
22. ibid., p.73.
23. ibid., p.74.
24. ibid., pp.218–19.
25. ibid., p.201.
26. ibid., p.220.
27. ibid.
28. ibid., appendix, p.510.
29. ibid., p.593.
30. ibid.
31. ibid., p.306.
32. ibid.
33. ibid.
34. ibid.

35. ibid.

36. ibid., p.97.

37. ibid., p.183.

38. ibid.

39. ibid., p.398.

40. ibid.

41. ibid., p.148.

42. ibid., p.149.

43. ibid.

44. ibid., pp.150–51.

45. ibid., p.299.

46. ibid.

47. See Arnold White, ed., *Letters of S.G.O.*, London: Griffith & Farren, 1890.

48. *Parliamentary Papers*, Report of the Capital Punishment Commission, Vol. xxi, 1866, p.412.

49. ibid.

50. ibid., p.112.

51. ibid.

52. ibid., p.121.

53. ibid., p.223.

54. ibid., pp.405–6.

55. ibid.

56. ibid., p.255.

57. ibid.

58. ibid., p.222.

59. ibid., pp.xli–xlix.

60. ibid.

61. *The Times*, 26 January 1866, p.8.

62. ibid.

63. *Analysis and Review of the Blue Book of the Royal Commission on Capital Punishment*, p.24.

64. *The Times*, loc. cit.

65. ibid.

66. See Thomas Beggs, *The Royal Commission and the Punishment of Death*, London: Society for the Abolition of Capital Punishment, 1866; *Analysis and Review of the Blue Book of the Royal Commission on Capital Punishment*; Humphrey Woolrych, *On the Report of the Capital Punishment Commission of 1866*, London: Society for the Abolition of Capital Punishment, 1866.

67. Woolrych, op. cit., p.9.

68. 'Anecdotes from the Blue Books', *Temple Bar*, Vol. xvii, February 1866, p.57.

CHAPTER 7   THE END OF PUBLIC HANGINGS

1. *The Times*, 24 March 1866, p.5.
2. ibid., 25 November 1867, p.9.
3. ibid.
4. Great Britain, *Annual Register*, 1868, pp.1–2.
5. *Hansard*, Vol. CLXXVIII (1865), col.455.
6. ibid., Vol. CLXXX (1866), col.915.
7. ibid., Vol. CLXXXI (1866), col.1623.
8. ibid., cols.1625–6.
9. ibid., col.1627.
10. ibid.
11. ibid., Vol. CLXXXII (1866), col.837.
12. ibid., col.242.
13. ibid., col.243.
14. ibid., col.251.
15. ibid., col.257.
16. ibid., Vol. CLXXXIV (1866), col.453.
17. ibid., col.455.
18. ibid.
19. ibid., col.487.
20. ibid., col.459.
21. ibid., col.460.
22. ibid., col.461.
23. ibid.
24. ibid., col.1163.
25. ibid., col.363.
26. ibid., col.366.
27. ibid.
28. ibid., col.367.
29. ibid.
30. ibid., Vol. CXC (1867), col.996.
31. ibid.
32. ibid., col.1128.
33. ibid.
34. ibid.
35. ibid., col.1131.
36. ibid., cols.1131–2.
37. House of Commons, *Divisions: Session 1867–1868*, 5 March 1868, pp.11–12.
38. *Hansard*, Vol. CXC (1868), cols.1132–3.
39. ibid., col.1134.
40. ibid., col.1136.
41. ibid.
42. ibid., cols.1137–8.

43. ibid., col.1142.

44. ibid., Vol. CXCI (1868), col.1040.

45. ibid., col.1041.

46. ibid.

47. ibid.

48. ibid., col.1047.

49. ibid., col.1057.

50. ibid.

51. ibid., col.1063.

52. ibid.

53. *The Times*, 22 April 1868, p.6.

54. Elizabeth Longford, *Queen Victoria: Born to Succeed*, New York: Pyramid Books, 1965, p.360.

55. *Hansard*, Vol. CXCI (1868), col.1337.

56. *The Times*, 3 May 1868, p.11.

57. *Morning Herald*, 4 May 1868, p.11.

58. *The Times*, 8 May 1868, p.8.

59. ibid.

60. *Hansard*, Vol. CXCI (1868), col.1879.

61. *Annual Register*, 1868, pp.16–17.

62. ibid.

63. Joseph Irving, *The Annals of Our Time, 1837–1868*, Macmillan & Co., 1869.

64. ibid., p.656.

65. *The Times*, 27 May 1868, p.4.

66. *Morning Star*, 27 May 1868, p.5.

67. *The Times*, 27 May 1868, p.6.

68. ibid.

69. *Daily News*, 27 May 1868, p.6.

70. ibid.

71. *The Times*, 27 May 1868, p.6.

72. 31 Vict. c.24. An Act to provide for the carrying out of Capital Punishment within prisons (29 May 1868).

73. W. A. Munford, *William Ewart, M.P., 1788–1869: Portrait of a Radical*, London: Grafton & Co., 1960, p.156.

74. *The Times*, 14 August 1868, p.8.

BIBLIOGRAPHY

PRIMARY SOURCES

MANUSCRIPTS

British Museum, *Gladstone Papers* MSS.44374–5.

PUBLIC DOCUMENTS

PUBLIC RECORD OFFICE

Commissions of Inquiry, August 1857–December 1868, Home Office 74, No.3.
Daily Registers, 1841–1909, Home Office 46.
Entry Books, 1816–1898, Home Office 41.
Home Office 45, No.15681.
Private and Secret, 1798–1864, Home Office 79.

PARLIAMENT

House of Commons, *Divisions: Session 1867–1868*, 5 March 1868.
Hansard's Parliamentary Debates (1st, 3rd and new series).
Capital Punishment Amendment Act (31 and 32 Vict. c.24).

PARLIAMENTARY PAPERS

Report from the Select Committee appointed to consider of so much of criminal law as relates to capital punishments in felonies, Vol. VIII, Cmnd 585, 1819.
Second Report from His Majesty's Commissioners on Criminal Law, Vol. XXXVI, 1836.
Report from the Select Committee of the House of Lords to Look into the Present Mode of Carrying into Effect Capital Punishments, Vol. VII, 1856.
Report of the Capital Punishment Commission, Vol. XXI, Cmnd 3590, 1866.

PRINTED BOOKS AND PAMPHLETS

Analysis and Review of the Blue Book of the Royal Commission on Capital Punishment, London: Society for the Abolition of Capital Punishment, 1866. Reprinted from the *Social Science Review*, May and June 1866.
Beccaria, Cesare Bonesana. *An Essay on Crimes and Punishments*, Philadelphia: Philip H. Nicklin, 1819.

Beedle, Susannah, *An Essay on the Advisability of Total Abolition of Capital Punishment*, London: Nichols & Son, 1867.

Beggs, Thomas, *The Royal Commission and the Punishment of Death*, London: Society for the Abolition of Capital Punishment, 1866.

Bentham, Jeremy, *The Works of Jeremy Bentham*, ed. John Bowring, 11 vols., New York: Russell & Russell, 1962. Originally published 1843.

Blackstone, William, *Commentaries on the Laws of England*, 15 edn, 4 vols., London: A. Strahan, 1809.

British Museum, *Murders (A Collection of Broadsides Containing Accounts in Prose and Verse of Murders and Executions)* (folio), London and Edinburgh, 1794–1860 and 1830–55.

Brixton, Charles, ed., *Memoirs of Sir Thomas Fowell Buxton*, J. M. Dent & Sons, 1925.

Broughton, Lord (John Cam Hobhouse), *Recollections of a Long Life*, ed. Lady Dorchester, J. Murray, 1911.

Bryant, G. E., and Baker, G. P., *A Quaker Journal: Being a Diary and Reminiscences of William Lucas, 1804–1861*, 2 vols., Hutchinson & Co., 1933.

Cox, Rev. J. Charles, *Three Centuries of Derbyshire Annals*, 2nd edn, 2 vols., London and Derby: Bemrose & Sons, 1890.

Creighton, Mandell, *Memoir of Sir George Grey Bart, G.C.B.*, Longmans, Green & Co., 1901.

Croker, John W., *The Croker Papers. The Correspondence and Diaries of the Late Right Honourable J. W. Croker*, 2nd rev. edn, 3 vols., ed. L. J. Jennings, John Murray, 1885.

Crook, G. T., and Rayner, John L., eds., *The Complete Newgate Calendar*, 5 vols., London: Navarre Society, 1926.

Dexter, Walter, ed., *The Letters of Charles Dickens, 1845–1847*, 3 vols., London: Nonesuch Press, 1938.

Dexter, Walter, ed., *The Unpublished Letters of Charles Dickens to Mark Lemon*, London: Halton & Truscott Smith, 1927.

Dickens, Charles, *Miscellaneous Papers*, ed. Bertram Waldron Matz, 2 vols., Chapman & Hall, 1908.

Dymond, Alfred H., *The Law on Trial, or Personal Recollections of the Death Penalty and its Opponents*, London: Society for the Abolition of Capital Punishment, 1865.

Fielding, Henry, *An Enquiry into the Causes of the Late Increase of Robbers, With Some Proposals for Remedying this Growing Evil*, London, 1751.

Forster, John, *The Life of Charles Dickens*, 3 vols., Chapman & Hall, 1873.

Gathorne-Hardy, A. E., ed., *Gathorne Hardy, First Earl of Cranbrook: A Memoir*, 2 vols., Longman & Co., 1910.

Greville, Charles Cavendish Fulke, *The Greville Memoirs: Second Part: A Journal of the Reign of Queen Victoria, 1837–1852*, ed. H. Reeve, 3 vols., Longman, Green, 1885.

Hanging Not Punishment Enough for Murtherers, Highway Men and House Breakers, Offer'd to the Consideration of the Two Houses of Parliament, London, 1701.

Hill, Frederic, *An Autobiography of Fifty Years in Times of Reform*, ed. Constance Hill, London: R. Bentley & Son, 1894.

Hill, Frederic, *The Substitute for Capital Punishment*, London: Society for the Abolition of Capital Punishment, 1866.

Hodder, Edwin, *The Life and Work of the Seventh Earl of Shaftesbury*, 3 vols., Cassell & Co., 1886.

Hogarth, Georgina, ed., *The Letters of Charles Dickens, 1833–1870*, 3 vols., Chapman & Hall, 1909.

Holyoake, George Jacob, 'Public Lessons of the Hangman', London: Farrah, 1864. From the *Morning Star*, 16 November 1864. Printed as a one-penny pamphlet.

Holyoake, George Jacob, *Sixty Years of an Agitator's Life*, Unwin, 1893.

Irving, Joseph, *The Annals of Our Time, 1837–1868*, Macmillan & Co., 1869.

Kingsmill, Joseph, *Chapters on Prisons and Prisoners and the Prevention of Crime*, 3rd edn, Longman, Brown & Green, 1854.

Kirwan, Daniel J., *Palace and Hovel*, London: Abelard-Schuman, 1963. Originally published 1870.

Lehman, R. C., ed., *Charles Dickens as Editor. Being Letters Written by Him to William Henry Willis, His Sub-editor*, London: Smith, Elder & Co., 1912.

Martineau, Harriet, *The History of England During the Thirty Years' Peace, 1816–1846*, 2 vols., London: Charles Knight, 1849.

Mayhew, Henry, *London Labour and the London Poor*, 4 vols., London: C. Griffin & Co., 1861.

Mayhew, Henry, and Binny, John, *The Criminal Prisons of London and Scenes of Prison Life*, London: Griffin, Bohn, 1862.

Mill, John Stuart, *Essays on Politics and Culture*, ed. Gertrude Himmelfarb, New York: Doubleday & Co., 1962.

Molesworth, William N., *The History of England from the Year 1830*, 3 vols., Chapman & Hall, 1874.

Montagu, Basil, ed., *Debates in the Year 1810, Upon Sir Samuel Romilly's Bills for Abolishing the Punishment of Death for Stealing to the Amount of Forty Shillings in a Dwelling House, for Stealing to the Amount of Five Shillings Privately in a Shop, and for Stealing on Navigable Rivers*, London: Society for the Diffusion of Knowledge Respecting the Punishment of Death and the Improvement of Prison Discipline, 1810.

Montagu, Basil, *The Opinions of Different Authors Upon the Punishment of Death*, 3 vols., Longman, Hurst, Rees & Orme, 1809.

Mozley, Thomas, *Reminiscences Chiefly of Oriel College and the Oxford Movement*, 2nd edn., 2 vols., Longmans & Co., 1882.

The Newgate Calendar, or Malefactors' Bloody Register, London: Capricorn Books, 1961.

Ollyfe, George, *An Essay Humbly Offer'd for an Act of Parliament to Prevent Capital Crimes, and the Loss of Many Lives and to Promote a Desirable Improvement and Blessing in the Nation*, London: J. Downing, 1731.

Peggs, James, *Capital Punishment: the Importance of its Abolition*, London, 1839.

Phillips, Charles, *Vacation Thoughts on Capital Punishment*, London: W. & F. G. Cash, 1856.

Ray, Gordon N., ed., *The Letters and Private Papers of William Makepeace Thackeray*, 4 vols., Oxford University Press, 1945–6.

Raymond, John, ed., *Victoria's Early Letters*, 2nd edn, New York: Macmillan & Co., 1963.

Reid, T. W., *The Life, Letters and Friendships of Richard Monckton Milnes, First Lord Houghton*, 2 vols., Cassell & Co., 1890.

Rogers, James Edwin Thorold, ed., *Bright's Speeches on Questions of Public Policy*, 2 vols., Macmillan & Co., 1869.

Romilly, Samuel, *Memoirs of the Life of Sir Samuel Romilly, Written by Himself*, ed. by his sons, 3 vols., J. Murray, 1840.

Romilly, Sir Samuel, *Observations on the Criminal Law of England as it Relates to the Capital Punishments, and on the Mode in Which it is Administered*, London: McCreery, 1810.

The Royal Commission and the Punishment of Death, London: The Society for the Abolition of Capital Punishment, 1866.

Russell, John, *An Essay on the History of the English Government and Constitution from the Reign of Henry VIII to the Present Time*, rev. edn, Longman, Green, Longman, Roberts & Green, 1865.

Smith, J. Barnett, *The Life and Speeches of the Right Hon. John Bright, M.P.*, 2 vols., Hodder & Stoughton, 1881.

Smith, Sydney, *The Works of the Rev. Sydney Smith*, Longman & Co., 1869.

Spedding, James, Ellis, R. L., and Heath, D. D., eds., *The Works of Francis Bacon*, 14 vols., Longman & Co., 1857–74.

Tallack, William, *A General Review of the Subject of Capital Punishment*, London: Society for the Abolition of Capital Punishment. 1866.

Tancred, Sir Thomas, *Suggestions on the Treatment and Disposal of Criminals*, London: T. Hatchard, 1857.

Taylor, John Sydney, *Selections from the Writings of John Sydney Taylor*, London: Charles Gilpin, 1843.

Three Papers on Capital Punishment: Webster, Edward, 'Remarks of Capital Punishment in Cases of Murder'; Dymond, A. H., 'Capital Punishment Practically Considered'; Mayhew, Henry, 'On Capital Punishment', London: Society for Promoting the Amendment of the Law, 1856.

Wakefield, Edward Gibbon, *Facts Relating to the Punishment of Death in the Metropolis*, London, 1832.

Wakefield, Edward Gibbon, *The Hangman and the Judge, or a Letter from Jack Ketch to Mr Justice Alderson*, London: Effingham Wilson, 1833.

Wakefield, Edward Gibbon, *Terrorstruck Town*, London: Steill, 1833.

Walling, E. A. J., ed., *The Diaries of John Bright*, Cassell & Co., 1930.

White, Arnold, ed., *Letters of S.G.O.*, London: Griffith & Farren, 1890.

Woolrych, Humphrey William, *On the Report of the Capital Punishment Commission of 1866*, London: Society for the Abolition of Capital Punishment, 1866.

NEWSPAPERS AND JOURNALS

Daily News, 1846–50, 1864, 1868

Morning Advertiser, 1837, 1868

Morning Herald, 1824, 1846, 1864

Morning Post, 1841, 1849, 1864

Morning Star, 1856, 1864, 1868

The Times, 1824, 1840–68.

All the Year Round, 1849, 1868

Eclectic Review, 1848–50

Fraser's Magazine, 1840, 1850–64

Gentleman's Magazine, 1850–60

Good Words, 1849, 1865

Journal of the Statistical Society, 1864

Law Magazine, 1850

Punch, 1850–68

Spectator, 1849–68

Temple Bar, 1866

Transactions of the National Association for the Promotion of Social Science, 1857–84, 1886

Westminster Review, 1868

SECONDARY SOURCES

PRINTED BOOKS

Appleman, P., Madden, W. A. and Wolf, M., eds., *1859: Entering an Age of Crisis*, Bloomington, Indiana: Indiana University Press, 1959; Oxford University Press, 1959.

Aspinal, A., *Politics and the Press, 1780–1850*, London: Home & Van Thal, 1949.

Atkinson, Charles Milner, *Jeremy Bentham: His Life and Work*, Methuen & Co., 1905.

Ausubel, Herman, *John Bright, Victorian Reformer*, New York and Chichester: John Wiley & Sons, 1966.

Bleackley, Horace William, *The Hangmen of England*, Chapman & Hall, 1929.

Bleackley, Horace William, *Some Distinguished Victims of the Scaffold*, London: Kegan Paul, Trench, Trubner & Co., 1905.

Blom-Cooper, Louis, ed., *The Law as Literature*, Bodley Head, 1961.

Briggs, Asa, *The Age of Improvement*, Longman, Green & Co., 1959.

Brown, Ivor, *Dickens in His Time*, Thomas Nelson & Sons Ltd, 1963.

Burn, William L., *The Age of Equipoise: A Study of the Mid-Victorian Generation*, New York: W.W.Norton & Co.,1964; Allen & Unwin,1968.

Calvert, Roy, *Capital Punishment in the Twentieth Century*, Putnam, 1936.

Calvert, Roy, *Executions*, London: National Council for the Abolition of the Death Penalty, 1926.

Christie, Octavius F., *Dickens and His Age*, London: Heath, Cranton Ltd, 1939.

Cole, George Douglas Howard, and Postgate, Raymond, *The British Common People: 1746–1946*, Methuen, 1961.

Collins, Philip, *Dickens and Crime*, Macmillan & Co., 1962.

Cowherd, Raymond J., *The Politics of English Dissent: The Religious Aspects of Liberal and Humanitarian Reform Movements from 1815 to 1848*, New York: New York University Press, 1956.

Dicey, Albert Venn, *Lectures on the Relation Between Law and Public Opinion in England During the Nineteenth Century*, 2nd edn, Macmillan & Co., 1914.

Gardiner, Gerald, *Capital Punishment as a Deterrent and the Alternative*, Gollancz, 1956.

Gash, Norman, *Mr Secretary Peel: The Life of Sir Robert Peel to 1830*, Cambridge, Mass.: Harvard University Press, 1961.

Gash, Norman, *Reaction and Reconstruction in English Politics, 1832–1852*, Clarendon Press, 1965.

Halévy, Élie, *The Growth of Philosophic Radicalism*, Boston, Beacon Press, 1955; Faber & Faber, 1954.

Halévy, Élie, *A History of the English People in the Nineteenth Century*, 2nd rev. edn, 6 vols., Ernest Benn Ltd, 1961.

Hammond, John L., and Foot, M. R., *Gladstone and Liberalism*, London: English Universities Press, 1952.

Hawes, Frances, *Henry Brougham*, Jonathan Cape, 1957.

Hindley, Charles, *The History of the Catnatch Press*, London: C. Hindley the Younger, 1886.

Hooper, William Eden, *The History of Newgate and the Old Bailey*, London: Underwood Press, 1935.

House, Humphry, *The Dickens World*, 2nd edn, Oxford University Press, 1960.

Jorns, Auguste, *The Quakers as Pioneers in Social Work*, New York: Macmillan & Co., 1931.

Koestler, Arthur, *Reflections on Hanging*, Gollancz, 1956.

Laurence, John, *A History of Capital Punishment*, New York: Citadel Press, 1963.

Longford, Elizabeth, *Queen Victoria: Born to Succeed*, New York: Pyramid Books, 1965. *Victoria R. I.* (abridged edn), Pan Books, 1966.

Maccoby, Simon, ed., *The English Radical Tradition, 1763–1914*, London: Nichols Kaye Ltd, 1952.

Marcus, Steven, *The Other Victorians*, New York: Bantam Books, 1967; Corgi Books, 1969.

Mills, Joseph Travis, *Bright and the Quakers*, 2 vols., Methuen, 1935.

More, Thomas, 'Utopia', *Ideal Commonwealths*, ed. Henry Morley, New York: Colonial Press, 1901.

Morley, John, *The Life of Richard Cobden*, 10th edn, London: T. F. Unwin, 1903.

Munford, W. A., *William Ewart, M.P., 1788–1869: Portrait of a Radical*, London: Grafton & Co., 1960.

Newsam, Sir Frank Aubrey, *The Home Office*, George Allen & Unwin, 1954.

O'Connor, Irma, *Edward Gibbon Wakefield: The Man Himself*, London: Selwyn & Blount, 1928.

Oakes, Cecil George, *Sir Samuel Romilly: 1757–1818*, George Allen & Unwin, 1935.

Owen, David E., *English Philanthropy, 1660–1960*, Cambridge, Mass. and London: Harvard University Press, 1964.

Phillipson, Coleman, *Three Criminal Law Reformers: Beccaria, Bentham, Romilly*, J. M. Dent & Sons, 1923.

Plumb, J. H., *England in the Eighteenth Century, 1714–1815*, Penguin Books Ltd, 1959.

Radzinowicz, Leon, *A History of English Criminal Law and its Administration from 1750*, 4 vols., London: Stevens & Sons, 1948–68.

Radzinowicz, Leon, *Sir James F. Stephens and his Contributions to the Development of Criminal Law*, London: B. Quaritch, 1957.

Rolph, C. H., *Common Sense About Crime and Punishment*, Gollancz, 1961.

Rose, Gordon, *The Struggle for Penal Reform: The Howard League and its Predecessors*, London: Stevens & Sons, 1961.

Spielmann, Marion Harry, *The History of Punch*, Cassell & Co., 1895.

Somervell, David Churchill, *English Thought in the Nineteenth Century*, 5th ed, New York: David McKay, 1965; Methuen, 1964.

The Times, The History of the Times, 5 vols., The Times, 1935–52.

Tobias, J. J., *Crime and Industrial Society in the 19th Century*, New York: Schocken Books, 1967; Penguin Books Ltd, 1972.

Trevelyan, George M., *The Life of John Bright*, Constable & Co., 1913.

Tuttle, Elizabeth Orman, *The Crusade Against Capital Punishment in Great Britain*, London: Stevens & Sons, 1961.

Walpole, Spencer, *A History of England from the Conclusion of the Great War in 1815*, new and rev. edn., 6 vols., Longman & Co., 1890.

INDEX

References to 'capital punishment' and 'executions' should be taken to refer to execution by hanging unless otherwise stated, though a few references cover discussion of more than one method of execution. 'Capital punishment' is generally abbreviated in sub entries to 'c. p'. Page numbers, in italic type refer to illustrations.